"[Lischer's] storytelling is quite effective . . . a worthy addition to the literature."
—*Kirkus Reviews*

"Vivid, funny, and compassionate. Again and again Lischer deftly illustrates that the simplest of human stories can also be the most profound."
—*News and Notes*

"Out of the unlikeliest material, Richard Lischer has produced a genuinely *exciting* book. Again and again I was amused, enlivened, nourished, and deeply moved by the truth of the tale he tells with such authenticity and wit."
—Frederick Buechner, author of *The Sacred Journey*, *The Hungry Dark*, and *The Eyes of the Heart*

"On these lively pages, sin, pettiness, gossip, and betrayal are kissin' cousins to faith, hope, and charity."
—*Spirituality and Health*

"The ministry used to be called 'The Cure of the Souls,' and that is what comes to mind in this candid, compassionate, and at times quite funny account of a young pastor's first church. Part Garrison Keillor and part Reinhold Niebuhr, this memoir of innocence and experience is destined for classic status."
—Rev. Peter J. Gomes, author of *The Good Book*

"With honesty and humor *Open Secrets* discloses the growing pains of a young, highly educated pastor. Colorful."
—*CBA Marketplace*

"*Open Secrets* is about gaining respect for one another and somehow finding the presence of God in dreary everyday life. By the time Pastor Lischer leaves New Cana, he's learned something valuable about life, humility, and the beating hearts of others. This honest book reads like silk."
—*Monthly Book News & Reviews*

Open
Secrets

RICHARD LISCHER

BROADWAY BOOKS
New York

Open Secrets

A Memoir
of Faith and
Discovery

BROADWAY

A hardcover edition of this book was originally published in 2001 by
Doubleday, a division of Random House, Inc. It is here reprinted by
arrangement with Doubleday.

Broadway Books titles may be purchased for business or promotional use or for
special sales. For information, please write to: Special Markets Department,
Random House, Inc., 1540 Broadway, New York, NY 10036.

PRINTED IN THE UNITED STATES OF AMERICA

BROADWAY BOOKS and its logo, a letter B bisected on the diagonal, are
trademarks of Broadway Books, a division of Random House, Inc.

Visit our website at www.broadwaybooks.com

First Broadway Books trade paperback edition published 2002

Designed by Nicola Ferguson

The Library of Congress has cataloged the hardcover edition as follows:
Lischer, Richard.
Open secrets: a spiritual journey through
a country church / Richard Lischer.
—1st ed.
p. cm.
1. Lischer, Richard. 2. Lutheran Church—United States
—Clergy—Biography. I. Title.
BX8080.L57 A3 2001
284.1'092—dc21   00-060271
[B]

ISBN 0-7679-0744-2

1 3 5 7 9 10 8 6 4 2

For TKL

Almighty God, unto whom all hearts are open, all desires known, and from whom no secrets are hid: Cleanse the thoughts of our hearts by the inspiration of thy Holy Spirit, that we may perfectly love thee, and worthily magnify thy holy Name; through Christ our Lord.

—*Book of Common Prayer*

Love is stronger than death—that stands within your books.

—Georges Bernanos,
The Diary of a Country Priest

CONTENTS

Open
Secrets

1

Egypt

 I had a parish in a small town in southern Illinois, not far from the confluence of the Mississippi and Missouri rivers, where the Missouri shows brown and the Mississippi foams yellow, and the two make a big river the color of cream soda. The farms in my parish rested on the American Bottom at the southernmost tip of the great Illinois prairie. The land was flattened by a prehistoric ocean several millennia ago, then smoothed by a glacier, and finally turned black as onyx by the rivers.

The Chippewas called it *Mechesebe*, the Great River, and it is great. But before you romanticize it, you have to see and smell its twenty-three miles of huge interceptor sewers that, along with a network of smaller pump stations, retrieve the raw waste pumped into the river. Twenty-nine locks on the Upper Mississippi convert the mighty waterway that once offered freedom to Jim and Huck into a carefully regulated series of steps for barges bearing the names of great oil and chemical companies. Near St. Louis, monstrous levees attempt to channel the river's capricious power away from the city and its suburbs. You have to squint like an Impressionist or frame the scene with your hands in order to block out the ugliness of the river. Gazing on the *Mechesebe* these days makes you want to feel sorry for the river, the way you do a circus elephant or a caged gorilla.

I myself grew up only a few miles from the Missouri, just west of where it joins the Mississippi, but I never saw the river as anything but an odd and somewhat ominous extension of the suburban sprawl to which my parents and I, like millions of other city dwellers, had migrated in the early 1950s. The backwaters of the Missouri were explored by boys far more adventurous than I. On the rare occasions when I went along to go crawdadding, I did not know what to make of the crayfish. I knew positively that I would not eat them. Swimming in the Missouri always seemed dangerous to me, and I did it reluctantly out of peer pressure. Many of the boys brought firecrackers to set off on nearby Pelican Island, and a few brought guns, which was one of those details from which a humane only child shields his parents.

The land around the rivers is incredibly fertile, and there have always been farmers to work it. The Mississippian peoples settled the land about a thousand years before the coming of the Teuton Lutherans. They grew many of the same crops our farmers planted: corn, squash, tobacco, and beans, though by the size and complexity of their cities they did it more successfully than we. They organized a culture more sophisticated than any that has since appeared on this land. Their plazas and temples would have put our shopping malls to shame. The explorer DeSoto claimed they worshiped the sun, but archaeologists have found numerous masks and earrings commemorating a mysterious, mutating being known as the Long Nose

God. The Mississippians apparently used their god for progressive purposes as a ritual symbol of unity between the tribes that lived and farmed together.

At some point in the sixteenth or early seventeenth century, the Mississippians were swallowed whole by history. They all disappeared, every last one of them, probably due to a European virus to which they had no immunity. By the time Marquette and Joliet arrived in 1673 all that remained of the Mississippian culture were two hundred mounds used for sacrifice and burial.

My parish lay above "Egypt," which is the name later settlers gave to the region where the Mississippi and Ohio rivers make a delta, like the Nile, and head toward the Gulf. Like so much of the American South, our Egypt beheld itself in the mirror of the great civilizations of the ancient world. Many of its cities like Goshen, Thebes, and Cairo (pronounced *Kay-ro*, to rhyme with *Pha*-raoh) were named after cities well known in antiquity. Its burial mounds, though not so splendid or famous, were no less mysterious than the pyramids of Egypt.

The entire region is still densely Southern in character with cypress swamps and water moccasins in the Cache River valley and wild orchids everywhere. The backwater glades are filled with ferns and moss and sumac. Canadian geese winter in our Egypt every year. Only a century and a half ago the woods were noisy with green-, red-, and yellow-striped parakeets.

North of Egypt lay the tenements and deserted packinghouses of East St. Louis, a community shadowed by its history of racial insurrection and poverty. A 630-foot stainless steel arch on the west bank of the Mississippi adds gratuitous insult to the misery of East St. Louisians. Then come the steel mills of Granite City, the refineries and stench of Wood River, and finally the quintessential river town of Alton, which tumbles down the bluffs into a heap of slag and soot in the flats along the Mississippi.

The first time I saw my church was across a field of glistening Mississippi mud and corn stubble. I had been looking for it all afternoon. Like one of

Joshua's spies, I had come to reconnoiter the town and the church to which denominational officials had assigned me. New Cana was the town, and Cana Lutheran Church was the congregation, but to the locals I learned it was all one: Cana or the Cana church. I could not find the town on any map of Illinois, but I knew it was "just out of Alton."

I drove my brand-new yellow Pinto across the Mississippi north of St. Louis through the immense floodplain between the rivers, past the year-round fireworks stands, past a few catfish joints and windowless nightclubs made of painted block, built low to the ground like bunkers. Then into Lower Alton and the flats along the river.

In the flats, wooden taverns were sandwiched between volcanic mills, glassworks, waterworks, ironworks, sheet metal shops, tool and dye operations, junkyards. The shops were dwarfed by a twelve-story grain elevator with an enormous American flag painted on it.

I drove up the steep hills of the business district into Upper Alton with its genteel homes and college buildings. A life-sized, nine-foot statue of a smiling, doomed young man named Robert Wadlow seemed to wave from a park. He was the tallest person in the history of the world and was affectionately known as the Alton Giant.

Alton is saddled with more history than any city its size should have to bear. If Chicago is the city of big shoulders, Alton is hunched and worried like a man looking for work. The city watches over the river but does not commune with it or enjoy it the way New Orleans, St. Louis, or even Dubuque enjoy the Mississippi. But it was not always so. In the 1830s it was Alton, not St. Louis, that was destined to be the great city on the river. But one hundred thirty years later, when all the newspapers and media people were looking for a pithy phrase with which to describe James Earl Ray's hometown of Alton, they settled on "decaying river town."

In 1831 a young newspaperman named Elijah Lovejoy was converted in the First Presbyterian Church of St. Louis by an antislavery evangelist. Upon his conversion, Lovejoy promptly enrolled in Princeton Theological

Seminary in New Jersey and within a year and a half returned to St. Louis to publish a religious newspaper.

Missouri was a slave state, and soon Lovejoy's defiant abolitionism made it necessary for him to relocate his newspaper across the river in Alton, where he resumed his editorial work and pastored the Upper Alton Presbyterian Church. Illinois was a free state, but in the small towns of southern Illinois hatred for Negroes was no less intense and violent than in the slaveholding states. Planters in southern Illinois envied the free labor enjoyed by their Missouri competitors and in the 1830s petitioned unsuccessfully for the reintroduction of slavery. Twenty years later southern Illinois supported the states' rights candidate over the unionist Abraham Lincoln.

Lovejoy's presses were repeatedly destroyed and dumped into the river while the Alton police stood by. Newspapers in St. Louis fueled the hysteria by advocating violence and declaring open season on Elijah Lovejoy. His opponents accused him of being an "amalgamist," a person who favors the blending of the races through marriage. Lovejoy's readers gnashed their teeth when he reminded them of the true source of amalgamation: the white man's abuse and rape of black women. No one had ever dared print such a thing.

On the evening of November 7, 1837, with Presbyterian church bells sounding a frantic alarm throughout the city, a proslavery mob attempted to burn a warehouse that held Lovejoy's new printing press. The young editor stood by the press to defend it and was shot and killed. When his body was brought out on a horse cart the next day, a mob danced about it in celebration.

His murder made him the first American martyr to freedom of the press, and it made Alton a byword for racism and violence across the nation. A newspaper in Massachusetts editorialized, "Who but a savage or coldhearted murderer would now go to Alton? Meanness, infamy, and guilt are attached to the very name. Hereafter, when a criminal is considered too bad for any known punishment, it will be said of him: 'He ought to be banished to Alton.' "

The city went into a precipitous decline. It quickly fell out of consideration to be the state's capital. Its reputation for lawlessness made it unattractive to new commercial ventures. River traffic favored St. Louis and other towns. For its part, Alton's civic leaders and newspapers refused to acknowledge the crime that had shocked the nation. The city grew paranoid and resentful, as if its sins had been blown out of proportion. When a monument was finally dedicated to Lovejoy sixty years later in the city cemetery, its base was simply inscribed, "Alton Slew Him." It might as well have read, "He slew Alton."

Twenty-one years after Lovejoy's murder, Stephen Douglas and Abraham Lincoln arrived in Alton aboard the steamboat *City of Louisiana*. They held their seventh and final debate in an outdoor setting not far from the warehouse where Lovejoy was killed. Only Douglas mentioned Lovejoy, and that only to reproach Lincoln for harboring the same fanatic notion of the Negro's equality with whites. Lincoln responded courageously by attacking Douglas's position "as having a tendency to dehumanize the Negro, to take away from him the right of ever striving to be a man," but he had too much political sense to invoke Lovejoy's name in Alton.

Alton is far from Egypt. Egypt is prehistory and the faded splendor of ancient civilizations. Alton represents *our* history of slavery, debate, riots, and murder, and now farm foreclosures, rusting steel, resentment, and welfare. Egypt is dying slowly; its life is measured out in geologic and mythical time. Alton flamed out one day in *our* time when the steamboats disappeared and the railroads chose other cities.

My parish was a speck on this map of myth and history. Its days of heroic struggle with the land belonged to the mythology of Egypt. We, and other churches like ours, were more like medics who stay behind the lines to tend the wounded. My parishioners lived near a port once destined for greatness. They farmed the blackest and richest earth in the country. The city had squandered its destiny in violence, and my farmers couldn't make a decent living no matter how hard they worked. By the time I arrived, most of them had either lost their home places or were moonlighting at the steel mill or the glassworks in Alton. You couldn't go to Alton to work or shop without tasting an ash or two of defeat. I didn't know that on my first drive through, but I soon learned.

Out of Upper Alton you pick up a state road, or "the hard road" as it was called, and move through geometrical patterns of corn and soybeans. At this time of year, however, there was no corn or soybeans, but only their remains, and the wheat had not been seeded. The road had no curves or bends, only ninety-degree lefts and rights. In twenty miles or so I turned east on the New Cana Road, though no sign called it that, and headed toward a community of about two hundred fifty people.

New Cana reminded me of nothing I had ever seen or imagined. It lacked the traditional accessories that make a town picturesque—no courthouse, town square, or ivy-covered cottages. The few white picket fences I saw were in disrepair and were obviously placed to keep the chickens in the yard. New Cana's appearance did not resonate with any longings I could remember or any needs I had repressed. Nothing was awakened in me when I saw the place for the first time. No Grovers Corners in *Our Town* or folksy Mayberry beckoned to me. My first look at the town reminded me that I was from a city and probably belonged in a city. New Cana had several blocks of white framed houses, a semidetached post office and grocery, a prefabricated town hall, a Texaco station, and a tractor store. That was it. I didn't even slow down. Outside the town, the paved road turned to oil covered with dirt.

Heading east again and then sharply north, I passed several clapboard farmhouses nestled in shelters of leafless oak and walnut trees. Each farmhouse was enveloped in a campus of faded barns and outbuildings, ribbed gray silos, and spidery machines in various stages of disassembly like grasshoppers with their legs off. Beside every home place stood a modern brick rancher, looking to the outsider like a tract home plucked from the suburbs and plopped into a rural setting where it didn't belong. A day in the country—this was not a novel experience for me but an alien world. I might as well have been touring Nepal as motoring through the dead cornfields of Illinois.

The entire landscape of fields and farms had faded badly in the late November sun. Its bleached stillness reminded me of a scene from an Ingmar Bergman movie: Swedish winterlight exposing rot and depression in rural Lutherans. It worried me that I thought of a Bergman film as I beheld my parish for the first time.

From above, Bergman's camera would have revealed a landscape the color of unglazed pottery disturbed by a single, moving bead of yellow. The car came to a T, turned left on the Cana Church Road, though no sign called it that, and idled before a country church and parsonage. From the camera's point of view, Cana and its parsonage would have appeared to teeter at the very edge of a flat planet. In front of the church, the alternating pattern of disked-over corn and soybean fields repeated itself from one farm to the next as far as the eye could see.

Behind the church, the terrain changed dramatically. A cemetery with a gravel track fell off a hill behind the parsonage. Back of the church and to the west, the land resembled an English heath. Its disorder ruined any notion of rolling waves of wheat or Midwestern infinitude. There were roads that ran behind the church—one skinny loop of a road, really—that descended so deeply into the heath that not even an aerial photographer could have traced it. That road followed a dry gorge tangled with willows and matted vines. It led to trailers and shacks with porcelain appliances out front and even narrower lanes to country taverns with screened-in porches. All roads seemed to disappear into the underbrush. From the front, the church stood alone on the prairie as a symbol of strength. But from the back, the dense and twisted heath threatened to engulf both church and parsonage in its own natural darkness.

When you pull up to your first church, it's a moment of truth, like the first glimpse of a spouse in an arranged marriage. It had been twelve years since I'd blurted out my secret at the family dinner table: "I'm going to be a pastor. What do you think of that?" This meeting had been a long time coming.

I felt something flop in my stomach. Then, a crushing sense of disappointment. *So this is what has been prepared for me*, I thought, as if something surely *should* have been prepared for me.

I saw no signs of life around the church or parsonage. The only sound was that of a breeze whistling through flagless stalks of pampas grass that separated the lawn from the road. They were as brittle and noisy as wind chimes. I studied the house first, for, after all, I would move a wife and child into that house, and soon a new baby. So this is where we would make our life. What kind of life would it be?

The parsonage looked to be about fifty years old. It was a story-and-a-half prairie bungalow, white clapboard, with triple dormers and a porch that shaded the entire front. Its two entrances, one to the pastor's study, the other to what appeared to be a small parlor, gave it the look of a duplex. There was nothing fine about the house, not a hint of character or charm. Its boards and frames might literally have come from a Sears Roebuck catalog. You couldn't say it was English, Dutch, or French, only American vernacular or Early Depression. The porch and steps were made of crudely formed concrete, scrubbed and bare of the hopeful signs of tricycles, dolls, or Frisbees. With no chimney in view, the house evidently was warmed by no fireplace. Its garage was a shed. Everything needed paint.

After I completed my study of the house, I turned my attention to the church. When I was a younger man, I once saw the cathedral at Chartres shimmering in the morning mist across a field of new-mown hay. It was a revelation, a sudden disclosure of the heavenly world. Like my church, the cathedral lay in an ordinary field on ordinary country roads near ordinary farmhouses, but with its foundation of mist and its towers of stone it was so supernaturally beautiful that it appeared to descend from heaven. I remember an American tourist exclaiming to no one in particular, "Now *that's* what I call a church!"

My new church definitely did *not* shimmer in the gloomy November light or appear to descend from any height at all. Instead, its faded red bricks appeared to grow up out of the soil. The twin lanterns beside the entrance were bizarre touches that might have been added by a ship's chandler. In place of a great tower, the building sported a peeling cupola and a steeple with a copper cross from which one arm was mysteriously missing.

I could not see anything fine about this church of the one-armed cross. What I'm sure the parishioners would proudly claim as stained glass was painted art glass decorated by cartoons of holy symbols with Latin labels. The double doors were painted a sickly salmon. I suspected the floral arrangements in the cemetery out back were plastic. How had this happened to me?

I wasn't so put off by the physical appearance of the church as I was by its obvious irrelevance. My seminarian friends and I reveled in the social and religious ferment of the 1960s. We never tired of posing as progressives and announcing like JFK that we wanted to "make a difference." We had skimmed Augustine's *City of God* but devoured Harvey Cox's best-seller, *The Secular City*. His book reminded us that there was a secular world out there yearning to be liberated from religious superstition, and theological activists like us would be the agents of its redemption. The *city* was where the action was, not in suburbs such as the one I grew up in, and certainly not in country churches like this one, with its broken cross and flourishing graveyard. Two minutes on this lonely road was a clarifying experience. The spiritual heroics of the secular city had passed me by.

I could have turned off the engine and gotten out of the car. I might have tried the church doors or stopped by a neighboring farmhouse and introduced myself. "Hello, I'm the new pastor here. My name is Richard. Friends call me Rick. Came out from St. Louis to see the place. I'd love to look around."

But no, I couldn't even open my car door because that would have been an admission, if only to myself, that this assignment was acceptable. Any gesture of regard might have seriously compromised my own superiority to parochial backwaters like this. The church of the one-armed cross did not fit my own personal profile. I knew who I was and, with a brand new Ph.D. in Theology already in hand, I had mapped out a distinguished career for myself: a cutting-edge pastoral appointment in a socially conscious but not unaffluent congregation, followed by a professorship in our denomination's flagship seminary, capped off by the presidency of the seminary and—why not?—of the whole church body, which to me was the sum of my whole world. By that time my hair would be streaked with silver and contrast stunningly with my black suit and gleaming clerical collar.

Of course I knew Christendom needed unstrategic little churches like this one, but I bitterly resented the bureaucrats who had misfiled my gifts, misjudged my obvious promise, and were about to place me in rural confinement. Whoever they were, they hadn't even bothered to get to know *me*. That's the way I felt, and my resentment came quick and fully formed.

I sat there in the car for a few minutes, no doubt with a pickled look on my face, and inhaled the scene with my eyes. Then I exhaled, threw the Pinto in gear, and headed back the way I had come, toward Alton and St. Louis and civilization.

2

The Secret History

 Exactly why I had arrived at my first call with such a developed sense of entitlement, I'm not sure. Nothing in my history would have led me to expect a more sophisticated way of life than the one I had enjoyed with my parents in our suburban tract house or later in a succession of tiny church colleges. Nothing in my denomination's history promised innovation or excitement. Any sociologist could have predicted that an earnest young Lutheran from St. Louis might easily land among earnest, somewhat older Lutherans just across the river in southern Illinois. There is nothing more exasperating than to discover that the precious choices of one's secret history merely illustrate an older and predictable story.

My ancestors came from Saxony in the 1830s to escape the Enlightenment. They were heroically opposed to the use of reason in the interpretation of the Bible. They refused to accept error in religion or to break bread with those who did. That remains the authorized story of our emigration. But if you read the literature of the German emigration carefully, you can also detect the usual stirrings of adventure and greed. Travel brochures prepared for unhappy Germans promised fertile land with opportunities for wealth and leisure beyond imagination, especially in "the wonderful plains and valleys of the Missouri and the Mississippi."

The brochures notwithstanding, the church on the Mississippi was born in poverty and conflict. If the first settlers worried about free thought and tolerance, they needn't have, for they eliminated both by placing themselves in total subjection to a group of autocratic pastors led by the infamous Martin Stephan, who was later deposed for embezzlement, adultery, and other high crimes and misdemeanors.

Stephan was a Svengali to the rest of the settlers, especially the women. While still on the high seas aboard the German ship *Olpers*, four pastors consecrated Stephan a bishop and later signed a "Pledge of Subjection to Stephan." They hoped to establish a Zion on the Mississippi, an ideal Christian community in a fabulously fertile valley. Instead, they became a sect ruled by a powerful man who presided over a lavish house in St. Louis, consorted with women (the history gets a little vague here), and introduced the odious practice of kissing the bishop's hand.

When Stephan's autocratic ways became too much for the colony to bear, he was sent away to a desolate place in southern Illinois named Horse Prairie, where, as the story goes, he died without repenting. Horse Prairie wasn't far from the place where my congregation would be founded thirteen years later.

Stephan was a scapegoat. *All* the pastors had coveted a share of power over the sect, and all had pledged themselves to the bishop as to a god. In the official histories of the church, however, the pastors are portrayed as resisters, and Stephan alone as the evil seducer. The sins of the whole community—its arrogant leaders and its sheeplike followers—were heaped upon the head of one malefactor who was banished to a lonely prairie.

My church body has lived with this secret for nearly two centuries. We sublimated our shame into mission crusades, family feuds, and interminable quests for "pure doctrine." My branch of Lutheranism—the *Olpers* crew—separated itself not only from other Christians but from other Lutherans. We haughtily refused to receive communion with Norwegian, Swedish, or Finnish Lutherans, who themselves were not famous for free thought or liberalism. In some situations we even avoided saying table grace with them, all in the name of purity. We remained resident aliens long after the English, Scots, and Swedes had rolled up their sleeves and taken over the city halls and public squares of the Midwest. We could never be clean enough because the original stain had not been removed.

Already in the early decades of our history, one can see the shadow cast by our church's secret. Reports from the New World struck a note of exaggerated horror in the face of immorality and unbelief. One Lutheran missionary wrote home of the cruelty of his fellow German immigrants, whose hearts had been hardened not only by backbreaking labor but also by the absence of the word of God, the sacraments, and the guidance of a shepherd. "The people," he said, "look as wild as the landscape." They prefer the saloon to church, and they do not listen to sermons willingly. Their children are savages, unbaptized and uncatechized. "Just imagine," he said, daring to put the unthinkable into words, "*German heathen!*"

It was Lutheran karma that the immigrants would establish their own system of schools for the education of the clergy. While other denominations were busy founding colleges for the general public, these would serve only the elite, the special boys who were selected for leadership in the church. Our schools would be separate from those of the other immigrants and would be governed by a hierarchy of pastors. They would instill purity of doctrine in little boys who in time would grow up to become powerful teachers of righteousness and enforcers of purity in their churches.

Our high schools and colleges reproduced the old German system of education with all its virtues and faults. It took a boy out of his home and grammar school, away from his church and community, and focused his entire twelve-year education on preparation for the ministry. It excluded girls and young women, who were restricted to teachers' colleges or hospitals for nurses' training. The system had been transplanted whole from the high culture of Saxony to nineteenth-century America, where it was presumed it would work among farmers with manure on their boots. It was the only way my ancestors knew to make pastors.

When I was a boy in St. Louis, happy with daily baseball games and the humid mysteries of adolescence, my parents sent me to one such school in Milwaukee, Wisconsin. The secret history would continue in me.

I never held it against my parents for sending me to Milwaukee. In fact, it really isn't accurate to say that they sent me, for we were such a tight little unit—I was an only child of two only children—that we thought and acted as one.

My parents' lives were shaped and sheltered by the church and the intensely ordered culture of the near-north side of St. Louis. My father met my mother by means of one of the great pickup lines of their era. After a social at the church, he followed her down St. Louis Avenue along the park to the streetcar stop. When he caught up to her he said with the savoir-faire of a Lutheran Cary Grant, "Say, do you go to movies during Lent?"

We had an understanding, my parents and I, that one could do no more nobly with one's life than to be a pastor. The word *pastor* means shepherd, but in the German vernacular it meant leader, head, boss, and beloved dictator. It was the most traditional word in my childhood vocabulary. Although we never spoke of my vocation, my mother had a way of coding her conversation with wistful religious longings and reverence for all pastors. She held ill-concealed aspirations for me. She was never as aggressive as the professional Catholic mother who single-handedly wills her hapless son into the priesthood and then makes a saint of "my Tony the priest," but she could play in that league.

My mother inherited her piety from the Baptists and Methodists of Kentucky before she "converted" to Lutheranism as a teenager. She loved to regale me with her preconversion stories of Methodist circuit riders and Baptist preachers and to sing hymns like "In the Gloaming" and "Shall We Gather at the River?" which she promised we would never ever hear in a Lutheran church. She hadn't forgotten how to sing,

> Shall we gather at the river,
> Where bright angel feet have trod,
> With its crystal tide forever
> Flowing by the throne of God?

Her father filled her head with stories from his Kentucky boyhood, of straitlaced Methodist circuit riders and Baptists so narrow-minded they could look through a keyhole with both eyes. He always told his stories etiologically, as a means of explaining the rough spots in his own behavior or justifying his disenchantment with preachers and "organized" religion.

My grandfather and his little brother hated it when the circuit rider came to town, because, since their daddy was a deacon in the Methodist church, the visiting preacher always stayed at their house and they had to shine the old bugger's boots. The circuit rider preached the same sermon every time he came, pummeled the same vices of drinking and card playing, even wiped his brow at the same climactic moment every time. One Saturday night, after the two boys had shined the preacher's boots, they carefully arranged a half-deck of cards in his handkerchief and put it in its regular place in the breast pocket of his frock coat. The next morning in church, just as the preacher was beginning to work up a sweat against card playing, he whipped out his hankie to wipe his righteous brow, only to have a little cloud of playing cards—jacks and aces, hearts and diamonds and jokers too—come fluttering to the floor like leaves on an autumn day. Their father the deacon was sitting in the front pew. As the cards fell at his feet, he arose with great dignity and walked up the center aisle, motioning to the two boys to follow. He had his belt off before he reached the back door. My grandfather said the look on the preacher's face made the strapping worthwhile and if he had the chance, he'd do it again.

My mother told her stories with such good humor that I could have never guessed the misery in which they originated. When she was nine years old, her mother came down with influenza and died. She didn't die of flu, but she was in the final stages of recovery when in her weakened condition she fell in the bedroom and struck her head on the corner of the dresser. All my mother remembered about the incident was the sticky mass of blood oozing through her mother's long blond hair. At the funeral one of her cousins lifted her over the casket to kiss her mother's lips one last time. That experience produced a trauma from which my mother never fully recovered.

My mother's father was a railroad man on the old L&N. He was gone for days and nights at a time. At an age when other girls were playing with dolls my mother was left to cook, keep house, and otherwise occupy herself while he was away.

One evening she was home alone, as usual. It was a typically hot St. Louis summer night, and she went down the street to the neighborhood Baptist church where they were having a revival. At first, she just sat in the back pew and watched the goings on. Up front there was a large pool of the coolest and most inviting water you could imagine, and right there in that sweltering church people were splashing and diving beneath its surface. When the preacher strapped on his waders and cried out, "O sinners come to the river of life,"

the beautiful, the beautiful river,
that flows by the throne of God

it was more than she could stand, and she bolted toward the water and was baptized. I don't think she ran forward because she thought she was a sinner but because she was lonely. The only stain she ever wanted to wash away was the one at the base of her mother's skull.

The next night it was even hotter, so she went back and did it all again. And the night after that, too.

Her father was a dashing fellow with a dangerous wave of black hair over one eye. He was the kind of rogue that men quickly see through but women never do until it is too late. My grandmother, who was ten years younger than he, fell head over heels for this dark Englishman who knew the rail lines of Kentucky like the back of his hand. When he and his beautiful young conquest ran away together, her brothers followed them onto the train with the intention of killing him. My grandfather had the presence of mind to hide in the ladies' toilet and escaped harm.

My grandfather was also a drunk who was often embroiled in battles with the family and the state over custody of my mother. She told the story of one trial in a St. Louis courtroom, when as a little girl she dramatically refuted the social workers and chose her father to keep her over an uncle and aunt. Her father, usually three sheets to the wind and weeping all the way, would sing "Me and My Shadow" to her when he took her walking in Fairgrounds Park.

And when it's five o'clock,
We climb the stairs.
We never knock,
'Cause nobody's there.

Later, after he remarried, every payday her stepmother would enlist her to finagle his check away from him—to roll him—before he spent it all in the tavern.

She told these things without a hint of shame or sadness. She did not draw morals or religious lessons from them. But in the context of our family prayers, her stories helped me understand what God can and cannot do.

God cannot stop your mother from dying or your father from being a drunk. God can help you survive. I never heard my mother complain about her father, poverty, sickness, or even her own impending death. I think it was my mother's childhood that radically reduced her expectations of life.

Whenever I raised my sights or put on airs, it was my mother who reminded me that we were "middle class." Thank God we had not descended to whatever it was that yawned ominously beneath the middle class, and not even in fantasy could we rise to a higher station. Socially, we were governed by two countervailing laws: Everyone in our family worked, and we would never be rich. "Middle class" functioned as code for the bounded territory in which God intended for us to live, work, marry, and die. Both my parents seemed completely satisfied with my father's low-paying job as an accountant, with their tract house to which they never added so much as a back porch or a garage, their neighborhood, their church, and their one and only child.

My father was a lot less complicated than my mother. He had been raised the only child of two middle-aged only children in the same neighborhood of identical walk-ups and scrubbed brick sidewalks. His father was a shopkeeper who did not drink to excess, travel on trains, or run after women. His mother was the salt of the earth.

My father was always the smallest boy in his class, to which I attributed his marvelous sense of humor. His instinct for irony was that of a person who is surrounded by people who are bigger but dumber than he. In his old age he added a public persona of great caution and reserve. Secretly, however, he wrote stories for his grandchildren in which he always figured as the hero, made jokes, and even did impressions of our friends, especially those who aspired to rise out of the middle class.

My father's life was not marked by tragedy or even uncertainty as he grew older but no richer. Whereas my mother viewed life as from a precipice, my dad observed it from his vegetable garden, where he grew approximately thirty times the number of turnips consumable by a family of three.

It was odd to me that someone with such a developed sense of the ludicrous was also so easily embarrassed. Only after I was grown did my mother confess that their church wedding had been a sham and that they had run away in a fever four months before it. My father simply couldn't bear for me to know that he had once succumbed to his passions.

He was unemployed, having recently lost his job as a cub reporter in the St. Louis office of *The Wall Street Journal*. It was the depths of the Great Depression, and he and my mother wanted desperately to be married. If their marriage license had been noted in the *St. Louis Post-Dispatch*, my mother would have been fired from her secretarial position, because married women were prohibited from taking jobs away from men. With my father piloting a borrowed Model A, they crossed to the Illinois side of the river and to the sleepy town of Waterloo. There they drove straight to the only Lutheran church, where after much explaining they persuaded the young pastor to perform the ceremony. He did it in the parlor of the parsonage, and his wife and children served as witnesses.

Afterward, they returned to St. Louis and checked themselves and their cardboard luggage into the Forest Park Hotel for what must have been quite a weekend. The doorman, my mother thought, "saw right through" them. They also felt sinful, she said.

My mother and father were approaching middle age when I was born. They had been trying for a long time, and when the family doctor confirmed the good news, my father took my mother to a Cardinal game at Sportsman's Park to celebrate. My dad had the lifelong habit of topping off the important events of his life with the *summum bonum* of life itself, a baseball game—preferably a doubleheader against the Dodgers.

My mother was not above interpreting her pregnancy in the mirror of the Bible and dramatizing my approaching birth with a promise to God. She never came out and admitted it, but I always suspected that she had cut some kind of deal with God along the lines of, "You give me a son, I'll give you a pastor." When I eventually announced my plan to enter the ministry, I noticed a curious lack of surprise in my mother's eyes.

I credit my parents' overinterpretation of my birth with a sense of destiny I carried through my youth and young adulthood. It is not bad for children to believe that they have an important reason for living. However, this sense of destiny can run to extravagance in clergy, who have a tendency to dramatize their inner states anyway and to interpret their thankless tasks and small salaries in terms of very large designs. I myself was not a remarkable child, either in achievement or imagination, only a very private boy who was secretive and sometimes lonely. But thanks to my parents' dramatic construction of me, I never doubted some special purpose for my life.

My mother and father were not educated people. They were endowed with their generation's sort of intelligence, a quality of literateness acquired in an era when grammar schools held commencements and a college education was not the norm. They thought clearly and expressed themselves articulately; they wrote beautifully balanced and interesting letters with excellent penmanship. My mother loved poetry and knew Poe and Longfellow by heart. She was the salutatorian of her high school class but refused a college scholarship in order to help support her father. No one on my father's side had ever graduated from high school.

My parents were not zealous for the Truth in any orthodox sense, and my dad was less likely to talk about God than my mother. They both simply and fully *belonged* to their neighborhood and its great stone church, and both gave absolute respect to the pastor. My mother often told the story of how, when she was a teenager in a church play, the pastor insisted that she change her red dress for a color "less mature." In fact, whenever they told stories of our church's pastors, the punch line was usually related to some awesome demonstration of their authority. On the morning of Pearl Harbor, for example, Pastor Sieck looked through his monocle with a steady eye and took as his text Psalm 46:10, "Be still, and know that I am God." God's word ruled that morning through our pastor.

When I was a boy I occasionally sat in the front pew of our church and fantasized on the incredibly narrow span that lay between me, an ordinary Christian, and the sacred space occupied by our minister. Sometimes I literally counted the rows of tiles in the floor. Only a few feet separated me from the richly tapestried altar and the mysterious folds of stole upon surplice and cassock. It is embarrassing to remember such thoughts, but at the time it seemed to me that only God's call could foreclose the enormous distance between me and the divine courts.

These feelings intensified during Lent in the Wednesday evening services. Then the church would be darkened except for the spotlighted cross, and our pastor would wear only a black cassock with an ivory crucifix on his chest. He was normally a distant if not gruff person, but during Lent he changed. Something in his voice reproduced the vulnerability and suffering of the Lord. Occasionally he wept in the pulpit. He had made the Passion of Jesus his own and was time-releasing it to us in weekly installments. He was never one for cute sermon illustrations, but during these dark hours of Lent he forsook all distractions entirely and followed the scent of death like a bloodhound.

When I got a little older, I migrated to the balcony with my pals. We sat on the front row where we took in the whole spectacle of our sin and its atonement with feigned nonchalance. Half the time we played a game in which we made bets on the exact moment our pastor would say Amen in his sermon. We knew the pacing of his sermons and the pattern of his voice so well that we were willing to risk a dime or two from our offering money to win the game. At the precise second we thought the sermon would end, we would whisper *Amen* and slap a dime onto the balcony rail.

That was half the time. The rest of the time I actually listened to what our pastor had to say about Jesus. Not that his sermons instructed me or persuaded me to believe. There are no arguments that will satisfy a twelve-year-old boy. I simply absorbed whatever it was that was there in the shadows offering itself to me.

The call came, undramatically as it turned out, well away from the atmospherics of Lent, on a Saturday morning after catechism class when I was alone in my room. It came in the form of the considered reflections and dedicatory prayer of a thirteen-year-old boy. I was trying to memorize my assignment in the blue catechism, which consists of the commandments and articles of faith followed by Luther's explanation of them, the two linked by the question *What does this mean?* It was nothing special in the creed or in Luther's explanation that captured me, but it was the question, repeated over and over on each page: *What does this mean? What does this mean?* It was the question that got me, as if addressed to me and no one but me. Ask it often enough, and *everything* begins to mean and glow with discovery.

I experienced the quiet clarity of that moment as a call, which I accepted on the spot and never doubted for the rest of my life.

By deciding for the ministry I was about to step across the line that for generations had separated our family from the authority of pastoral leadership in the church. When my parents took me to Milwaukee and we attended the opening service of the college, I was as filled with emotion as they.

3

Slow Boat to Cana

 Our church officials called the Lutheran academies like the one I attended "prep schools." Of course, our academies had nothing in common with real prep schools like Andover, Lawrenceville, or Choate. These other schools temporarily isolated boys from the world in order to prepare them for mastery of it. They taught their boys to be comfortable with power, money, privilege, and beauty. Our schools isolated us from the world, too, and taught us to be comfortable with German, Latin, Hebrew, and Greek.

Our prep school consisted of a high

school and a two-year college, which was followed by two years at a senior college and four more years of seminary at another location. The whole arrangement was affectionately known as "the System." My pastor was also a product of the System. The best and only advice he ever gave me was, "Try not to think about all the years," which, amazingly enough, I didn't.

The academy in Milwaukee followed the Old World fashion of enumerating the classes in Latin according to the number of years remaining until graduation. A freshman was a "sextaner," or a sextie, a sophomore a "quintaner" or quinta, and so on until you finally reached the crown of your education: prima. In any other school primaners were nothing but college sophomores. However, in the culture of a Lutheran prep school, they were accorded an exaggerated measure of dignity.

Primaners could tell sexties to eat dirt and frequently did so. The school was held together by an infrastructure of arrogance, hazing, and authoritarianism presided over by well-meaning but mostly inept professors, all of whom had at one time or another served as "effective" Lutheran pastors in places like Frankenmuth, Michigan, or Altenburg, Missouri. Our study of the humanities and languages was considerable, but nothing was undertaken that was not associated with and subservient to the Bible. The senior college offered a far more liberal approach to Christian humanism, but by then we had already been formed in the old ways. We were already finished.

My classmates and I were trained in a system of thought called Lutheran orthodoxy, which arose in Germany as a defense against the authority of the pope and the free thought of the Enlightenment. Our training provided us with a complex set of rules for faith and life. The Germans built an edifice of truth as symmetrical, rational, and unsurprising as a burgher's house, then boxed it up and shipped it to America and to prep schools like the one I attended.

Our teachers began from the premise of an infallible Bible whose evidences of perfection we were trained to defend. From the Bible we deduced dogmatic axioms in Latin. We might as well have netted the Almighty and pinned his wings for display. Our taxonomy of faith included the attributes of God, the algebra of the Trinity, several species of sin, the two natures of Christ, the three modes of his presence, and many other formulas. My religious education appeared to be unrelated to whatever it was I had experienced in the dark Lenten services and in my room after catechism class. College religion reminded me of confirmation class, but without the girls, the spit wads, or the afterglow of discovery.

One day my professor called on me to explain the "nonlocal mode of subsistence by which our Lord was enabled to pass through locked doors," and I replied insolently, "Christ in the woodwork?" My professor laid down his yellowed lecture notes and addressed me with contempt. "Mr. Lischer, are you aware of the creatures that, as we say, come out of the woodwork?" I made no answer. "It's not a rhetorical question, Mr. Lischer. Let's see if you can name some."

I was too humiliated to speak, for I knew I had just been exposed for the theological brat that I was. I couldn't articulate what I found wanting in the traditional terms, not to this professor and in front of the whole class. So I sat there hot in the face and speechless.

We also learned that truth comes with enemies, like shadows on a sunny day. Our teachers vilified all heretics, including the Roman Catholics, who teach that heaven is earned by good works, the Calvinists, who deny the real presence of our Lord in the bread and wine, and, worst of all, the "Enthusiasts," or Pentecostal types, who think our house of doctrine is built on an earthquake fault. That the Spirit might not be bound by our rules was the most pernicious heresy of all. We got the system by rote, the way science students memorize the periodic table. Most of us knew there was something wrong with our education, but we couldn't name it. We weren't clever enough to rebel intellectually, so we rebelled by drinking beer and wasting time in endless bull sessions and epic poker games.

The oddness of my education in Milwaukee, which I sensed but could not analyze, was enough to make me a spectator of my own society. I passed through prep school on a moral holiday, smart enough to master the fundamentals of orthodoxy, but vacuously free of passion or even opinion on most issues.

Whatever it was that was shaping and neutralizing our spirits passed unnoticed by us, partly, I think, because we were distracted by the genuine nuttiness of our professors. Most of our teachers did not hold Ph.D.s and, therefore, had not been academically broken and groomed. Their eccentricities subtly reinforced my personal suspicion that religious education had absolutely nothing to do with normal people or the secular world. I was convinced our teachers could not have survived three days in the world as insurance agents, bank tellers, mechanics, or professors in a real college.

My biology teacher, Korn, spent most class periods declaiming against evolution and vitamin pills. He also showed many movies, like a coach.

My "physics" teacher, Zilber, believed on biblical grounds that the earth was the center of the universe. He also fell off the lecture platform at least once a day. He was reevaluating his Ptolemaic worldview in light of John Glenn's recent mission but died before he got it worked out.

My English teacher, Gunther, said the words "isn't it?" at the end of each sentence, no doubt a relic of the Germanic tic *nicht wahr?* ("isn't it so?") We learned not to flinch when he said, "In 1066 the Normans invaded the British Isles, isn't it?" I was one of his pets and, therefore, frequently invited to read my compositions in class, where they were sullenly received by my classmates.

My German teacher, Herr Hecht, had been a translator at the Nuremberg trials after the war. Nuremberg was the pinnacle of his life and had obviously rendered his present occupation insignificant, with the result that we learned nothing of the German language in his class. He missed the Second War terribly. His key signature phrase was, "So, I said to Goering, 'Look, Hermann . . .'" Herr Hecht was also half-blind, which meant that by the end of the hour he was usually lecturing to a handful of boys, the rest having crawled out on their hands and knees after answering a question or two.

Our Dean of Students, Axelmann, was a former police instructor in the Chicago Police Department. He was a bullet-headed man and had a bullhorn for a mouth. He regularly referred to sexties and quintas as "little shits." He preached in chapel once a year always on the same text from

Proverbs: "My son, if sinners entice thee, consent thou not." I never took sin so seriously as after one of Dean Axelmann's sermons.

My official education was subverted by a little man with black snapping eyes named Harold Henrichs. Every morning at eight o'clock he bounded into a room of thirty boys and let fly a Greek aphorism, which we chorused back to him. Professor Henrichs lived with his mother, and all we knew of his private life was that the two of them ate lunch every Sunday in the cafeteria and then took a walk around the neighborhood. He always wore a natty double-breasted suit with pin stripes. His hair was like the coxcomb of a twelve-year-old, not quite mastered by enough pomade.

"*Kairete, ho ti kalon philon aei,*" he would shout, his eyes darting and rolling up in his head. " 'Hail, a thing of beauty is a joy forever.' " With that began a wonderful hour of Greek banter in which he parried our thickness with a remarkable love for us his students and the Greek language. At the beginning of the course, the aphorisms were as simple as *Gnothi seauton,* "know thyself" or "Man is the measure of all things." "*Metron ariston,*" he would beam, "Right, men? Moderation is best. We follow the middle way, don't we, boys?"

We had no idea.

By the end of the year we were chanting in Greek,

Some say the Muses are nine. How careless!
Lo, Lesbian Sappho is the tenth.

We sang the declensions of *potomos,* "the river," recited verb forms like Chinese schoolchildren, and read and translated from the classics. We *played* in a way I suspect no one in Saxony or St. Louis ever imagined was possible in a ministerial academy. We began with the simplest of classics, Xenophon's *Anabasis ("The Journey"),* which told the story of a wandering regiment's long march home. "*Thalatta! Thalatta!*" "The sea! The sea!" we cried out in unison, as if we, too, were a lost company of hoplites and had just caught sight of our home waters. In a year or two we had graduated to Plato and Aeschylus. By the time we reached seminary we had come full circle to the easy stuff, the Gospel of John and the rest of the New Testament.

Some of my classmates didn't like Greek and refused to learn it. When called to translate in class, they kept an English Bible open at their feet and read off their translations as if producing them on the spot. One boy translated with great stammering concentration, " 'The wind bloweth where it,' h'mm, let me see, 'where it listeth,' I believe it is, sir, 'and thou hearest the sound thereof, but canst not tell whence it cometh, and wither it goeth . . .' "

How dumb *is* it to use the King James Version as a pony? Professor Henrichs just laughed with the rest of the class at the boys who cheated, as if he felt sorry for them. He probably did.

By learning Greek we were exposed to the labial extravagances of classical culture. We met characters like Antigone and Clytemnestra, whose outsized passions did not fit into the familiar stories of our patriarchal tradition. We discovered that some sins, like Clytemnestra's gory defiance of the gods, are so large that they are unattainable by the German middle classes.

To our chagrin, we realized that much of the New Testament is written in a style of Greek resembling that of a modern travel brochure or government pamphlet. In some small way, all this knowledge subverted the aims of the System.

It was our four years of Greek before seminary that taught me to love the possibilities of beauty in God's world. In most seminaries today, the study of Greek is an optional burden; for us it was a lifeline. In my later years when I met Protestant seminarians who had skipped Greek, I pitied them.

Many of the boys in my school were members of the founding families of the church body. Not a few had the same family names as those who sailed on the *Olpers* and other ships that brought Bishop Stephan and his followers to the New World. When it came to the lore of the church, they seemed to be more in the know than I, more securely embedded in the tradition. The reason gradually became clear: These were the sons and grandsons of pastors. It was not necessary for them to learn *about* the tradition; they *were* the tradition.

I soon discovered that many of my classmates had not been called to prep school by God the way I had been, but were sent there, as to a penal colony, by their fathers whom they desperately resented and against whom they acted out endlessly. They alchemized their resentment into a perfect hatred for the school, the church, God, and themselves. I have never again experienced the nihilism I met in the dormitories of my religious prep school.

In my first college dorm—a tenement, really—we lived in three-bedroom suites in a converted apartment house. Most of the inmates in the suites were carryovers from high school, which meant that a new boy, if he wasn't sharp, could have a rough row to hoe.

We had a new secunda on our floor, a shy, eggshaped boy afflicted with nearsightedness. His name was Thomas. Thomas had arrived from a dairy farm north of Wausau with a brand-new set of luggage. He seemed not to understand things that any normal seventeen-year-old should have known. He was backward in ways that entertained our floor for days. To make matters worse for him, when he opened his mouth he sounded exactly like Lawrence Welk. By the end of orientation week Thomas had been dubbed "Turkey" and made the butt of countless jokes.

Turkey was a revelation to me; I had never met anyone like him. But an even greater revelation was the cruelty of his suite mates toward him. He must have represented the piety and naïveté they never had, for they delighted in making his life miserable. On the evening of our inspirational opening service, two of his suite mates, a tall, greasy-looking intellectual named Krueger, and his pal, a blond boy with a perpetual squint, named Zwick, came in drunk. They entertained themselves for a while by baiting Turkey but became bored with it. By the end of the evening Zwick had urinated in Turkey's new Samsonite suitcase. Not long after midterm, Turkey went home and never came back. I carefully observed Turkey but never lifted a finger to help him.

Although I was never the butt of jokes, Turkey and I had a lot in common, beginning with the vocation-shock we both experienced among our classmates. We had arrived in Milwaukee inspired by our call to the ministry, as had many of our fellow students. Once safely deposited by our parents in the dorm, we encountered routine alcoholism, though I would have never called it that, the usual carousing with student nurses, which I wouldn't have minded joining had I been invited, and a number of openly homosexual relationships, which I recognized as different but could not define with a name.

The most difficult adjustment for me proved to be the noise of dormitory life. Our living arrangement was about as far removed as one could imagine from a monastic or contemplative environment. Of course, I knew nothing of the contemplative life, but I harbored the romantic notion that preparation for ministry would be carried out in relative *quiet.* Instead, we studied, prayed, and tried to sleep in the acoustical equivalent of a bowling alley. Our apartment building was made of block with ugly exposed pipe everywhere. Its system of suites created warrens of racket and made privacy impossible. Everyone's pre-Beatle music crashed into everyone else's; boys yelled at one another through the night and into the morning. Enormous, open air shafts communicated the noise from floor to floor.

Our dormitory was located in a shabby neighborhood of closely spaced, wooden houses and towering elms, not far from the old Miller brewery. In the early autumn evenings you could almost taste the yeast in the air drifting through the trees. Loneliness, falling leaves, and the sweetness of fermenting hops was my first formula for the spiritual life.

It was on the sidewalks in our neighborhood that I learned how to pray. I was so lonely that I needed the sound of my own voice to keep me company. Night after night I walked the blocks around my dormitory speaking through the tops of the trees. I told God everything. *Learning three languages at one time is impossible,* I said. *Living in this noise is killing me. Plus, I do not have a friend,* I admitted. *Getting used to blasphemy is breaking me down,* I confessed. But most frequently I told God how cut off from the world I felt, how badly I missed my parents, the solitude of my own room, and the familiar places in my hometown. *I may not become a pastor,* I suggested.

I also gave thanks on those walks, for God was clearly present to me. With neither skill nor experience in talking with others about my unhappiness, God became the secret outlet for everything bottled up within me, the Big Ear to my big hurt. I grew so close to God that it would have been sacrilege to confide in anyone else. Yet this was also the God I was meeting in the Bible and studying in class, the God of Abraham, Isaac, and Jacob, the Father of Jesus. *That* God made a covenant with me in Milwaukee, of all places, never to forsake me no matter what. I drew courage from that promise for a long time.

One of the results of my praying was transference. Something of the communion and triumph experienced in the solitude of prayer is transferred to another, more complicated realm of life. That's what began to happen for me in prep school. I took my newfound serenity into the nihilistic atmosphere of my dorm, into the stale worship services, the bratwurst-infested dining hall, and the orthodox lectures. I perfected the art of abstracting my spirit from any meanness or unpleasantness in my environment. I discovered that once you understand what God can and cannot do, your praying will fill up the emptiness around you and within you. Although I did not realize it at the time, my mother had survived her whole childhood by the same method.

An adolescent crisis is a poor substitute for spirituality. Its strength is also its greatest weakness: The intense privacy of your communion with God excludes others from life's most critical moments. You practice intimacy with God but avoid it like the plague in human relationships. You dramatize your stages of belief and, like a good Protestant, chatter endlessly about your doubts, all at the expense of the greater dramas of history and the suffering of others.

Some of my education occurred in my efforts to get home on weekends, which wasn't very often, because the school did not allow us to go home but twice a semester. The only traveling I had ever done was in the backseat of a 1940 Chevy coupe my dad bought after the war and, later, in our gray '53

Dodge. The only place our family ever went was to a primitive fishing camp in the Ozarks, except for one epic journey across the desert to California. Although we lived near the airport, the thought of boarding an airplane had never entered our minds.

One Friday afternoon I hitchhiked out to the Milwaukee airport, which wasn't much bigger than a good-sized bus station, and bought a ticket on a green and silver DC-7 to St. Louis. The flight was full of salesmen on their way home for the weekend. They wore white broadcloth shirts with loosened ties, chewed on unlit cigars, and boisterously joined in the airline's game of guessing the combined weight of the stewardesses. The pilot flew as low as a crop duster along Lake Michigan so that we could take in the fall foliage, or so he said, but I suspect the lack of a pressurized cabin had something to do with our altitude. We followed Charles Lindbergh's old mail route over the small farming towns and checkered fields of Illinois, crossing the two rivers near Alton before descending into St. Louis. I hadn't bothered to tell my parents I was coming home, which added to the pleasure of my first flight. At seventeen and surrounded by obviously successful businessmen, I felt I was a man of the world.

My family couldn't afford air travel, however, and I usually went back and forth to Milwaukee by train, on the old GM&O, changing at Union Station in Chicago each way. There was nothing like the luxury of reclining in a padded rail car with a good book, nibbling on sandwiches and cookies from home, and watching the world fly by.

On my way back to Milwaukee after Christmas vacation, the train's brakes locked somewhere north of Peoria, and we sat frozen to the tracks for about five hours until they were repaired. That meant that I missed the last train out of Chicago for Milwaukee. There was nothing to do but find a comfortable bench to curl up on until morning.

At about 4 A.M. I opened my eyes and looked into the face of a middle-aged Negro man who was leaning over me as if to wake me or confirm that I was asleep. His wife and teen-aged daughter stood behind him and looked over his shoulder.

"Excuse me," he said politely, "we are looking for our niece. She telephoned us in Milwaukee to tell us her train had got in late. Said she was in the station in Chicago, and hung up, not knowing there are *six* stations in Chicago. We're making the rounds. Have you seen her?"

I hadn't, but it seemed like a worthy adventure, so I joined them in searching Union Station. It was a pretty sleepy place at 4 A.M., and it didn't take us long to eliminate Union from consideration.

When the man discovered that I was bound for Milwaukee, he said, "If you don't mind trailing around with us, when we find her we'll drive you back, too." I was happy to agree, and I joined the expedition. The four of us must have presented an odd sight, traipsing from rest room to rest room and bench to bench, peering under newspapers that doubled for blankets, looking for the lost girl.

We drove to the Dearborn Station but with the same result. Its cavernous spaces were filled with drowsy travelers—but no niece from Milwaukee. Before we left for the LaSalle Street Station, in a city that was now beginning to stir, the man called his home in Milwaukee only to have his niece answer the telephone. She had taken the bus!

Relieved and tired, we drove north toward Milwaukee just as the sun was coming up. After we had cleared the last Chicago suburbs, I remarked, somewhat casually, that this adventure had given me an appetite for breakfast. I was hungry. We were all hungry. We had just driven beneath one of several Fred Harvey restaurants located on the overpasses between Chicago and Milwaukee, and I was ready for juice, pancakes, bacon, and coffee.

The car got quiet until the father said, "That's fine with us. You can take our order."

His remark did not register on me at all.

At the next Fred Harvey we pulled into the parking lot, and each member of the family gave me a detailed order for breakfast, which I wrote down on a piece of notebook paper. I entered the restaurant, gave the order, and brought it out in bags and paper cups with plastic utensils. With other travelers around us locking their cars and pouring into the restaurant, the four of us ate breakfast in the parking lot as the sun rose above the interstate.

By the time we got to Milwaukee, it was a beautiful morning, and the circumstances of our breakfast had finally begun to register on me—me, the unfinished product of segregated schools, churches, libraries, swimming pools, and restaurants. I had never eaten in a diner where the customer at the counter beside me was black. Never worshiped in a church where the Christian in the next pew was black. Never had a high school or college teacher who was black. Never a friend who was black. The banality of the arrangement was obvious. How routinely the Negro family incorporated this indignity into its daily system of life, like an old wound one learns to live with.

The family dropped me off at the college to resume my theological education where I had left it three days earlier. Except it could not be the same. The Negro family left me grateful for the ride, but thoroughly chastened by my brief course in segregation. I would never survey my lily-white life with quite the dumb satisfaction I had before. A whole new world of sin was opening before me and offering to educate me. I could feel my new knowledge in my stomach and chest.

I arrived on campus just as classes were beginning for the day. There was no time to go to my room to pick up my new texts and notebooks. I was still carrying my suitcase when I sprinted to my first class of the new semester.

I took my last two years of college on another campus, followed by four years of seminary. Senior college and seminary added sophistication to my knowledge, but, God help me, my ship was launched in prep school.

Over the years, the cast of characters changed little in the schools I attended. Krueger remained the self-conscious intellectual he was when I first met him, though he had shifted from medieval to analytic philosophy. Zwick's basic cruelty never fully disappeared. Terry Henke remained the gifted athlete and alcoholic he was in prep school. Nels Fryonyard (our only Norwegian), designated by himself *ho sophos*, the wise one, skipped classes, and held court in his room at seminary much as he had six years earlier in Milwaukee. Dickie Burgel, who as a primaner was famous for keeping student council minutes in Latin, continued to shine as a linguist in his seminary years. A few dropped out to become teachers or lawyers, and a couple died in Vietnam, but most stayed with the System like passengers on a slow-moving but reliable freighter.

As the years passed, I moved through the System, too—or it carried me forward—in the company of the same young men. It was like being aboard the *Olpers* with no land in sight. We were even seated alphabetically in the same arrangement year after year and in school after school. I formed some lasting friendships in those years but also developed claustrophobia in the presence of people who had hemmed me in too long. Once, in the dining hall at the senior college, I remember suffering an allergic reaction to the chronic presence of a boy from Iowa. I had to leave the table and rush from the room. He was an ordinary person as bland as cottage cheese who had never done me a wrong, but in that odd moment I realized that his open, homely face had become a part of the wallpaper of my life. I had to get out of there.

I didn't ride through eight years of education on a crisis, nor did my co-travelers in the System. We put one foot ahead of another as if following snowprints through a Wisconsin woods, but with no horizon in view. Some of us emerged from the journey open to new learning and experience, and some fancied ourselves as completed ministers of the gospel. But all of us were missing something. Our education taught us to speak the System's language, but it did not disclose the language that "speaks us" by possessing our spirit and shaping us as human beings. It is not a question of how did we survive the voyage. Surely, at one time or another every boy in that school must have fought through a crisis as quietly as I did mine. The real question is, how did those long years open a path to ministry?

There's a New Yorker cartoon in which a pompous-looking doctor hands a prescription to his patient and says, "Take this. It will either cure you or kill you." I'm afraid my education was something like that. It didn't attend to the gifts of the Spirit, such as love, joy, peace, patience, and long-suffering. It did not help me develop Jesus' instinct for compassion toward the outsider or outrage toward injustice. Our professors didn't invite us into the agony of race or war; they never intimated that God could grieve over the poor or that Jesus really cared about the fate of women. Perhaps it was the substructure of Greek humanism that kept us to the middle way, which caused us to overlook God's grief and anger and the essential excesses of Christianity.

The spirituality imparted to us was the safe spirituality of structure but not of passion or abandonment. The theological categories we memorized would either stifle true spirituality for the rest of our lives or provide the skeleton for a growing and adapting organism. "We've given you a vocabulary," my teachers seemed to say, "Now, what are you going to do with it?"

Likewise, the enforced chapel services into which we dutifully filed morning and evening could either kill you or make you well. If you paid too much attention to the sermons of Dean Axelmann and others, you might die in the spirit. But we also sang Matins every morning, and four hundred male voices chanting the *Te Deum* couldn't be wrong:

> *To You all angels cry aloud,*
> *The heavens and all the powers therein.*
> *To You cherubim and seraphim continually do cry,*
> *Holy, holy, holy, Lord God of Sabaoth!*

Take that prescription five mornings a week for eight years, and it just might save your life.

What my classmates and I learned to sing in prep school we at last engaged intellectually in seminary. In the combustive 1960s, we all read the gospel as "freedom." We reveled in Jesus' remarkable freedom to stir things up and violate social and religious rules. We were exhilarated from afar by Martin Luther King, Jr., who preached freedom and eloquently traced it out like a figure in a tapestry all across the nation.

In my final year at seminary I took two courses with theologian Robert Bertram: one entire course on Luther's interpretation of Galatians, the "magna charta of Christian freedom," and the other on the philosophy of history, in which Marxist notions of the future were brought into dialogue with Christian hope. Bertram was as orthodox as they come, but, unlike my prep school teachers, he had a big picture of the world. He knew how to turn every statement of doctrinal truth into a declaration of power that did not exclude those who had come on other boats. He held the tradition up to the light, like a jeweler who patiently turns a stone until it yields its greatest brilliance, and he did it with low-key Socratic patience. By the time one of Bertram's classes ended, we were often passionate about truths we hadn't even suspected at its beginning.

By the mid-1960s, our seminary faculty and many of the students, like me, were already in rebellion against the aridity of religious orthodoxy. A new spirit—and an inevitable split—was moving through the church. We had begun our theological pilgrimage in the last placid years of the Eisenhower regime. We were ending with the bang of Vietnam, civil rights, the sexual revolution, assassinations, and the invasion of Cambodia. Everything had changed. A few classmates and I watched the 1968 Democratic convention in Chicago on a little black-and-white portable TV in my apartment. We were astonished to see clerical collars among the mob of dissident Democrats storming the gates of Mayor Daley's organization.

We identified our theology with the artisans of a new humanity wherever we could find them, in whatever discipline or sphere of life. Our heroes were John XXIII, Camus, the Kennedys, the Berrigans, Lennon, Marcuse, Dubček, and King. When Bob Dylan sang,

The slow one now
Will later be fast,
As the present now

Will later be past,
The order is rapidly fadin'.
And the first one now
Will later be last,
For the times they are a-changin',

we thought we heard the rasping echo of prophecy. We were already living in "the world come of age" that Dietrich Bonhoeffer had predicted from his Nazi prison cell. Religion was being synthesized into something deeper and more comprehensive than the formulas that had been drummed into our heads.

In the late autumn of my final year in seminary, Thomas Merton died in Bangkok while exploring the Zen tradition of Buddhism. Earlier Paul Tillich had died after a lifetime of doing theology on the boundaries between religion, art, and psychology. Our seminary mourned their passing, but only *un*officially in the commemorations of a few students and bold teachers.

I myself had inexplicably developed an interest in the Christian-Marxist dialogue. I say "inexplicably" because what's a nice bourgeois Lutheran from St. Louis doing at a meeting with Communists or writing a doctoral dissertation on Marxist and Christian anthropology? The young Marx's humanistic manuscripts had recently been discovered, the Prague Spring was in full bloom, and Christianity's rapprochement with secular humanism seemed a religious and historical certainty. The Soviet invasion of Czechoslovakia in August 1968 put an end to "Marxism with a human face" everywhere except in college philosophy departments and my doctoral dissertation.

In our infatuation with dialogue, many of us overestimated the saving possibilities of psychotherapy and socialism and other popular models of redemption. We neglected the distinctive qualities of the church's story and took for granted the ordinary practices of the Christian life. After all, we had grown up with sermons, sacraments, and church suppers. What was special about them?

We also assumed dogma had to be as gray and oppressive as Milwaukee in midwinter. The point, we thought, was to *translate* the gospel into words like "authenticity," "freedom," "solidarity," and other political slogans. We were sure we could expose the kernel of truth in the Christian message while shucking off its embarrassing myths, rituals, and, above all, the quaint piety of its adherents.

The endless years of our education had opened a breach between the naive religious faith with which my classmates and I had entered the System and the even more naive secular faith with which we exited it. Without fully realizing it, some of us were quietly canceling the terms of our call. My friends and I accepted assignments like the Cana church because eight years of theological education had rendered us uncertain of our identity and, like our professors, unemployable in the real world. After years of grooming, we were no longer sure what it meant to be a *pastor* or if we wanted to be one. Whatever it was that once called us and shaped our spirits now eluded us. Reluctant voyagers, we had neither the imagination nor the courage to jump ship.

4

The Next Thing I Knew, We Were Married

 I sat on an unpacked box and looked out the parsonage windows at a long line of headlights on the prairie. It might have been a funeral procession or an invasion of aliens. *They are coming for me,* I thought, *my time is up.* The service of installation would begin in thirty minutes.

"They don't expect you to stay, you know."

"What? Why would you say that?"

"Only because it's true." Reuben Braun was the senior pastor of our circuit. He was a handsome old man who had given his life to ministry in several towns on the circuit, including East Alton, Cherry Grove, Blaydon, and now Two Rivers. His job was to oversee the congregation during the vacancy and to help it choose a new pastor. He seemed amused that a young Ph.D. from the University of London was about to take the reins of the smallest and most isolated parish in the district.

"They're quite open about it. They think you've got bigger fish to fry. They know the rules. You've got to get your three years of parish service in before you're eligible for a teaching position. If they get three years out of you, they will have gotten their money's worth."

"What are you saying, that I've come to a church with an inferiority complex?"

"I've never called it that—or anything—but now that you mention it . . . *Cana* is a kind of byword in this county. You have to wonder about settlers who would name their town and church after a village, and one that's still buried under a pile of rubble at that. I don't know how it got started, but if you want to say somebody's backward, just say they come from New Cana. If something's small or a bit outdated, it must be from New Cana. You get the idea. They're proud of you, actually. I mean, they don't know you yet, but here's a young *doctor* of theology in New Cana, of all places. They need *something* here."

"Well, they shouldn't feel that way. I am glad to be here. I'm looking forward to this ministry."

"Of course you are." Then, sounding like the death-row chaplain in *I Want to Live*, he added, "Let's go over. It's about time."

It was about time. It was high time. The leaders at Cana held a peculiar notion of what a pastor could or could not do before his installation. As it turned out, I was not allowed to perform any public duties of the ministry before my official swearing in. Even though I had been ordained, I wasn't allowed to preach or preside at the communion table. I would maintain my virginal state until the wedding day.

The one preinstallation event I attempted had turned out less successfully than I had hoped. In fact, it was a minor disaster. I invited the leaders of the church to the parish hall for an informal supper followed by small-group discussions. With several of the women's help I arranged card tables around the room and covered them with plastic checkered tablecloths. The idea was that for one evening we would turn the dreary parish hall into an intimate bistro. We would have a spaghetti supper after which we would break into small groups where we would get to know one another and share our vision of the congregation's future. Each group would have a trained facilitator. I would rotate from group to group.

The evening went well until we broke into small groups. The members of my first group treated one another with stiff formality as though they were strangers and not cousins and neighbors. They introduced themselves for my benefit but none of the participants expanded on their name and the location of their family's farm. A few smiled at me sheepishly.

I meant to break the ice and perhaps demonstrate a little leadership when I asked the first group, "Why do you want me to be your pastor?" I admit the question was ill-conceived, but its point was to generate a conversation about our new partnership in ministry.

The first to speak was a man named Leonard Semanns. He said rather cheerfully, "Well, I didn't vote for you, but I know we will have a very good church with you as our pastor" or some such thing. His wife studied the carpet intently, as if she had dropped a contact lens. The next man—only the men spoke in this exercise—said without a hint of embarrassment, "I didn't vote for you either, but I agree with Leonard." I looked anxiously to the next person in the circle, a serious young man in a starched cowboy shirt and a string tie, and when he flushed and averted his eyes from mine I knew my plan had been a mistake.

The participating clergy were gathered in the tiny sacristy beside the chancel. There we would vest and then walk around the exterior of the church in the frigid January air and make our procession from an even smaller narthex. I was meeting my fellow pastors for the first time. My initial impression of them was that they all looked like my father—silver-haired, lots of widow's peaks—like Reuben Braun, handsome old men.

I peered through the door at the gathering congregation, and there was my father with my mother in their usual place in any church, about four rows back on the lectern side. This habit reflected my father's conservatism. He did not sit in the front row for fear of vaunting himself above others, nor in the back because the last pew in any church is reserved for ushers and noisy children. My father would not betray his game face in church; I never saw him laugh or express any emotion in the sanctuary of any church because it was *church*. There he was—this man to whom as a child I had related solely through the rhythm of a baseball endlessly tossed and caught—now planted with his arms folded and his jaw set, waiting for the new pastor to appear.

Only a month earlier, my call to this church had been the occasion of the worst argument my father and I ever had. We were in the backyard of my parents' house trying to shore up the sagging limb of the sweet gum tree. Tornado-like winds had brought one side of the tree dangerously low to the ground, and now we were trying to get a couple of two-by-fours under it for support. The tree meant something to both of us because twenty years earlier I had "helped" him plant it, though neither of us mentioned it or would have admitted that the tree stood for anything other than a tree.

The official invitation from the congregation, as dictated by the denomination's board of assignments, had arrived weeks earlier, but I had not been able to bring myself to accept it. Now, straining under the limb of the sweet gum, my father wanted to know why. It was uncharacteristic of him to probe beneath simple events and to explore motives or emotions. I wasn't prepared for the depth of his feelings.

"Have you answered this call yet?" he asked.

"You know I haven't."

"You're damn right I know you haven't. What's the holdup?"

One little "damn" from my father meant more than a hundred goddamns from lesser men. It was not a casual utterance. It signified anger and not annoyance. If I had been thinking clearly, I might have remembered that my father blew up at me only when he thought I was endangering something in my own nature or venturing into self-destructive territory.

Defending, I answered, "There is a chance that Christ Church in St. Louis will call me. If I can hold off Cana and wait it out, it could work out . . ." I almost completed the sentence, "to my advantage," but wisely let it go and began anew.

"I am looking for a significant ministry. Cana is very nice but is it significant? That is to say . . ."

"Significant," he repeated, as if I'd just said "Communist" or "lunar." "You have been preparing for this"—we both knew what "this" was—"for more than ten years. You've piled up more schooling after high school than most people accumulate in a lifetime." (He meant himself, who had no schooling to speak of.) "How many languages have you learned? Three? Six? These people are saying, 'Come, we've been waiting for you. You can be our pastor,' which is what you said you wanted all along. And now it has to be *significant*? Isn't the ministry significant? I thought it was. All of it. Everywhere."

"Yes. Right. Yeah. I guess I want to have an impact on people's lives."

"There are people in New Cana, in case you hadn't noticed."

"I know there are people . . ."

Then to gain traction he dropped the argument into a lower gear. "You have a wife, a child, another on the way. You are twenty-eight years old and do not work. Have never worked. High school, college, seminary, Ph.D., but no work. Books and degrees, professors and big ideas, but no work. You don't even *know* that you don't work. You think books are work. You don't even miss it. These people are offering you work, and you are too—what, special?—to take it."

When I was a kid, one of the tapes my parents ran through my head was my father's willingness to do any kind of work during the Great Depression. "Your father sold bug powder," my mother said. "It certainly was discouraging. It was not what he wanted, but he did it. He also operated an elevator. He could never open the door level with the floor, but he was not ashamed."

Work, work, work.

"You don't understand what I want. I am weighing this offer, but it has to be right for me."

"It's not an offer, it's a call," he interrupted.

"Your whole generation was out of work for a decade. I don't have those kinds of insecurities."

"You are right about one thing," my father admitted. "I don't understand you." And then of the sweet gum he said, "Leave it on the ground."

If he ever thought again of our conversation, my father never let on. For all I knew, he was reprising the whole tirade in his head while we waited for the prelude to end. I would never know. But between us, there would be no further probing into my vocational uncertainty.

Then the procession began.

The aisle of even the humblest church can appear long and forbodingly grand to a bride on her father's arm, a widow behind a casket, or a candidate for ordination. I remember an old relative of mine who lived in a nursing home who spoke of the corridor on which she lived as her "street" and of the other inmates as "my neighbors across the street." The whole world and everything in it had come indoors. It worked quite well for her.

As we began to process down the worn maroon carpet, we followed the cross, two candles carried behind it, and a Bible-bearer down what now had become a long and mysterious path toward the chancel. My universe had just come indoors, and my place in it was being revealed to me.

High on the east wall of the sanctuary the Trinity window glimmered with the help of some jury-rigged outdoor lighting. Three bare light bulbs out back, corresponding to the three divine persons, were trained on the window. A good deal of the church building appeared to be in disrepair, but the Trinity window was in splendid shape.

Beneath the window the cross of the Victorious Christ was mounted to the wall. The crucified Jesus was robed in royal vestments and giving a two-fingered benediction from the cross. The wooden altar was dressed in red brocade for the fire of the Spirit and the blood of the martyrs. On the nave-level of the floor, centered beneath the accumulated symbolism of the Holy Trinity, the crucifix, and the crimson altar, sat my chair, which was actually an easy chair borrowed from someone's parlor, that tonight and only tonight would serve as the seat of honor for the new pastor.

I was moved when I saw that alignment of things. I could only imagine the mysteries of all our lives and how they would unfold beneath the cross and our orthodox window. It didn't concern me that the acolytes had mismatched outfits or that the crucifer was wearing black high-topped sneakers, that the three lights behind the window were a little too specific, that the chair was not a *cathedra*, or that the aisle really wasn't all that long or impressive. Because it wasn't an aisle at all anymore but my road to the chair and to my call and my truest self and to the ministry of Christ's church.

Along the road lay various way stations through which I had passed: the damp privacy of my call, my parents' love, loneliness at prep school, the ghosts of Turkey, Krueger, Zwick, and the others, the pleasures of Greek ("a thing of beauty is a joy forever!"), and even the hard argument with my father. I was about to cross the line I had dreamed of as a boy.

The words of the service struck me as archaic and hollow. I promised to adorn the doctrine of Christ with a godly and holy life, and the congregation promised to receive with meekness the engrafted word—whatever that was supposed to mean. Intoned with pious solemnity, the words themselves made little impression on me. The music, on the other hand, redeemed the spoken word and touched my spirit. When we sang

> Let my prayer be set forth before thee as incense,
> And the lifting up of my hands as the evening
>   sacrifice,

my head momentarily filled with the voices of my classmates in Milwaukee singing Vespers. I could almost see the church's callused hands cradling my uncertain prospects for ministry and lifting them to the Lord above.

A few days earlier the yellow Pinto had pulled up to the parsonage once again, this time behind a U-haul truck driven by a friend. The trustees had offered us five hundred dollars for moving expenses with the proviso that if we could move ourselves, we could keep the money—a typical country-church deal. Of course, we leaped at the money.

Now my very pregnant wife, Tracy, was taking her first look at the parsonage with our daughter, Sarah, chattering in her car seat. As we looked at the house from the road, faces of church members peered out from every front window. The men had completed painting the interior, and the women were sorting through our boxes, unpacking them, and putting away their contents. It made us feel good to see the faces. The scene was like a Breughel painting or a fun house at a country fair. We were touched by their welcome but a little unnerved by our lack of privacy. Already our pitiful possessions had become public knowledge in New Cana. Someone must have noticed, "The preacher has a painting of a naked lady with a cat. I wonder where *that* goes?" And of Tracy's bikini briefs, "It's gonna be a little chilly in this house for *these!*"

Now, with the entire congregation, including the 49.5 percent who evidently had *not* voted for me, singing

> We bid thee welcome in the name
> Of Jesus, our exalted head,

I felt properly welcomed but no less strange. The cloying lyrics only reinforced the exaggerated formality of the occasion.

In his sermon the bishop compared my installation to a marriage. If that was true, it was an arranged marriage, for this bride and groom had not fallen in love or chosen one another. My spaghetti debacle had already proven that.

The congregation and I were insignificant figures in a larger and older pattern. The church has always identified its potential leaders, indoctrinated them, and then rudely inserted them in some setting or other where they almost never belong. At seminary we brooded over the mysteries of God for four years, only to turn up later as chaplains to covered-dish suppers and car washes with the youth. One part of the church goes to great expense in order to prepare a theologian for another part of the church that wants a guitar player. Like misshelved books, we are *there* waiting to be used, but will anyone ever find us? As partners in an arranged marriage, my congregation and I might fall madly in love, which, in this creaky old church already seemed unlikely to me, or we could accommodate ourselves to what, if we were honest, each of us knew to be a mismatch.

When I knelt before the bishop, the white-haired pastors formed a circle around me like a coven of witches. They placed their hands on my head and shoulders, shrouding me in the long folds of their surplices. But instead of intoning *Double, double toil and trouble,* each in his turn spoke a blessing or recited a Bible passage prefaced by, "Brother Richard . . ." except for Reuben Braun, who said sweetly, "My dear Rick."

Finally, the bishop asked the congregation, "Are you willing to receive your pastor as a minister of God and show him love, honor, and obedience in the Lord?" They said, "I do" or words to that effect, and the next thing I knew, we were married.

Afterward, at the reception, my new flock circled around me and eyed me warily. Everyone seemed ill at ease, which was odd since we were meeting for the second time on their turf, in their decrepit parish hall, around their antique punch bowl, surrounded by the daguerreotypes of their former pastors. No small groups this time. I was struck by how closely my new parishioners resembled one another, not merely in style of dress and silver-rimmed eyeglasses, but in their tentative way of smiling, as though apologizing for something. "Don't worry," they seemed to say, "this will be over soon."

While I was making mental notes of the occasion's incongruities, I failed to notice the biggest incongruity of all. That would have been *me.* My very presence had produced an awkward situation. My new parishioners were expected to welcome an inexperienced, twenty-eight-year-old stranger into a community that was as tightly sealed as a jar of home-canned pickles. The church had decreed that henceforth I would be spiritual guide, public teacher, and beloved sage to people whose lives and work I couldn't possibly understand. With a stroke of his wand, God—or the bishop—had just made me an expert in troubled marriages, alcoholism, teen sex, and farm subsidies. *Of course* my new parishioners were standoffish! They knew better than I that we were not really persons who were meeting for refreshments; we were social roles awkwardly dancing around one another but, who knew? perhaps destined to grind against one another. I'm glad I didn't understand the absurdity of my installation.

If I failed to catch the essential madness of the occasion, I also missed the goodness it represented. Who could have invented a job called *pastor*? What CEO would create a task force in which savvy and self-sufficient farmers subject themselves to the authority of a recent graduate student? The role was simply *there*, waiting to be filled. It had been in New Cana for a century, and, like an old reliable well, it would remain long after I was gone. The Germans referred to ordination as "office-grace," but that term would have made little sense to me as we loitered about the punch bowl on my first evening as *Herr Pastor*.

I was attended to by a friendly couple named Leonard and June Semanns, who were apparently leaders of the church. It was Leonard whose cheerful "I didn't vote for you" had set off the string of uninvited confessions a couple weeks earlier. As it turned out, Leonard was the president of the congregation and June was in charge of the Sunday School. They introduced me to the few brave souls who were willing to hazard a full-frontal conversation with the new pastor.

I noticed a threesome standing apart from the rest in the shadows. A boy about ten years old was tethered to a great bull of a man with a red face and a flat head. Another, older boy stood to one side. With a rehearsed smile and a permanently arched eyebrow, the little boy appeared unnaturally pleased to be stuck at so dull a gathering. The older boy had lank bleached hair and wore many chains. He did not appear pleased to be at the reception. The man, presumably the boys' father, looked like an enlisted man who had wandered by mistake into the officers' club and was overcome by the splendor of it all. Leonard didn't introduce them to me, but the little boy and his flat-headed father grinned across the room at me.

I remembered something Reuben Braun said to me before the service. "Tonight you can count on meeting your most supportive lay leaders. Also your biggest headaches. They'll all be there."

5

A Week of Signs

 On the Tuesday morning after my installation Leonard Semanns came by my study in the parsonage to orient me to the community. He brought along the elders, three men who were charged with the spiritual oversight of the congregation, which in practice amounted to making sure that Sunday services ran on time and that Confirmation instruction was provided. As I would learn in succeeding weeks, they gathered every Sunday in the sacristy for ritual kibitzing before and after each service.

The trustees, on the other hand, were in charge of the church's physical properties, which lately included the vexing problem of how to fix the broken cross on top of the steeple. They were not required to possess the spiritual aptitude of the elders. Unlike the trustees, who were almost always old and retired, and unlike the members of the cemetery committee who were even older—older than the dirt they supervised—the elders tended to be middle-aged, the sons of trustees.

That morning Leonard and his cousin August Semanns, or Gus as he was called, spread out a hand-drawn map of the parish with each house and farm noted and labeled. Members of the church were marked in red. The two of them, along with elders Bud Jordan and Ronnie Semanns stood in their overalls in a respectful circle around my desk. Their running commentary reminded me of a "talking map" I had once seen at the Gettysburg National Battlefield. Press a button near the site of a particular battle, and a recorded voice begins explaining it. I had been heard to complain that the church kept no roster of its members. How can you organize a church without a list? I wanted to know. With their talking map they were remedying the situation.

As Leonard gave me the rundown on each of our households, he confirmed a suspicion that had been growing in me since the ill-fated spaghetti supper: Approximately 75 percent of my members bore the same last name, Semanns.

"That would be Milfords' place. Him and Clara moved there when his dad quit farming. You want to see a man plow a straight furrow, you watch old Ben." Leonard and Gus exchanged knowing looks. Then they shared the same look with Bud Jordan and Ronnie Semanns, who passed it between them like a secret handshake. "You want to see the crookedest furrow in county, then I believe you'd have to visit Martin's place in the spring." The four laughed uproariously. They were not bothering with last names and may have noticed my confusion. "Milford's Clara and Martin's Clara are both Dullmanns—of the Cherry Grove Dullmanns. Their mothers were cousins. Semanns and Dullmanns have been clost."

"Tell me this," I asked. "Since there are so many Semanns, why isn't the town named Semannsville instead of New Cana?" I had to laugh at my own clever use of the name, which in my own mind was always spelled Semen. (I knew a fellow by that name in prep school, though with an *a*, who suffered considerably for it.) Ronnie started to explain, but I cut him off. "Anyway, Semanns is the right name for farmers, isn't it," I said. "You know, since it means *seed* in Latin." The four looked at me without expression.

Leonard continued as if I hadn't spoken. "So you can see, Pastor, that every house on the Loop Road belongs to a member."

"What's the blank space behind the church?" I asked.

"That ain't nothin' but the Brush," said Ronnie.

"And the road?"

"There's another loop called Snake Road, which also leads to a back way to Dempster and, if you know what you're doin', another loop to Cherry Grove. Nobody goes that way. We don't have any members from the Brush. That's mainly Irish and Hoosiers back in there. No church people."

"Hoosiers?"

"You know, Trash," Gus clarified.

"Have we ever had members from the Brush?" I asked. The only non-Semanns in the group, Bud, who worked as a plumber when he wasn't farming, recollected something. "There was one, an immigrant . . ." Then he stopped mysteriously and gave no indication that he would continue any time soon. I wanted to say "I thought we were all immigrants on this prairie," but held my tongue.

"Let me ask you about somebody else," I said. "The big man at the reception with the two boys. Where are they on the map?"

"That'd be Buster Toland. He works at the garage. The young'un is Max. Poor Bust owes everybody. And Max, well, he's slow, Pastor, real slow." Gus Semanns elongated the sentence's duration as if to make his point. "It's not all there. The big kid is Lacy. He's nothin' but trouble, him and his motorcycle. There's a little girl, too. Angela. They call her Little Angel. And she is, too. How she's a Toland, I'll never know."

"Does Buster have a wife?" The foursome sighed as if about to tell me that I needed a new fuel pump.

"He does," Ronnie said regretfully.

At this point Leonard took command. "That family would have a chance at being a decent family—only a chance, mind you, what with them boys' problems—if they had a woman who was solid. But she ain't. Beulah went mental after Little Angel come along and stayed mental. Plus, she's on dope."

"Dope!" I exclaimed.

"Yes," he replied adamantly. "I call it dope. She's got every doctor in Alton, Blaydon, and Cherry Grove prescribing her pills. And Medicare pays. You and I pay!"

The subject was getting reframed in a hurry, so I asked again, "Where are they on the map?"

"Next to Buford's Garage where Buster works."

"I don't see a house for them."

"They're renters."

Later that afternoon I stopped by Ronnie's dad and mom's place. Bertie was a former trustee who had moved up the ladder to the cemetery committee. Lois once had a leading role in the congregation that roughly corresponded to June Semanns's. Now she was content to keep their little house, quilt on Wednesdays in the church basement, and look after Bertie. Bertie was too frail to plow, but that did not stop him from dressing as if he were about to jump on the tractor at any minute. He was dressed like a farmer doll in a freshly ironed pale blue workshirt under a pair of gray denim overalls with a narrow blue stripe. The red kerchief around his neck was knotted to the side the way the film actor David Niven might have done.

The senior Semannses lived in a tiny ranch-style bungalow beside the home place now occupied by their son's family. When I arrived I was greeted by an angrily barking German shepherd. The dog insisted I remain in my Pinto with the windows up until Bertie appeared in the doorway and with many good-natured gestures invited me to get out of the car. He motioned me to a side door that led directly to the basement to which I was accompanied by the dog, now hoarse with barking, whose sport I had become. In fact, I had become sport to any who witnessed my panicked entrance to the house. I was already promising myself that I would never set foot on this property again. And I never did, because of the dog and other reasons.

Bertie and Lois cordially guided me through the mudroom and led me down the half-stair to a paneled rathskeller where several of the older men of the congregation were gathered in a semicircle. Over the years I would learn that the back door was the entrance of choice and the basement the usual place for entertaining guests in New Cana.

After the introductions, the men and I sat and exchanged a series of formal statements about the weather, about my hometown of St. Louis, about the treacherous condition of the county road (due to wet dirt over fresh oil), and about the broken cross, but mostly we looked at the linoleum floor in silence. Occasionally one of the men would exhale in the shape of a word, "Yeah" or "Well," the way an old dog sighs before going to sleep, but for my part it seemed like a game of who could go the longest without talking.

Finally, at what I am tempted to call a lull in the conversation, Bertie fixed me with his cagey blue eyes and asked offhandedly, "Pastor, will you have a beer?"

Everyone looked at me, and with only an extra second's hesitation—just enough to make it an unnatural response—I said, "Sure."

Bertie went to a refrigerator filled with Budweisers. He selected exactly one bottle, opened it, and brought it to me. The seven old men watched me intently as I drank it. "You're not having one?" I asked.

"Naw," Bertie replied in a tone that seemed to ask, "What kind of man would drink a beer at two in the afternoon?" His eyes almost smiled as he said it.

The point of the exercise? The new pastor is either one of the boys or a moral slacker. I left knowing I had been tested, but unsure of my grade.

My first week brought a tumble of pastoral duties. Although I had yet to preach my first sermon or celebrate my first public Eucharist, I brought communion to one of my parishioners in the hospital. His name was Alfred Semanns and he was dying of complications resulting from admission to the dingiest American hospital I had ever seen, Prairieview General. Its only ward reminded me of a dorm I had slept in as a boy at summer camp. There were twelve beds, one nurse, and no private or semiprivate rooms.

Alfred and I had the place pretty much to ourselves as I prepared for the momentous event of my first Eucharist. Only the community rightly celebrates communion and when private distribution is necessary, the pastor should bring the consecrated elements from the community's Sunday meal. But Alfred was sick, dying, and through his daughters and son he had asked for the Eucharist. He apparently didn't mind that it was a stranger who would bring him the Bread of Life.

I brought my kit, which included a tiny paten and a screw-together chalice, a seminary graduation gift. We made the confession and absolution together and recited Psalm 46, "God is our refuge and strength; a very present help in trouble." His gruff voice betrayed no emotion as he recited the words, which he uttered like a man breaking rocks with a sledge.

We were making Eucharist on a hospital tray on wheels. I poured some wine into my little chalice and set it before him, but when I reached farther into the kit I discovered to my horror that I had forgotten the wafers. "I don't have any bread," I said. Then, as if he were deaf as well as dying, I repeated myself more loudly, "*No bread.*"

Alfred looked deeply into my face and sighed like the men in Bertie's rathskeller. His eyes quickly surveyed the ward, as mine had done a split-second earlier, in hopes of spotting a stray scrap of bread on a lunch tray. No such luck. He said in his same rough voice, "Well, why don't you get some bread . . . *Pastor.*" He stressed the last word of the sentence in order to remind me of something about me. "I'll be here."

The hospital kitchen was closed until 5 P.M., so I drove into town to the nearest Lutheran church where I humiliated myself before one of the old men who had helped install me and borrowed a few communion wafers. I then sped back to the hospital and entered as though nothing had happened.

Take eat. This is my body given in death for you, I said for the first time in my life. Receive this host. Jesus is the host at every sacramental meal, no matter if it is celebrated at the high altar of a great cathedral or in the deserted ward of a country hospital. Jesus hosted our little meal, too, and did not forsake Alfred. I was his stand-in on this bleak occasion, but I had proved less than hospitable. With ten years of theology under my belt, and a passing acquaintance with many mysteries and much knowledge, I had scrambled awkwardly to produce a scrap of God's body for a dying man.

One of Billy Semanns's daughters was waiting for the new pastor. She was ready to have a proper wedding. This word was only relayed to me by telephone, as Billy himself, who was perennially between jobs and wives and lived alone in a camper east of Prairieview, had had nothing to do with the church ever since someone from Cana had asked him for a financial pledge. That had been fourteen years ago.

"The church is only interested in my money," he had complained, implying that this church, like all the rest of them, was preying on his vast wealth in order, say, to build a marble campanile in the parking lot or to support the voluptuous lifestyle of a missionary in East St. Louis. According to the grapevine, the previous pastor had offended him by saying, "Billy, you don't *have* any money. What would we want with you?"

The daughter and her intended arrived at the parsonage promptly at five, he having taken off a few minutes early from his job as an asphalt man on the county's roads. Leeta and Shane were seventeen and eighteen years old respectively. Aside from the family's trademark smile, she bore no resemblance to my imaginary picture of her oafish father or to anyone I had already met in the family. She was darkly, even beautifully, beetle-browed, a feature that lent determination to her young face from the first hello. Shane was a serious sort of young man with close-set eyes and a curly page boy that was already thinning on top. Thirty seconds into the interview, she seemed strong, he seemed weak. Together, they were so nervous that they couldn't even slouch. Teenagers simply do not sit as straight as those two were sitting in front of my desk.

"Shane and I want to get married, and Shane wants to take adult instructions, don't you, hon? I'd come with him every time. I promise," she said to Shane, and smiled sweetly at both of us. "We want to do everything right. Same goes for Shane's baptism. We won't wait forever to have that done, will we, hon? We could start studying up on the baptism anytime soon."

Then, in a move that seemed rehearsed, she opened her pea coat to reveal what I'd known was in there the moment she had entered the room, a little Semanns about six months along. She pulled her coat back the way an amateur stickup man flashes his piece in a 7-Eleven. Leeta was wearing a white polyester shift, awkwardly high on her legs and tight across the midriff. The two of them had come to rehab what little they had of a past and to begin a new future. They wanted to get off on the right foot—two poor, uneducated teenagers, one of them pregnant, the other unbaptized, both of them scared and excited at the same time. It appeared that I could combine premarital counseling with adult membership instruction along with some lessons in baptism for both of them. These two would be the first beneficiaries of several semesters of training in pastoral care and counseling.

"My practice is to meet at least six times with the couple before the wedding so that we can go over the service and discuss all the issues pertinent to Christian marriage. We'll do a modified version of the Meyers-Briggs Personality Inventory. At the rehearsal . . ." Why I said "My practice" I have no idea, since I had never performed a marriage, had no "practice," and did not understand the futility of trying to prepare anybody for marriage, let alone two teenagers:

You can't imagine this, Shane and Leeta, but let me tell you a little about your future: at twenty-eight, Shane is drinking eight or ten beers a day and already daydreaming about retiring from his job on the second shift at the glassworks. Leeta is so exhausted from caring for a little boy with cystic fibrosis that she is making desperate plans. Your parents are all dead, including Billy, who got drunk and burned up in his camper one night. You two don't say grace at meals, or kiss each other good morning, good night, or good-bye. You do not engage in the ritual tendernesses that make an ordinary day endurable. And did I mention that Leeta thinks she's pregnant again, and is seriously considering a trip to Chicago where something can be done about it? Yes, let wise Pastor Lischer prepare you for married life.

Leeta stood up in front of the desk, this time in an unrehearsed way, and gave me a distinctly unSemannslike smile, as if to say, "I have news for you." (She really *was* determined.) "Honey, give the pastor the license."

Shane and I stood up, as two men will do when they are about to close a business deal or fight a duel. In a voice that a boy might use when asking a girl's father for her hand, he said, "Could you do it tonight? This here's the license. We done passed the blood test with fly'n colors, didn't we, babe? We can't wait no longer, Pastor. It's time."

I thought of my own mother and father, she in her best organdy dress, he in his double-breasted olive suit, both of them trembling as they made their vows in the parlor of another Lutheran parsonage. I bet it was like mine, with dark woodwork and lace curtains and the smell of diapers. Still, I felt years of training slipping away from me in a matter of minutes as I agreed to the "wedding." All my pastoral actions were occurring outside the lines and away from the sanctuary—an unauthorized Eucharist in a hospital, a pickup wedding in my house. I invited them to walk over to the church, but they politely but firmly declined on the tacit grounds of their own unworthiness.

"Witnesses," I said, "we must have witnesses," again, with no earthly idea of the truth or falsity of the statement. I walked down the short hall to the kitchen where my own pregnant wife was fixing supper with Sarah wrapped around one of her legs.

"I need you," I said.

Soon our little tableau was in place. Leeta and Shane stood before me,

Tracy at Leeta's side, our Sarah gazing in from the doorway, trying not to smile at the strange goings-on.

The bride, six months pregnant, in her white Venture Mart shift, looked dark-eyed and radiant. The matron of honor, eight and a half months pregnant, in a Carnaby Street mini-maternity dress, nervously brushed her long blond hair away from her face. The women were smiling and blooming with life; the men were trying not to make a mistake. The groom appeared pale but steady, a little moist beneath the nose. The minister was wearing bell-bottomed corduroys and a wool sweater over which he had draped a white stole. He kept his eyes in his book. To an outsider peering through one of the large windows in the study, the scene might have been borrowed from a French farce or a Monty Python skit.

At the book-appointed time, I laid the stole across Leeta and Shane's clutched hands and onto her belly, read the right words, and the deed was done. Shane and Leeta got themselves married. They left in a rusted El Camino, seated well apart from one another like an old married couple. They looked sad beyond knowing.

Two nights later in that same interminable week the telephone rang at about 3 A.M. "Pastor," the voice on the other end said, pronouncing it *Pestur*, "Ed Franco. My Doral is here in St. Joe's. Gall bladder's rupturin'. It ain't good. It ain't good at all. We're goin' to have surgery in thirty, forty minutes. We need you here—if you can."

"Of course," I said. "St. Joe's?" Did I understand the difference between the Front Way and the Back Way out of town, he asked. I didn't, and he explained. He gave me clear directions from the driveway of the parsonage over the Back Way to the hard road, then to 140 directly into Upper Alton and to St. Joseph's Hospital. I was into my clerical gear and out of the house in five minutes.

The leafless trees along the canopied Back Way were dripping with fog and deep darkness. I caught only glimpses of the Davidson place and the Gunthers' peeling outbuildings as I flew by. An ancient haying machine was eerily backlit by the Gunthers' security light; propane tanks stood awkwardly like foals on skinny struts. But in the night and fog everything had become strange to me again. A time for goblins to shriek out of the forest. As I slowed near the Felder's curve an enormous German shepherd roared out of nowhere and scared the hell out of me. I felt like a spy or an astronaut on a dangerous mission. Of course, if it was dangerous, it was only because I was driving like a maniac on unfamiliar roads, and my mind was racing with yet another *adventure in ministry.*

At three-thirty in the morning one does not easily walk into a small-town hospital. The doors were locked, and it appeared that everyone had turned in for the night. This was an unassuming place, more like a neighborhood B&B than a full-service, Ramada-type hospital. My clerical collar finally got me into the building, but by the time I arrived at Doral's room she was nowhere to be found.

I raced down toward the OR, passing through a couple of NO ADMITTANCE doors, and found the Francos strangely alone in a laundry alcove next to the operating room. Through the crack of the OR door the light blazed harshly, but in the alcove the light was mercifully dim. The only decoration on the wall was a picture of Joseph the Carpenter with the boy Jesus, who was lighting his father's workplace with a candle. A red fire extinguisher was hung in an arrangement beside the picture. Doral and her gurney were parked to one side. Ed hovered above her, nervously petting and patting her.

The Francos were a childless, middle-aged couple who, although she was a Semanns and they never missed a Sunday, were not prominent members of the church, perhaps because Ed not only came from Blaydon but was, according to my Tuesday rundown with Leonard and the elders, of "foreign extraction." Doral was as thick and bouffant as Ed was skinny and bald. You could feel their love for one another in the shadows of the alcove.

"Are we glad to see you," Ed said, as though I was about to make a difference.

Once I came face to face with them I realized that I hadn't brought a little book or any other tools for ministry. I wasn't sure what was expected of me. If there was a ritual for this sort of situation, I didn't know it. But I did take a good look at Doral, her hair slightly undone, expressive eyes moving from my face to Ed's and back, her face and arms pasty with sweat. She was the most frightened person I had ever seen.

They looked at me expectantly, but I didn't know what to say or how to open a conversation. I didn't know the Francos. They corresponded to a *type* of parishioner I had in my head, but nothing more. I must have known people like them in my boyhood congregation. Surely, we had a great deal in common, but at the moment what we had was silence. It was very quiet in the alcove.

What came, finally, was the fragment of a shared script. I said,

The Lord be with you

to which Ed and Doral replied in unison, *And with thy spirit.*

I said, *Lift up your hearts.*

They said, *We lift them to the Lord.*

And suddenly the *Lord* himself became as palpable as Ed's love for Doral. What was disheveled and panicky recomposed itself. The Lord assumed his rightful place as Lord of the Alcove, and the three of us wordlessly acknowledged the presence. It was as if Ed and Doral and I had begun humming the same melody from our separate childhoods.

This was no longer me alone, desperately talking toward the treetops in Milwaukee. That night the Spirit moved like a gentle breeze among us and created something ineffable and real. We prayed together, then recited the

63

Lord's Prayer; and whatever it was that happened came to an end as quickly as it had begun. My little part in the drama was over.

My first week had been a week of signs.

I took the drive home from the hospital at a more leisurely rate of speed, returning via the Front Way through town. A delicate line of pink neon extended across the eastern horizon. Each pasture gently overlapped its neighbor like a becalmed, gray-green sea until the folded pastures met the sky. The town was silhouetted against this dawn with a narrative sweep. At least one light shone in every home place. The little houses, in which the old folks were stealing an extra hour's sleep, remained dark.

Soon I entered my own dark house, slipped into my own bed warmed like an oven by my pregnant wife, and stole an extra hour myself.

6

The Real Presence

 From the very first week in New Cana, my preparation for worship began at the Sacred Burning Barrel. There was no garbage pickup in our part of the county, just as there was no newspaper or, for the first year, home mail delivery (to say nothing of pizza), which meant that we burned our own trash in a big rusty barrel at the southwest corner of the property. My wife and I playfully invested this lonely but beautiful place with transcendent meaning and a holy name. If God showed up on the Plain of Midian in a burning bush, why not here in a creosote-stained trash barrel? At first it was a joke between us, but soon we were vying with one another to see who got to burn the trash while the other minded the baby.

I don't know what Tracy thought about when she stood in the freezing cold before the flames and watched the sun setting behind the heath-like Brush. I made the experience a time of preparation, when I reflected on the events of the past week and planned my Sunday sermon. As time went on, I began praying for individual parishioners at the Sacred Burning Barrel.

On my first Sunday morning I was taken aback by a ghastly sight in the sacristy. A dying man was sprawled on a chaise lounge in the center of the room. He was white as snow and as cold to the touch. His total hairlessness, I was soon to learn, was the result of an experimental drug therapy. He was dressed in a cassock, surplice, and stole. A hymnal lay open across his lap.

Erich Martin was the former pastor of the church. He was so weakened by cancer that he couldn't sit in a pew. He worshiped in the sacristy with the door to the chancel wide open. From his lounge chair he could also keep an eye on me, and from anywhere in the chancel I had him in view. Since no one could see him but me, he constituted my private audience of one, a second congregation. Whenever I stood in the pulpit during those first months, Erich was a barely living blur to my right. If I was tempted, as preachers occasionally are, to replace the proclamation of the gospel with affable chatter, the presence of a liturgically vested, dying man in a chaise lounge never failed to dissuade.

Long after he was gone, I could not step into the pulpit without instinctively checking the sacristy door. Although Erich never played the lovable, crusty old mentor toward me, his presence, at first intimidating, grew to be a source of reassurance. If we are "surrounded by so great a cloud of witnesses," as the Book of Hebrews promises, here at least was one I could keep my eye on.

The old academy system of education had forged Erich with a discipline that was foreign to me. I never met a person so utterly controlled by the patterns and duties of the ministry as he. Even among farmers, who are not famous for their introspective nature, I never met anyone less absorbed in himself or driven by a personal agenda than Erich. Unlike the therapeutically trained cleric, Erich did not compulsively insist on being a friend or a pal to his parishioners. He was not, as one of my friends says of Protestant ministers in general, "a quivering mass of availability." He did not personalize his every act of ministry. Unlike ministers who make a career of getting along with people, Erich's approach was to do his duty, and to let the duties symbolize something larger and more important than his own personality.

Erich had been seasoned by many years of ministry in India, where he and his wife had lost a son to malaria. New Cana was just another mission field to him. No one who has buried a child in Jabalpur can be beaten by a little loneliness or a few stubborn farmers in Illinois.

No doubt owing to his background as a missionary, Erich's practice had been to refuse his paycheck until the monthly mission allotment had been paid. He never made an issue of it, but in a small town word gets around. It was solely due to his example that in good years and in bad an ingrown rural congregation gave away one half its income. Everyone respected him, but if someone were to ask, "Did you like Pastor Martin?" they would say, "*Like?*" then look quizzically at one another and reframe the question.

With Erich a constant presence to my right, I was physically linked to the authority of tradition. But I soon recognized other fixed positions in our small-town sociogram. Most of the older generation sat on the pulpit side of the church; their grown children and families sat on the other side of the aisle. This probably represented a vestige of the old days when the men and women sat on opposite sides of the church. Most people clustered to the center of the church, which might have been a memory of the enormous potbellied stove that once sat in the center aisle, around which parishioners would toast one side of their bodies and freeze the other while the whole room slowly filled with smoke. Only the young teens, giggling and elbowing one another like hockey players, sat in the first couple rows. Their position represented their first adventurous separation from their parents.

Leonard and June Semanns always sat in the fourth row on the lectern side. Buster Toland and (when she came) Beulah, along with the smiling Max, Angela, and the lank-haired Lacy, usually sat farther back by the window. Buster, his neck bulging out of a filthy dress shirt with loosened tie, sweat popping through his flattop, was always hoping to catch a little breeze on steamy summer days. Lacy, for all his surliness toward anyone in authority, tended his little sister more like a young father than an older brother. She responded by laying her head on his shoulder with theatrical sighs of fatigue.

The ushers usually began the service standing officiously at the rear in the tiny narthex, but as the hour wore on they would slyly inch their way backward out the door for a smoke. Even the reclusive Henry Dire had his appointed spot. He sat in the darkest corner of the sacristy and pretended to monitor the PA system, which, as everyone knew, didn't work. Each member had a place in this congregation and, in summer, everyone swung a fan provided by Metz's ("Be-in-Time-for-Eternity") Mortuary of Cherry Grove.

Ernie Semanns was once a trustee whose responsibilities dictated that he and his family sit in the front row on the lectern side, from which position he could easily exit if the toilets flooded the downstairs hall, as they frequently did, or if any other physical calamity occurred. For example, one Sunday early in my ministry, a little girl threw up onto the dark wooden floor in front of her pew. I was about two minutes into my sermon at the time and decided to demonstrate my professionalism by continuing to preach. A trustee (not Ernie, by the way) immediately sprang up to attend to the stiffening puke. He surveyed it and within minutes returned to the scene pushing a bucket on wheels with rollers and a mop. The wheels and rollers squeaked noisily. I found it possible to preach through this distraction, and after a few minutes of squishing, mopping, and squeaking, he and the vomit were gone.

Several moments later, however, as I moved persuasively into my next point, the trustee returned to the scene of the mishap, this time with a can of scented air freshener. *Psss-psss-psss.* Pause. *Psss-psss-psss.* And for good measure: *Psss.* Suddenly the whole church smelled like an alpine forest gone slightly off. That was the first time I heard laughter in the church.

Ernie and Darlene had had one child, a son who was enrolled in the agriculture program at Carbondale and would some day make the family farm a success. One night Ernie Junior was killed in a wreck out where 140 T's into the hard road. I had heard the story from several parishioners. "He died on the road, Pastor," Leonard had said in the formulaic pattern that everyone in New Cana seemed to use:

> Took forever to get an am-bu-lance.
> We're on our own out here.
> He was a good boy
>   but hell on wheels.
> He died on the road.

It took Ernie and Darlene a long time to come back to church, and when they did Darlene spent most of her time helping in the nursery, counting offerings in the parish hall, or preparing coffee in the kitchen. Ernie took up residence in the last pew on the lectern side, as far removed from the word of God as is physically possible, and never moved. He became an expatriate in his own church while his old pew remained empty.

Early on I noticed a young stranger to the community who sat in the back row on the pulpit side. Every Sunday she wore the same floor-length, Aquarian dress with (I could only imagine) beaded anklets and sandals. From a distance of sixty feet, all I could make out was long, dark brown hair and powerful, Mongolian cheekbones. That was all I knew of her in those first few weeks, for she always vanished between stanzas of the final hymn. My mystery woman invariably arrived late and left before anyone could greet her, though I never actually saw her walk out. Why did she come? What did she have in common with the farmers? The best I could do was arc my voice toward the back pew in order to include her in the sermon and liturgy.

Within the physical pattern of our worship several movable parts stood out, like Elmer Branson's uncanny ability to pop up like a cheerleader a split-second before the entire congregation for the *Gloria*. Like eighty-year-old Lydia Semanns's practice of kneeling at her pew on the hardwood floor after receiving communion. What made the practice even more remarkable was that she knelt with her back to the altar, head bowed, with her hands folded on the seat of the pew.

When I asked forty-five-year-old Leonard why he thought she did that, he replied, "Well, *we all* did that fifty years ago for confession. Must've been the peculur'ist sight to the preacher: hunert 'n fifty *backs* facing him as he got us ready to confess our sins."

"Why did *you* stop?" I asked, getting into the swing of his corporate sense of identity.

A shrug. "Hard to say. Maybe we don't feel *that* sinful anymore. Ha!"

"When did it stop?"

Another shrug. "Couldn't tell ya."

Because Erich had been sick so long, the elders, and others appointed by the elders, had assumed helping roles in the worship service, which was an irregular practice in our pastor-centered tradition. Elders distributed the wafers in communion, and other laypeople read the lessons. The elders seemed to think that the new pastor would want to reclaim control of the service. They were pleasantly surprised when I showed no interest in asserting my clerical rights.

It was the practice in our churches for the pastor to place the wafer into the opened mouth and onto the tongue of the communicant. The elders were uncomfortable performing this intimate sacramental act. Instead, they placed the wafer into the cupped hands of each recipient. They were clearly nervous whenever it was their turn to touch the bread.

Our elders had the thickest and most heavily muscled fingers I have ever seen. How they got a wedding ring over such enormous knuckles I can't imagine. Gnarled and callused hands, textured by manure and industrial grit in equal parts, gingerly pressed the Bread of Life into the uplifted palms of their neighbors, cousins, and parents. In a patriarchal church, the daintiness with which their monstrous hands handled the sacrament, like little girls laying a tea table, was our nearest brush with the femininity of God. Their role in the ritual reinforced our church's teaching on the "real presence." I was trained to believe that Jesus was really *there* in the bread and wine, but now I saw him with my own eyes in poor Erich to my right and in the calluses and knuckles of the servers.

Body of Christ. Body of Christ, they said robotically. They meant the body of Jesus, to be sure, but also the body of believers. All of us. Paul warned his readers in Corinth to "discern the body," which means to see Jesus' body in a new way. Not as a miracle of physics occurring in the elements, but as a miracle of community in which atoms of solitude are re-created into new families and friends. Christianity is a body religion. I had only begun to discern it.

I took such pleasure in lifting the chalice—"the way the Catholics do it!" someone said—when I came to the words, "Do this as often as you drink it, in remembrance of me." Because, when the light was filtering through our art-glass windows or flooding through the open doors in back, I could just see the whole congregation reflected in the silver cup. And in the congregation, the whole church.

7

Help Me, Jesus

 I preached my first sermon in the Epiphany season on a bitterly cold morning with sleet pelting the windows of the church. The bell and the toilets had frozen up, but the church was full and warm as toast as if the old potbellied stove were still cooking.

When I was a seminarian I considered myself a good preacher, mainly because I could put words together and declaim them with Kennedyesque urgency—a legacy of mistaking myself for a liberal in prep school. I even arched my arm and stabbed the air with two fingers turned outward the way JFK did.

Like most preachers, I grossly overestimated the importance of my part in the sermon. When I thought of preaching, I did not consider it to be a congregation's reception of the word of God, but a speaker's command of the Bible's hidden meanings and applications, which were served up in a way to showcase the authority and skill of the preacher. In those days the gospel lived or died by my personal performance. My preaching was a small cloud of glory that followed me around and hung like a canopy over the pulpit whenever I occupied it. How ludicrous I must have appeared to my congregation.

In my first sermon I explained the meaning of *an* epiphany, not *the* Epiphany of God in the person of Jesus—no, that would have been too obvious—but the *category* of epiphanies in general. To this end, I drew at length on the depressing short stories of James Joyce in *Dubliners*. "Each of these stories has one thing in common," I said. "In each the central character comes to a deeper and more disturbing understanding of himself. Nothing really happens in these stories except that in the midst of the daily routine a character is unexpectedly exposed to the predicaments of estrangement in his own life. One man realizes that his wife has never loved him. Another recognizes that he is trapped in his vocation. Another finds himself to be a hopeless failure. The human condition is full of such epiphanies . . ."

Before I could talk about Jesus, I apparently found it necessary to give my farmers a crash course in the angst-ridden plight of modern man. With the help of clichés from Joyce, Heidegger, Camus, and even Walker Percy, I first converted them to existential ennui so that later in the sermon I could rescue them with carefully crafted assurances of "meaning" in a meaningless world. Along the way I defiantly refuted Marx's view of religion as an opiate that permits us to escape the hard realities of existence. It didn't concern me that the problem of *meaninglessness* had not occurred to my audience or that Marx's critique of religion rarely came up for discussion at the post office.

It's not that I minimize the importance of the major themes of modernity. No doubt my parishioners would have understood themselves better had they opened their eyes to the intellectual context of their lives. But they did not and could not. The giants of modern thought—Darwin, Marx, Nietzsche, Freud, Sartre—and the movements they unleashed, would never touch New Cana. My parishioners lived in a prison whose view was limited to the natural world and the most obvious technologies of the twentieth century. Aside from formulaic complaints about Communists, perverts, and radicals, they did not engage the modern world.

But then I did not bother to engage their world either. It did not occur to me that I needed a new education. I treated the rural life as an eccentric experience in ministry. I was a spectator once again, as I had been in college, watching a slide show of interesting scenes and odd characters. And since I was the viewer and they were the viewees, I was in control. When I preached, I always stood above my parishioners and looked down upon them.

Consequently, my sermons carried too many prerequisites to be effective. About 90 percent of my listeners had not graduated from high school; the majority of that group had not *attended* high school. There was no one with a four-year college degree in the church with the exception of a regular visitor named Darryl Sheets, our Lone Intellectual, who was principal of the high school in nearby Cherry Grove. Darryl regularly cornered me in long and fruitless conversations on the possible meanings of the Hebrew word for "young woman" in Isaiah 9:14 and how they all pointed to "Virgin." But the truth is, Darryl and his wife Marvel didn't drive all the way to Cana because of my expertise in Hebrew or the intellectual content of my sermons. Darryl was a tongue-speaking, fire-anointed charismatic who for some reason suspected that I might be one, too. It didn't take him long to figure out he was wrong, and then we saw quite a bit less of Darryl and Marvel.

My audience paid a heavy price for the gospel. The farmers had to swallow my sixties-style cocktail of existentialism and psychology before I served them anything remotely recognizable. I implicitly required them to view their world and its problems through my eyes. All I asked of them was that they pretend to be me.

The only person who appreciated my sermons was my wife, who, like me, lived from books. Tracy was completing her course work for a Ph.D. in English and, therefore, considered poetry and literary allusions to be the most natural of all forms of communication. What's a sermon without, "Perhaps Milton said it best when he wrote . . ." But among the *rest* of the congregation my preaching produced a standoff of sensibilities: If the idea for a sermon did not come from a *book*, I was not interested in pursuing it. If it did not emerge from *life*, my parishioners were not interested in hearing about it. In a few short months we had achieved homiletical gridlock.

That year some of the great Epiphany readings came from the letter to the Ephesians, which is Paul's vision of the grandeur of the church. Ephesians presents every small-town preacher with the marvelous opportunity of unveiling Jesus' presence in the midst of the common life of the congregation. "Look around you," Paul seems to say, "the church is magnificent!" It's hard to depreciate Paul's image of the "mystery hidden for ages" and its revelation in "the Body of Christ," but with the help of Joyce and Camus, I managed to whittle it down to size.

Why couldn't I see the revelation of God in our little church? In our community everyone pitched in and learned how to "pattern" a little girl with cerebral palsy. We helped one another put up hay before the rains came. We grieved when a neighbor lost his farm, and we refused to buy his tools at the auction. As a people, we walked into the fields every April and blessed the seeds before planting them. Weren't these all signs of "church" that were worthy of mention in the Sunday homily? Whatever lay closest to the soul of the congregation I unfailingly omitted from my sermons. I didn't despise these practices. I simply didn't see them.

It took me a while to improve as a preacher because no one in the congregation helped me. My first few sermons were carefully prepared, expertly given, and politely received, but my listeners maintained a studied indifference to my words, as if to say, "We *dare* you to move us. Just try it." The preacher was speaking into a dead microphone, but no one bothered to tell him.

The first time I got through to an audience was in a black church in East Alton. Before my experience at the Shiloh AME Church, I didn't know such communication was possible. One of my colleagues had organized a series of pulpit exchanges among congregations near his parish, but when it was his turn to visit Shiloh, he was ill, and I took his place.

The exchange entailed no extra work for the preachers; they simply repeated their Sunday morning sermon in the evening service. I did the same at Shiloh—but with very different results than in my morning sermon at Cana.

My first glimpse of the sanctuary and congregation reminded me of my own small church. *We* had simple art glass windows; *they* had simple art glass windows, too, theirs depicting the same Shepherd, lambs, and angels as ours. *We* had an electronic organ and a homemade altar; *they* had the same. *We* had old people who used canes and sat in the same pews every Sunday; *they* had old people, too, with canes, fans, and hearing aids, who took their place in church with the same proprietary air.

But at the point of the sermon, our churches parted ways.

When I launched into the reprise of my Sunday morning sermon, it took the people of Shiloh about thirty seconds to recognize a preacher in trouble. An old woman in the second row said softly, *Help him, Jesus.* The entire congregation was witnessing the painful spectacle of a careful young man failing to strike fire.

Soon, others were saying, *Well? That's all right, Preach! Make it plain,* and *Come on up!* At the time, I had no idea that each of these phrases encodes a specific opinion of the sermon and a method of encouragement for the preacher. For example, when someone says rather quizzically, *Well?* in the middle of a sermon, I think it means, "That's interesting, but what are you going to do with it?"

I came from a church where *Amen* always meant "the end." When the Amens started popping like firecrackers in the *middle* of my sentences, at first I resented the interruptions, but then quickly realized that for the first time in my life I was having a conversation from the pulpit. Not only that, it was a *rhythmic* conversation! I even flexed my body in the pulpit, something our teachers warned us never to do.

The people of Shiloh helped free me from the correctness of my manuscript. At Cana I was usually so overprepared that I forgot about my hearers, but now I was actually looking at them and timing my speech with theirs. Every time one of the deacons said, *Make it plain!* I found myself smacking my next sentence like a drum. I didn't say anything out of the ordinary, but I did *smack* it. By the end of the sermon I was on the typical white preacher's high in a black-church pulpit. I was drawing energy from their responses, and loving every minute of it.

I don't want to overstate the lasting effects of my one experience at Shiloh. The black tradition of the congregation's partnership with the preacher helped me that evening, though it didn't transform me into the charismatic performer I'd always dreamed of being. But I did learn to be more interactive with the congregation. And, on occasion, I aimed my sermons at their hearts instead of their heads.

Although my own audience remained as quiet as ever, I came to realize that their silence was not the equivalent of unresponsiveness. Among Lutherans, ecstasy may take the form of a slight twitch of the eyebrow or the pursing of lips in order to suppress a smile. Sometimes a knowing glance between farmers must pass for the "Hallelujah! Preach, brother!" that is in there all right, but will never come out in this life.

Shiloh gave me something to hope for. I was waiting for my audience to become a congregation.

One Sunday morning I was announcing the names of those in the community who needed our prayers. When I came to the name of my two-day-old son, Adam, my emotions betrayed me, and I bleated his name as though it were a cry for help. Which it was. I had never asked for anyone's prayers for myself or someone I loved. When I did, my petition must have sounded like an exit wound. Although I led the people in prayer that morning, the congregation was praying through me.

My wife had endured her second cesarean in fourteen months, this time in a hospital in St. Louis. Through the glass in the neonatal unit I could see a robust little boy lying on his tummy, ready for whatever life had to offer. Within seconds, gratitude gives way to pride, and the father begins a lifelong journey of foolish hyperbole about his son: Nine, five. Whoa! That's *big* (in *every* way, if you know what I mean). Long enough to be a six-footer. Great lungs. What a husky body! Look at all that hair!

Tracy and I talked for a few drowsy minutes until her Demerol kicked in, and I returned to stare through the glass. After a while I left to make a few telephone calls and to grab a sandwich and a cup of coffee.

Forty minutes later, when I returned to the nursery, the baby was gone. As soon as I saw the empty crib, I could feel in my stomach that something was wrong. It felt like I was on a free-falling elevator.

I found Adam in neonatal intensive care, battling for air, his ribs heaving and shuddering with every breath. He looked like a little Gulliver tied down with tubes and wires, unjustly imprisoned on his first day of life. Whatever endowments he had brought into the world he appeared to have lost in the time it takes to get a cup of coffee. Now he was not only scrawny, but he appeared to be turning yellow before my eyes.

I remember experiencing a surge of irrational guilt. *Why had I left him— and for what—to enjoy supper? If I had remained by his crib, this wouldn't have happened. I should have protected him!* And so begins a second, parallel journey, as foolish as the first. The parent begins to raise a totem of self-blame, a project that begins at the child's birth and does not end until the parent's death.

The pediatrician and I sat up most of the night in rocking chairs beside the crib. He was a Greek named Tsifonis, who, besides his great medical knowledge, possessed the knack of conveying terrible news in a reassuring manner. What I remember most from that long evening was how much this total stranger cared for my son and for me. He suspected hyaline membrane disease, a disease of the lungs that is a leading cause of death in infants. But we would have to wait until the morning to know for sure. And so we waited. And rocked. When he left at dawn we agreed to meet, along with the ob-gyn, at 9 A.M. in Tracy's room to confront her with the news.

If Tracy was alarmed to see a delegation of grim-faced men enter her room, she didn't show it. She was already hurting from a ten-inch incision and disoriented by a night of terrible dreams. She simply asked Dr. Tsifonis, "Do I have to worry that he will die?" He replied with words to the effect that there is no short answer to such a question. But he spoke to her so reassuringly that she closed her eyes and said, "Fine."

Adam rallied, his lungs slowly cleared, and the hyaline membrane disease did not materialize. But two days later everything caught up with me in this unexpected little breakdown in front of a church filled with people. After a moment or two, the prayers continued and the service ended, but I felt surprised and a little humiliated by my loss of composure. As the congregation filed out, each person ministered to me in his or her own way. No two words were quite the same. Each touch or handshake bore the special character of its giver. That day marked a beginning.

8

Our Best Window

 I am trying to find the best way into the Cana church. Sometimes windows work better than doors for that purpose.

All our windows came from a St. Louis catalog, except for our best window, which was made in a studio in Chicago. It was ecclesiastical boilerplate like the rest of them, but its brilliant colors and intricate design set it apart from the others. It was a Trinity window that sat high above the altar and dominated the east wall of the sanctuary.

Our Trinity window was a gorgeous piece of classical theology, nothing less than a diagram of God. At the center of the window was a triangular area in which was inscribed the word DEUS (God). In the area around the center were smaller triangular areas, one with the word PATER (Father), another with the word FILIUS (Son), and a third with SPIRITUS SANCTUS (Holy Spirit). These three were connected by three little highways running to DEUS, and on each highway was the word EST (is). Rimming the circle and connecting the three persons were more highways—between the Father and the Son, the Son and the Spirit, and so forth, and on each of these were the words NON EST (is not).

God is persons and nothing else. There is no waxy residue of divinity that is not wrapped up in these three persons, Father, Son, and Holy Spirit. That's who God is. God is (*est*) each of these three persons, but the persons are distinct from one another (*non est*). God is both: alone in majesty and at the same time forever radiating love through each person of the Trinity. Our window's geometric design seemed to say, "Any questions?"

We are only able to love each other because the Father loves the Son through the Holy Spirit. We want to be with one another as friends, lovers, and neighbors for the same reason. That's not an argument that would appeal to most theologians, but that's what the Trinity meant for us.

In Cana, we baptized our babies, celebrated marriages, wept over the dead, and received Holy Communion—all by the light of our best window. We believed there was a correspondence between the God who was diagrammed in that window and our stories of friendship and neighborliness. If we could have fully taken into our community the name *Trinity*, we would have needed no further revelations and no more religion, for the life of God would have become our life.

An aerial photographer once remarked that from the air you can see paths, like the canals on Mars, that crisscross pastures and fields among the farms where neighbors have trudged for generations, just to visit or help one another in times of need. These, too, are the highways among *Pater*, *Filius*, and *Spiritus Sanctus* grooved into human relationships. The word religion comes from the same root as "ligaments." These are the ties that bind.

The Trinity is a mystery, *the* divine Mystery, but it does not follow that the doctrine of the Trinity is irrational. Karl Barth once remarked that even in theology two plus two always equals four, and never five. When I remember our best window, I think of Flannery O'Connor's confession in a letter to a friend:

> I believe what the Church teaches—that God has given us reason to use and that it can lead us toward a knowledge of him, through analogy; that he has revealed himself in history and continues to do so through the Church, and that he is present (not just symbolically) in the Eucharist on our altars. To believe all this I don't take any leap into the absurd. I find it reasonable to believe, even though these beliefs are beyond reason.

Nobody in the church knew that believers had died (and, alas, killed) for what the geometric design of our window represented. No one knew that the Coptic father St. Athanasius had been exiled five times from his beloved Alexandria over the word *est* connecting the Son to the Father in order to defend the divine nature of Jesus. We only sensed that the design of our window stood as a witness against the religion "of our own sweet invention," as O'Connor put it in the same letter.

Who is the real God? Not long ago I heard of a Protestant theological student who was asked by his examining board to name an attribute of God. Genuinely stumped, he said, "Intimacy?" We are so accustomed to inventing a god in the image of our own needs that we cannot conceive of this lonely-yet-gregarious, geometric God.

Our best window said "God is for us," and lavishly so. We can only approach the Trinity via the love of Jesus and the experience of the Spirit. See how the little highways connect God to us, and us to one another? But the geometric God also lives in a realm of mystery beyond reason and analogy. You can't get there from here. You can't deduce the Trinity from religious experience or human relationships. No amount of windows and artwork and homely analogies (the skin, the pulp, the core—all an *apple!*) will produce the majesty of the Holy Trinity, who is alone in greatness and divinity, and as immutable as the eternal laws that govern the isometric triangle.

Without the *doctrine* of the Trinity, we are left with a terrifyingly capricious god, about whom a Masai chief once said, "When I meet that God" (that is, the "high god" who randomly visits suffering and natural disasters upon the earth), "I will run a spear through him."

Without the God of our best window, we would have found ourselves defenseless in a disordered world, pitting our meager resources of friendship and hope against the charismatic authority of random events, like car wrecks, unwanted pregnancies, heart attacks, anthrax, drought, and death. The window did not explain the senseless things that befell us, but as long as we were convinced that some *design* underlay the God we worshiped, it suggested a hidden design in our lives as well and, like an absurdly delicate barrier, held back the chaos of the years.

Regina Logan was the mother of a toddler boy named Darwin. They lived with Regina's mother, Rhoda, in a little house west of New Cana near the Prairieview Road. Without any men in the house, the two women relied on one another, which was just fine with both of them. The daughter relied more completely upon her mother because Regina did not think as clearly or move as quickly as Rhoda, who also held down a job at the library in Upper Alton. Regina was a quiet girl with kind eyes. Her mother was thoughtful in appearance, as befitting a librarian, but her shoulder-length red hair seemed a touch too glamorous, too *noisy*, for a sleepy little library. If Regina appeared young to be a mother, Rhoda was absurdly young to be a grandmother.

They rarely came to church, but one Sunday morning, to the delight of the congregation, I baptized a resisting, twisting little Darwin. At eighteen months, the little towhead was robust enough to crane his neck away from the baptismal font as if it were filled with pea soup, to whoop with displeasure, and to fight his regeneration all the way. Country people say, "That's the devil making his last stand."

I didn't talk with them again until several weeks later when I was summoned to the hospital in Upper Alton, where Regina and Rhoda were about to claim Darwin's body. It was a nurse who called me. She said she just thought "somebody else ought to be here."

Darwin had toddled to the only bulkheaded section of the little pond that adjoined his grandmother's property, fallen in, and drowned. Later, the medical examiner reported that he found very little water in his lungs. Apparently, the cold water caused Darwin's windpipe to spasm and close, which meant that he may have died of shock and asphyxiation. He also bruised his head and lips and the tissue around his eyes on the bulkheading or a submerged rock, but that was not the cause of death.

Darwin's drowning was a tragedy compounded by irony and further tragedies. His mother and grandmother had finally begun to "make it" as a viable child-rearing team—as a family. That struggle to be a family was probably what prompted them to have Darwin baptized. The water near their house was an ever-present danger, but one they recognized: Rhoda and Regina took turns caring for Darwin, watching him like a hawk. It was Rhoda's turn to watch him in the moments before he died.

It was too cold to sit on a lawn chair outside. *Who is going to sit on a frigid metal chair in the middle of November? Who even thinks about water this time of year?*

When it happened, Rhoda was alternating between the back porch and the kitchen, trying to keep one eye on the little one (*he wasn't going anywhere*) and the other on three sizzling pork chops.

Where's Darwin? Rae, Rae! My God, where's Darwin?

Rhoda had her daughter to look after, as well as Darwin, the house and most of the meals, her job in Alton, and, last of all, herself. Now she had lost Darwin, and was crushed with grief and guilt.

The nurses at St. Joseph's tried to comfort Regina, who was numb, and Rhoda, who was wild with grief. They wanted to give the two women a proper farewell with Darwin. When I got there, they had just finished laying out the child on the hospital bed and had carefully folded back the sheet across his legs.

The nurses had brushed back his sandy hair like a little old man's and dressed him in yellow pajamas with drums and sticks on them. His eyelids were blue with bruises, and his expression still bore a trace of consternation.

"You can hold him if you want," the nurses said.

Regina and Rhoda were keening in accents I had never heard, like primitive women who live on hilltops or deep in the Brush. They did a dance of grief around the child. They petted him and kissed him and spoke to him; they took awkward turns crushing him to their breasts; but they could not so much as change the expression on his face. This went on for about fifteen minutes, but it seemed much, much longer.

Finally, we joined hands, or I took their hands, knowing that if it did not stop, something else would break in all of us.

No more to build on there, the poet said after the death of a boy in the next village. Absolutely nothing to build on. We were breaking at the place where body meets spirit. You cannot build on a farewell ripped from the chest.

"We must pray to God," I said at last. "Father, Son, and Holy Ghost."

I asked God to gather up our grief and to absorb it into his own heart. I asked him to receive his own child, Darwin, water-baptized in the name of the triune God. I thanked God for Darwin. I thanked Jesus for dying for him. I asked the Holy Spirit to help us.

Then with a few more kisses we said good-bye.

When we left him there on the bed, it was the hardest thing any of us had ever done. We had commended him to God, but it still felt as if we were deserting him. *Won't he be afraid if he wakes up?* The nurses stood by his bed, one at each side, and followed us out of the room with concern in their eyes.

By the time we left the hospital, the day had grown lurid with noise and light. The sun was shining with an unnatural glare, as if something in the atmosphere had evaporated and left us unprotected. The whole world, if it had ever paused, had returned to its affairs. Rush hour was under way, and traffic had begun to thicken toward the beltway. We could hear the din of engines and radios and the blurred laughter of commuters who, *since they were not the one dead*, were in a big hurry to get home from work.

*S*he *said to* me, "There is something I haven't told you about myself."

"Really? I thought we knew everything about one another. We've talked so many times."

She was sitting in the new window seat with a flowered cushion along one wall of the back porch. They'd had the screen replaced with glass and the rest of the porch enclosed with cheap paneling so that the pond could no longer be seen. It was as if it no longer existed. The boy might have drowned fifty, sixty years ago. He might have been someone else's boy.

The two of us sat opposite one another like strangers on the subway, until she curled her legs under her body and paraphrased herself.

"There's something you don't know about me."

She shifted into the corner and drew her knees up to her chin, the way a child sits to hear a story. In the dusky shadows of the evening, all colors had faded except her brilliant hair. It was the Hour of Lead, a quiet time for both of us.

"What haven't you told me?"

"I know things."

"What do you mean?"

"I know things before they happen. I can see them clearly in my mind. Not like a photograph. More like a movie. I might have been an angel. It's impossible to know."

"What do you see?"

"I saw it happen to Darwin before it happened. I saw it all, Pastor."

"You saw him drown in the pond."

"Yes, I did," she whispered.

"No, no, you *think* you did. Of course, you think you did."

"I knew you wouldn't understand," she said factually, without a trace of reproach.

"You think that if you knew it all beforehand, it was a completed action. Which means that it *had* to happen. Someone had already decided that Darwin must die."

I might have added, "And therefore you can't be blamed," but that was no longer Rhoda's concern. She had moved beyond self-reproach to larger issues, to the necessity of what Is. Othello must kill Desdemona every time; they both know that. Judas must betray Jesus. The *Titanic* never slides safely by the iceberg. The passion plays must go on.

"No human person can know events before they happen," I said. "That would be a terrible gift. Only God sees everything."

"If God sees everything, then why did he let this happen to Darwin?" I was maneuvered to the corner of the board again in a game I had long since lost interest in winning.

"Oh, Rhoda, we've been over this a thousand times. You know my 'answer' . . ."

At night, when our Trinity window was illuminated by its three bare light bulbs, it appeared to have been designed by an ancient engineer or a wizard. The window mocked us with its complexity. *You are not God*, it seemed to say. *This is beyond your knowledge. Venture no farther!*

By the light of day, however, the window ignited in color and turned to poetry, which is the proper language of suffering and hope. Then it said, *God is for us, after all. See, even the crimson pain of Jesus travels the highway straight to the golden heart of God. The mystery of love is not irrational. There's your answer, such as it is.*

By mid-morning our window would resemble a web of reticulated silk, latticed and glistening after a morning's shower, showing off the colors of creation. But the Black Widow, the One who wove this gorgeous pattern through the secret hours of the night, was nowhere to be seen. All She left was her mysterious name, like three clues, written in lace for those with eyes to see.

9

Changing the Furniture

A white woman in a Native American church once helped me understand the importance of story and symbol in a congregation. She was giving me a tour through her church in Robeson County, North Carolina, one of the poorest and most racially-conflicted counties in the South. As we walked, she told me the terrible story of how her Lumbee husband and two of her sisters were killed in an automobile wreck. There she was, she said, like the Moabite Ruth, stranded in an alien community. She walked me over to an art glass window near the baptismal font. It was a memorial to her husband and her sisters. It portrayed two hands clasped beneath a cross.

"See?" she said. "Don't you see? This stands for all of us. When I married my husband, everybody warned me against a mixed marriage. A white woman and an Indian? Never. They said it couldn't work. I would never be accepted. But this congregation made us one. See, it's in the window."

It all begins with the symbols. They capture primal relations, like water and death, fire and purification, seeds and hope. The stories do not come before the symbols, but they emerge from them and bring them to life. The stories explain the symbols, and the symbols make the stories worth remembering and telling. The window in the Lumbee church said, "See, under this sign of suffering, we will accept one another as brothers and sisters." A congregation lives most deeply by its symbol-bearing stories. They tell us who we are.

Any cultural anthropologist would have warned me not to rearrange the furniture in our church. Of course, there *were* no cultural anthropologists in New Cana. Had there been, they would have reminded me that the physical focus of worship symbolically "freezes" the community's story into a sacred universe. Therefore, to shuffle the furniture in the chancel or to alter the ritual, say, by moving the flag or changing the music, is to offend against the stories and derange the universe itself.

Who knew?

I should have known not to try to remove the American flag from the chancel. To me, the national flag represented an intrusion into the sacred space of the congregation, an obvious symbol of civil religion. Theologically, the flag has no business beside the altar.

At one of our congregational "town meetings," I patiently explained that I had nothing against patriotism but that it was a short step from "God and country" to "God *equals* country." These were the last hours of Vietnam and the early days of Watergate. How can Christians minister prophetically to the country, I asked, if we embrace the nation's chief symbol and admit it into our sanctuary?

Leonard's brother Don, a farmer and a Caterpillar driver, rose to his feet and, without introduction, began to tell a story. "We had an uncle named Warren," he said respectfully, "who went like he was supposed to, and wound up near a place called Anzio. Never heard of it before n'r since. I was a kid when he left. Seemed like he was gone forever, which, in a way of speak'n, he was. I won't ever forget when that telegram come. 'Cause it come to our house first. We went with the man over to Aunt Mary's. Some of you remember that day. I know I will never forget it."

Then he sat down.

In typical Semanns fashion, he had elided the main points of the story as well as its climax. He followed the community's rule: Whenever possible, avoid taking anything head-on. Absorb all, allude strategically, address nothing directly. Everyone understood his speech, however, and I did, too.

The writer Isak Dinesen said, "Any sorrow can be borne if a story can be told about it," but some stories, like this one, are too painful to tell in detail. The flag, as it turned out, did not represent civil religion or any other abstraction, not, at least, for my congregation. It simply told a story that everyone wanted to remember but found too sorrowful to repeat.

The assembly then voted, as it usually did when faced with any controversial question, to table the motion to change the chancel furnishings. The flag stayed put.

The same "vote to table" awaited my proposal to move the altar away from the east wall of the chancel and make it free-standing. My idea was derived from the sacramental theology that had recently emerged from Vatican II, although in my formal presentation to the assembly I left the Catholics out of it. For too long the priest had turned his back on the people and, muttering a formula known only to him, performed the ritual as if by magic. "This is my body," we say furtively. *Hocus-pocus* and all that. Vatican II encouraged priests to celebrate the Eucharist from behind a free-standing altar, facing the people. In that way the sacrament assumes the character of a family meal, and the altar becomes a kitchen table.

My parishioners had a story, of course, with which to confound both me and Vatican II. To move that altar would destroy everything it stands for. And that cannot be. A former pastor named Rottman, who served at least twenty-five years before Erich Martin, built that altar with his own hands. One of the older heads then recited a long and tedious story of how the pastor brought his tools from Germany, found the ash on the old Jacobi place, hand-adzed it, sharpening his adze on Orville's grindstone, and oiled the wood for days on end. ("Imagine," my parishioner seemed to be saying, "a pastor who could handle *tools*.")

As the recital wore on, I knew the story had defeated me.

I didn't appreciate how comfortable everyone was with the carnage that is symbolized by an altar. A few months after the meeting, I happened to visit an old woman named Betts. She lived in the woods adjacent to the county gravel pile in a concrete-block cottage. Word had it she was the oddest and most self-sufficient woman in the county. My knock on the front door didn't raise a response, but there was an awful commotion out back. Someone in hysterics, I thought, a terrible argument in progress, maybe a murder.

Well, yes and no. It was only Betts preparing to slaughter a chicken. With her left foot firmly placed on the chicken's neck and her right arm raised with cleaver in hand, she bore a remarkable resemblance to "Mother" Bates in *Psycho*. When she brought the cleaver down, the blood sprayed in all directions.

The communion table exudes harmony and unity. It's a family-friendly piece of furniture. The sounds of the table are good conversation and the clink of sterling on china or at least the reassuring solidity of plastic against Styrofoam.

At the altar there is the squealing and braying of hogs, chickens, and other beasts. Their blood covers the floor and runs to the drain. Our table food does not come from a cellophane package in a supermarket or even a refrigerated truck, but a slaughterhouse.

At the table there is the security of family relationships. Everyone belongs at the table. Only for the worst of crimes is the child sent from the table. Even the most remote father or the busiest mother is accessible to the rest of the family at the supper table.

At the altar is the alien and austere presence of the priest, the intermediary, who is neither father nor mother nor friend. He can never simply be one of us because he has seen and heard too much.

Our table-oriented family relationships in the church are possible because behind the table looms the shadow of the guillotine. On Maundy Thursday, while sitting at table, Jesus considered himself a dead man and spoke of blood and betrayal and other indelicate subjects.

Why, my parishioners seemed to ask (as they once again deferred action on my motion), why would anyone want to reduce the altar to something as flimsy as a table?

It occurred to me that with all these *votes* I was abdicating my prophetic responsibility to lead the people of God. Some matters should not be brought to a vote. Our youth choir and its director, Billy Meyers, sensing that in me they had a pastor with a bit more flexibility than Erich, asked if they could perform "They Will Know We Are Christians by Our Love" in a Sunday service, accompanied by a guitar.

It was the early 1970s. Janis Joplin, Jimi Hendrix, and Jim Morrison were already safely off the scene. The nation had recently survived Woodstock. An upbeat group called the 5th Dimension had performed at an outdoor concert as near to Cana as Edwardsville with no ill-effects, and Tracy and I had boldly taken the youth group to see *Godspell* in St. Louis with only minor rumblings in the parish. Folk and soft-rock masses had already become passé in the church. It seemed like a safe bet. There would be no voting on this one.

I alerted the always-agreeable elders that on Sunday the Cana church would experience its first guitar player in the person of fuzzy-lipped Norbie Semanns, everybody's cousin or nephew.

The choir stood on the chancel steps, facing the congregation. Norbie sat on a folding chair not far from the front pew. They flailed the high notes, Norbie strummed furiously, and together they closed it out with a flourish:

By our love,
They will know-ow we are Christians
By our love.

The congregation seemed pleased with the youth and pleased with itself for tolerating the youth. In the half-second of absolute silence that follows any performance, something awful happened.

Ferdie Semanns, son of Alfred, who even his relatives referred to as a big, red-faced farmer, erupted in derisive applause, which, given the enormity of his hands, sounded like two hogs slapping against each other in a metal pen. His face was contorted with rage as he strode down the center aisle, still clapping, and walked out the back door past the smoking ushers.

It was an explosive performance. I was amazed at his behavior, but only slightly less astonished by the indifference with which it was received by the congregation. No one's face changed expression. Even his own children, two of whom sang in the choir, betrayed no hint of surprise or embarrassment.

After church, an air of crisis hung over my usual session with the elders. It was clear, however, that I perceived a greater crisis than they did. "We have to go to him," I said. "He's hurting and confused. We have to work through this with him and resolve the issues involved."

"Aw, *Pestur*," Bud Jordan slowly replied. "We don't have to do that."

"We don't?"

"*Naw.* Everybody knows Ferdie is a horse's ass."

The others nodded in solemn agreement.

With typical impassiveness, the entire community let it go. I never heard anyone speak of the episode again. It was absorbed into the communal memory, mulched, and reprocessed for use in another form, perhaps as a joke, or a cautionary tale for future pastors about voting before changing the worship service. I know I never brought it up to Ferdie, and Ferdie continued to treat me as he always had, with a mixture of fake respect and genuine contempt.

A couple months later when Ferdie's dad, Alfred, finally died at Prairieview General, I conducted the funeral. Afterward, Ferdie offered to pay me twenty dollars, but I politely refused. That turned out to be a happy exercise of pastoral ethics.

Three days later Ferdie rolled up to the parsonage in his pickup truck and off-loaded an entire side of beef—cut, packaged, and labeled: rib-eyes, sirloins, Kansas City, chuck, flank, round, ground—you name it. "Here you go, Preacher. Thanks for the words. Eat good this winter. He liked you."

"Your father?" I turned red at the thought of my first Eucharist *sans* bread.

"Yep."

Ferdie didn't add, "And I respect you, too," or, "*Say, about that crazy clapping . . .*"

He simply left the beef.

10

Gossiping the Gospel

 The fact is, everyone did know that Ferdie was a horse's ass. His pattern of behavior had been informally chronicled, his character sifted, and certain conclusions, mostly in proverb form, had been rendered. He had been properly gossiped.

The word *gossip* originally implied a spiritual relationship. A gossip was a sponsor at a baptism, one who spoke on behalf of the child and who would provide spiritual guidance to the child as it grew in years. A gossip was your godmother or godfather. Gossiping was speech within the community of the baptized.

For all its negative associations, gossip retains something of its salutary function in a small town. For example, our community had long ago passed judgment on Ferdie, but it did so by acquitting him of his outrageous behavior. Gossip is the community's way of conducting moral discourse and, in an oddly indirect way, of forgiving old offenses. In our town all desires were known, no secrets were hid, and every heart was an open book. Every life was gossiped by all, and all were gossips.

The continuous reworking of the community's stories, characters, and themes served two purposes. Gossip helps soften the edges of people who are simply too accessible to one another, who irritate one another to death, but who can't escape one another or their common history. Gossip also explains peculiarities, such as Ferdie's, and tells how they came to be.

Second, our gossip was common discourse. It contributed to a moral consensus on, say, what constitutes decent farming, honorable business, tolerable preaching, or effective parenting. Gossip was our community's continuing education.

One afternoon Tracy walked the kids a quarter-mile down the church road to one of our nearest neighbors, Tom and Lottie Semanns's place, where Lottie was in charge of all the kids and all the chickens. Tracy wanted to show our two-year-old Sarah the hundreds of baby chicks still under the incubator lights. When they walked into the shed, Sarah looked at the sea of chicks and said, " 'Lello!'"

Lottie quickly turned to her own five-year-old, Wendy Sue, whom Lottie always called "Miss Mouth," and, making as if to box her ears, said, "Look there, Miss Mouth, and you don't even know your colors. What's wrong with you?" Then she asked my wife, "How *does* that child know her colors? How does she know those chickens are yellow?"

Tracy said, "I teach her. You know, Lottie, I point to things like apples and rag dolls and name their colors. Then we repeat them together. See, I would say 'apple, red; wagon, red,' and so on."

"Oh," Lottie replied with a mixture of wonder and resentment.

Everyone in New Cana recognized the double-edged quality of gossip. I once began a sermon on Matthew 7:1–2—"Judge not, that you be not judged. For with the judgment you pronounce you will be judged, and the measure you give will be the measure you get"—by uttering two contradictory sentences. "There is something wonderfully wholesome about living in a small town. There is something terribly destructive about living in a small town." Everyone nodded and smiled uneasily, as if to say, "We understand the benefits and the risks of gossip."

When gossip serves the gospel, it exhibits historical, moral, and pastoral dimensions. It works like this: Let's say the teenage baby-sitter comes home from the parsonage where she has been minding Pastor and Mrs. Lischer's two kids, and reports to her grandmother that Mrs. Lischer does not really leave the property when she hires a baby-sitter. What she does is she puts on a bathing suit, takes a lawn chair and a stack of books out behind the garage facing the cemetery, and *hides* from the kids for hours on end while she reads books. Not only that, her poor daughter Sarah plays a game she calls *Dissertation* in which she puts her dolls down for a nap and then *she* pretends to read books.

The grandmother takes that story to the weekly quilting session held in the church basement and effectively disseminates it to the mothers of the entire community, who in turn report it to their husbands, who may be trustees or members of the cemetery committee, as well as to their daughters and daughters-in-law, who in turn convey it to *their* husbands, who will confer on the matter in the feed store, the post office, the church parking lot, or the poker game in Buford's Garage.

If there is a switchmaster in this process, it is Burley Means, not because he gossips more than anyone else but because he is in a *position* to gossip more than anyone else. He is the postmaster. From the same concrete-block building, he operates the post office and a tiny grocery store with tins of ham dating from late in the Truman administration.

By eleven o'clock one morning in the post office, Burley repeated verbatim to me something I had said in exasperation two hours earlier on the parsonage porch. Some trustees with chain saws had shown up unexpectedly at the parsonage. The trustees had a weakness for chain saws. They revved them up and banked them down like hot-rodders on the Snake Road. Put a chain saw into the hands of a God-fearing trustee, and he becomes a Visigoth. The trustees proceeded to "trim back" the trees until they were, to my eyes, grotesquely disfigured. By the time I got out on the porch, they had finished their work, and I was fuming. "They look like hell!" was all I could say, a phrase that Burley repeated back to me with pious accuracy two hours later.

"I hear your trees *look like hell*," he said.

Burley was the figurative successor of an actual switchboard operator, a woman named Hilda Semanns, who opened a telephone line for anyone wishing to place a call and monitored all conversations. Hilda Semanns really *did* know everything.

Anyway, *Mrs. Lischer hides behind the garage and reads books*. The community first asks the historical question, "Have we ever seen anything like this? Have any of our other ministers' wives hid behind the garage to read? Have we ever heard of this type of behavior?"

Morally, the community wonders, "What are we to make of her actions?" Does such behavior indicate anything about her fitness as a mother or a pastor's wife? *Must* one leave the premises if one hires a baby-sitter? The community attempts to attach a positive or negative valence to the behavior. It weighs this habit against other perceptions of Mrs. Lischer as mother, church member, and helpmeet: "She pedals those kids all over the county on that old bicycle Percy Heins sold her for five dollars. Yellow hair flying in the wind, the little girl on the bar, the baby in the basket. The three of them carryin' on like songbirds."

On the other hand: "When we invited her to join the altar guild, she asked what we do, and I said we wash and iron the paraments. She said, '*Oh no, an ironing club!*' "

And yet: "She asked Wilbur to plow for a garden—a big one. Says she wants to learn how to put up beets and corn. We can teach her something about that. We're starting her on zucchini."

And this: "The minister's wife has a beautiful voice. She belongs in the choir."

"We don't have a choir."

"With her, we could."

Pastorally, then, the community seeks to integrate a person whose behavior does not enjoy historical or moral precedents. It makes allowances and adjustments. It also asks how her habits might be affecting the minister and the performance of his duties. How can we help him work around her behavior, as it were—those awkward moments in which a grown woman and mother of two hides behind the garage and reads books? Gossip is always a painful business but, when it functions as speech in the community of the baptized, it can serve a constructive end. In my wife's case, the sifting of stories led to grudging appreciation of a "peculiar" sort of prairie wife.

When the pastoral dimension is omitted from gossip, it no longer serves the gospel and becomes tediously destructive. Beulah Toland's dependence on prescription drugs and Buster and Beulah's shrieking, pan-throwing, dish-breaking fights were the subject of unredeemed gossip. Especially since they lived in the middle of town, next to Buford's Garage, and fought it out where everyone could hear them. The town was generally sympathetic to Buster. No one seemed to know how to approach a figure as deeply neurotic as Beulah, any more than they knew how to intervene in Teddy Heins's alcoholism or the Bentons' chronic money problems. The result was a lot of sanctimonious talk but little pastoral care for the Tolands and others like them.

When a domestic quarrel or some hard drinking crossed the line, everyone read about it in the "Police Blotter" section of the *Cherry Grove Gazette*. There was no hiding place from the *Gazette*, a weekly that reproduced in excruciatingly factual detail the movements of people who were going no place special and who were up to nothing in particular. A trip to St. Louis fifty miles away to visit the zoo or to see a baseball game might elicit a half-column story.

The New Cana social column was a regular feature of the newspaper. In it you might learn that Mrs. Ethel Semanns dined at the home of Mrs. Dorothy Semanns on Sunday afternoon. The columnist neglected to inform the reader that Ethel and Dorothy were sisters who had lived across the street from one another for thirty years.

When we moved to New Cana, I was interviewed by the *Gazette*. Evidently, my graduate work in theology was not deemed to be good copy. My wife and I were amused but not totally surprised to read that we had served as missionaries to England for the past three years!

But it was the "Police Blotter" that captured everyone's attention, including mine, because in the smudgy-inked facts of public drunkenness, stolen tools, fistfights, and housebreaking, you could see how far we really were from the kingdom of God.

Our church's annual report, the *Cana Chronicle*, actually carried on in the tradition of the *Gazette*. Somehow we had gotten the idea that we could capture a year of grace by listing how many baptisms had taken place, how many "souls" had communed, and how many funerals had been conducted. No one ever attempted to render the *stories* behind the numbers. Perhaps we thought that if we were still generating statistics, we must be a church. Which was ironic because we lived as an organism, not an organization. The last thing we truly cared about was numbers.

Neither did we use religion to enhance our quality of life. We never measured the truth of our faith by the measurable psychological or social improvements it afforded us. I doubt that anyone in the Cana church ever said about Jesus, "He makes me feel better about myself" or "He helped me get close to my father." He did not help anyone stop smoking or lose weight. None of our alcoholics ever used Jesus to quit drinking, perhaps because none of them could bear to associate God with the shame of being a drunk.

God was there, like the Trinity window and the cemetery were there, but his Son was nobody's Personal Trainer.

Our congregation didn't want programs in family communication or systems planning like those I was trained to provide. They simply wanted to *be*. Religion was a matter of identity—who you are, who your people were, what you believe, and, ultimately, where you belong. That's why our annual report was such an anomaly. We lived by a sophisticated network of folk stories, proverbs, memories, and practical wisdom, but we could express ourselves only by means of dumb statistics.

There was no hiding place from the *Cana Chronicle* either, especially the financial report on the last page, which listed the contributions of every member or family—amounts *and* names. On the Sunday the annual report was distributed, you could see people turning to the last page first, as they strolled ever so nonchalantly to their cars. There was very little chitchat on those Sundays, as everyone looked to see who had been talking too-big-for-his-britches during the past fiscal year.

The *Chronicle* could never substitute for gossip, however, because gossip requires repetition and give-and-take. It relies on the nuanced reply, subtle changes, and intensification that occur in even the most scrupulously repeated message. These happen only in the spoken word.

The printed word emanates from a central power source in the town—the newspaper or the church newsletter. Gossip is decentered speech that belongs to the entire community. A newspaper's article cannot sift the stories and come up with a pastoral remedy for a delinquent teenager or a financially careless farmer. At best, the "Police Blotter" or the New Cana social column provided the raw material for the more productive and Christian work of gossip.

When I first came to New Cana, I fretted about all the gossip going on in the church—until I realized I couldn't carry on a decent ministry without it. I quit worrying about "privacy issues" and "privileged communication" and other supposedly moral protections, which finally only safeguard the individual's right to be left alone, lost, and miserable. "Privacy" is a smoke screen for the therapeutic model of ministry. It scatters the community's tradition of care into a series of personal problems and festering secrets.

There was a time when I equated religion with an intensely private faith. Sticky Lutheran piety suited my own introverted nature just fine. But I didn't find much piety in New Cana and certainly no privacy. Instead, I got myself apprenticed to a community, and this odd little warren of friendships, stories, rivalries, and rumors turned out to *be* my ministry itself.

11

Open Secrets

 One night my wife woke me and said, "I think there's somebody in the church. I heard a noise." It was one o'clock in the morning. No one could possibly be in the church, I assured her.

I took a flashlight and made my way from our house, around the front of the church, to the far corner where the new parish hall abutted the older building. With no security light on that side, I fumbled my way in and up the wooden steps to the sacristy (where Erich had so often lain). From there I would enter the chancel. I pushed open the sacristy door and shone my light around the altar and pulpit. To my astonishment, a pair of eyes gazed back at me from the darkness.

First eyes, then a face, then remarkably high cheekbones on the face. She was sitting in the sedile, the clergy chair—*my* chair—just behind the pulpit, facing the open sacristy door. By this time I was thoroughly spooked, but she seemed calm.

I immediately recognized her as the stranger who sat in the back pew on Sundays and disappeared before I could speak with her. Now that I had my chance, I was speechless.

"You . . . you. What are you doing here? In the dark . . ."

"I am praying," she said evenly.

"In a church? In the middle of the night? How'd you . . . ?"

"Through the window," she replied, anticipating my question. "I always come through that window right there. It's easy. After I jimmied it the first time, nobody bothered to shut it right."

"You mean you have been breaking into the church—to pray?" I knew I was beginning to sound like the police, but I couldn't help myself. It also felt weird sitting in the darkened church, me on the chancel step, she in my chair, holding a colloquy by the narrow beam of a flashlight. "But this is your church," I said.

"Of course it isn't," she replied in a way that closed that avenue of discussion.

"Well, you know what I mean. It *could* be your church. You worship here. You are free to pray here anytime you want. Just quit breaking in. What if the trustees find out?" Then I added generously, "Here, take my key. I can have a new one made. Go ahead, I give you the key to the church."

We sat there in the dark for quite a while that first night. Over the next few months, she would continue to break into the church to pray, usually on Saturday nights, and I would continue to offer her a key (the trustees would have died). But she never accepted it, because, as far as my mystery woman was concerned, the church was not a family to be joined but a fortress to be stormed. This church was for breaking into.

Her name was Teri, which was a Midwestern compromise between her mother's name, Terami, and her real father's choice, Theresa. She lived with her stepfather and two brothers in a mobile home in the Brush. No, this was not her church, but she was so beset by problems that she could find no other place to clear her mind and pray. At twenty-two, she was juggling night classes at Southern Illinois University in nearby Edwardsville, waitressing in Cherry Grove, tending bar, and staying out of her stepfather's way. And she was pregnant. "Some guy" she didn't care about had her carrying a baby she didn't want. Her mother was dead. Her stepfather customized vans for the local dealer and did occasional house painting, which meant that he worked a day or two a week. The rest of the time he drank Jim Beam and shot squirrels.

The fact is, Teri did have a connection to our church. Her mother had been engaged to a Semanns boy, but when she got pregnant his family "ganged up" on them both and forced him to drop her. At least, that's what she claimed.

"There's this story called 'The Lottery' . . ." she said. *Still freshman reading,* I thought, *after all these years.* "Every year the people in this nice little village choose one person to sacrifice, you know, to make the crops grow." She curled her lip and squinted, as if trying to help me see the connection.

"I know the story, Teri."

"Okay, it wasn't exactly 'The Lottery,' " she conceded, "but it was *like* it."

"That's better. The Semannses may be a prickly bunch, but let's don't make them characters in 'The Lottery'!"

"Fine."

She told me that her mother went off to Martinsville to get away from her heartbreak and to have the baby. When the baby arrived, she named the child after herself, Terami. The two Teris lived in Martinsville for about ten years until the mother married and the family migrated south again to the notch in the prairie northwest of New Cana.

"But who is it?" I asked.

"Who is who?"

"Your real father, of course. I must know him. He's a Semanns, right?"

"You don't know him. He's—he's—dead."

"So you don't care about your father?"

"Why should I? Besides, I told you he's dead."

Teri was smart enough to know that she had to get out of the Brush. But when you're poor, you don't up and move away from your poverty. She worked in the restaurant, tended bar on weekends, and enrolled in classes that were practically free to state residents. But there was no escaping the trailer and the beer bottles. Living with some guy in Edwardsville, where the university was located, was supposed to be her ticket out of the trailer and away from the Brush. But it took her only as far as another trailer, another small town, and another foul-tempered man. The move to Edwardsville hadn't worked out, so she was back in the Brush again, this time bearing her own little secret to whom she darkly referred as "the Thing."

When I confronted her in the church that night, Teri was looking for a home, though she wouldn't have put it that way. She needed a place to pray that didn't smell of stale beer and cigarette smoke. She was also considering an illegal abortion in suburban Chicago, though how she could have managed that without money, friends, or transportation was unclear. When her stepfather found out about the pregnancy—and it was only a matter of time—he would smack her. If he got wind of an abortion, he would shoot her like a possum or a squirrel.

She may have felt that she possessed a lineal right to the church building if not the community. She was desperate and depressed. I was always afraid she would hurt herself, and one night she did the unthinkable. Instead of raising her usual window, she impulsively jammed her arm through it and bled her way into the church.

That act proved to be the beginning of a more public relationship with the congregation. After all, the window had to be fixed. I informed the elders of special privileges for a young woman that would grant her access to the church at "odd hours." They seemed more concerned for my reputation than Teri's mental health.

I hadn't considered the ramifications of meeting a strange woman in a dark church. But that wasn't what concerned them, and I was left to guess their true intent. From that point, Teri began seeing me for counseling and prayer in my office at home, which seemed a relief to my wife, but made the elders no happier.

These were gray months for my wife and me. Our lives were as circumscribed by the Cana church as my parishioners', perhaps more so, for they at least got out in the fields and worked in the dirt. We seemed to be shriveling into people who haunted an old house and an older church. What had happened to the graduate students who once knew every bookstore and pub in Bloomsbury, who used to talk about ideas? In the space of a few months we had become creatures of the sanctuary, the parish hall, the drafty parsonage, my office, and the cemetery. On Sunday evenings we socialized with the youth. On Mondays we burned our trash. On Wednesdays we had *Kaffeekuchen* with the quilters. On Saturday evenings we mimeographed the church bulletins and later folded them while we watched TV. *Every* night when we finally turned in after the last feeding, we lay in the dark and listened for the reassuring snap of the mousetraps in the kitchen. In the morning we emptied them. Everything in our lives was occurring within a one-hundred-foot radius of our new washer and dryer.

Neither of us had grown up in a parsonage or benefited from the rules of parsonage culture. I had no ministers on my family tree, and Tracy had only been baptized as a senior in college. Neither of us had signed on for the sequestered life of a country parsonage. Tracy had received no lessons on being a preacher's wife, but she never complained about her role. She simply followed her own nature, which was to be positive, cheerful, and inquisitive.

She learned about gardening and putting up pickles, taught a Sunday School class, chatted up the quilters (no doubt inhibiting their gossip), and even joined the Ladies Fellowship, all the while reading Edith Wharton on the fly and trying to salvage a stagnating dissertation.

Her life was not made any easier by the self-importance with which I approached "my ministry." I had invested a decade's worth of grooming in this position, and I took it seriously, too seriously. I pointedly closed both sets of doors between my study and the rest of the house, as if to erect a wall of separation between my important work and the distractions of my family.

When my wife occasionally reminded me how small and undemanding my parish really was, I got angry and accused her of not understanding. She accused me of hiding in my study. "The way you hide behind the garage?" I asked.

She reminded me that I made plenty of time for whining parishioners and neurotic counselees but didn't have the time of day for her or the babies. "Let the most dysfunctional member of the Toland family show up, and you drop everything and roll out the red carpet," she said at one of our low points, "but you lock the door to us."

What would prevent her from finishing her last two courses at SIU while I watched the children? I agreed but only on the condition that we buy a second car—just in case of a pastoral emergency. We both knew that a second car, like a second TV or second winter coat, was out of the question on my meager salary. Point proved. I won again. In the same fight I coolly informed her that my work took precedence over her schooling because mine was a Calling and hers was—what?—a job.

When we were first married, Tracy and I lived on love and a few dollars a month. In England we managed nicely without a car, a TV, or a checking account. We assumed our mastery of the simple life would continue in the idyllic setting of a rural parish. How was it possible that this homely little church was pushing us to our limits?

A toddler and a newborn, as well as recovery from a second cesarean, added elements of fatigue to the first winter of our discontent. But now, compounding her exhaustion, Tracy was not resting during the day and couldn't sleep at night. When I noticed a bottle of Valium in the bathroom cabinet, it dawned on me that our disagreements were helping turn a problem into a crisis. How can two people drift apart in a farmhouse?

The Valium was a big deal to me, much more so than for Tracy, who simply finished the prescription and never refilled it. But the crisis we experienced was enough to frighten us both and help me see her desperation. In time, what was occluded between my wife and me slowly opened and, to our great relief, we began to breathe again.

Baby Adam turned out to be a happy child except every night and every morning when he cried continuously. Otherwise, perfect. When he cried at night he arched his back and could not be awakened to be comforted. He seemed to go rigid with terror, as if having a nightmare. But what could a five-month-old be afraid of? "He's a colicky baby," the mothers of the church assured us. We stroked and held him, and even sprinkled water on his face in an attempt to wake him from his bad baby dreams, only to feel guilty afterward. Eventually he slept, only to wake at dawn with more wailing. Those were noisy mornings in the country with all living creatures, including the turbulent Adam, invoking the sun, as if they had made it stand. The rising sun replied,

> *All you beasts and cattle,*
> *and all you flocks and herds,*
> *bless the Lord!*

One morning Adam and I peered through the splayed light and caught sight of a white-tailed deer drinking in our neighbor's pond. He stared at us intently between two casual drinks, and leapt into the forest. I occasionally carried Adam around the grounds or sat on the porch swing with him as our day began, waiting for the light, asking God to give us both a little peace.

By the time I met Teri, then, my new son had already given me a course in the trials of the night and the blessings of the morning. When it came to child rearing, Tracy and I had drawn on the wisdom of a few women in the congregation. I was hoping that the congregation would shoulder some of Teri's burden, too. However, she bore the handicap of being an outsider, a denizen of the Brush, which meant that even though she attended church and was working her way through SIU, she was nothing more than some kind of immigrant, a renter, a Eurasian hoosier, poor off-white trash, and could never be one of us. "Is she even *Lutheran?*" someone asked.

Most professed to know little of the outsider or her mother and their unhappy history. But a few knew. A few could remember back to 1950 or thereabouts, when a pregnant teenager quietly went away or, according to Teri's version of the story, was driven away. I knew they remembered, for the lovely sound of *Terami* set a few older jaws on edge.

Ronnie Semanns, Bertie and Lois Semanns's son, got testy whenever Teri's name came up at council meetings or in parking-lot conversations. He never failed to make a show of his resentment of what she had cost the church. And he should know, he said, because he was filling in as church treasurer, and it was his responsibility to cover the bills for her "common vandalism." He and his parents drew into a fist at the mere suggestion of help for this intruder. The family was beginning to chafe under an old debt—or so I imagined.

Teri was getting herself gossiped but, as far as I could see, not in a helpful manner. One evening Leonard and June Semanns treated Tracy and me to dinner at a catfish joint in the Brush not far from Dempster. It was a simple little tavern with a knotty-pine taproom and a Budweiser clock. Above the bar, General Custer and his men were getting slaughtered as usual. We sat in the screened-in porch on the side where they served fried catfish with sweet onions and beer. After dinner we drove into North Alton and strolled around the countrified Antique Village.

Leonard and I fell behind the women, and I put it to him. "About Teri, Leonard. It's in Bertie and Lois's family, isn't it?"

"What do you mean?"

"You know, Ronnie gets pretty tight whenever Teri's name is mentioned. What do they have to do with it?"

We stopped walking, and he turned toward me and said, "Once upon a time, somethin'. Now nothin'."

"What does that mean?"

"Ronnie had an older brother named Ted who killed hisself."

Hung hisself in his father's barn.
Because he didn't have a barn of his own.

Leonard was drifting into formulas in a way that would soon shipwreck genuine conversation.

"Tell me what you know, Leonard."

"Ted lived in Prairieview after he got out of the Army. Did mainly odd jobs. His wife, or widow, Billie, still lives there. She had Billie's House of Beauty, but that was a few years ago. They were once members here, but they never came."

Leonard went on. "But about Ted and Teri, I mean Teri's mom—Ted always denied it. There's two sides to that story. True, he did know her, and they did have a romance. Bertie and Lois didn't like it one bit. But . . . *but* Ted wasn't the only guy interested in her by a long shot. All these farm boys just home from service, Pastor. Let me tell you, Teri's mamma was one beautiful woman. She was something *Oriental*." He said it and paused, as if to give me time to fall away in a dead faint.

"What does that have to do with it?"

"Now? Nothin'. Then? *Everything*." Leonard moved to his summation. "All I honestly know, Pastor, is when she got pregnant she left, and with no husband going with her. There was more than one family that was glad to see her go. Ted stayed. Then he married Billie. Then he died."

"But what are the connections?"

"I dunno. Who does? Look, what happened to Teri's mamma was not all that unusual. If you think country girls don't get pregnant, you have led a sheltered life."

"But this was different."

"Yep yep yep. There was more talk about this one, I'll grant you that, 'cause of her race and her looks. Funny, what bothers one generation to death, the next one hardly notices." Leonard's voice trailed.

Then he added, "Billie don't get around here much."

"That's an understatement if I ever heard one. I've never seen her. I didn't know she exists." *Another expatriate in our community*, I thought.

You don't know him, Teri had said, which was her way of counseling, *You don't want to know everything*. Now Leonard's agnostic tone was saying the same. *You don't need to know. Because there are some things you are not allowed to know*. Memory is not a camera, it is a darkroom.

Was it Ted? And if Ted, then what about his parents? I couldn't look at Bertie and Lois every Sunday without wondering about their role in the disappearance of Teri's mother. Bertie was a revered figure in the community and a key member of the cemetery committee. His advanced age and frail appearance belied his continuing authority in the community. Unlike most of the Semanns men, he was small and flinty rather than tall and rawboned. Although he had farmed his whole life, he had the skin of a bank teller, so chalky, in fact, that the first time I met him I thought he was sick, like his brother Alfred.

Bertie had presided over my test when the Silent Seven watched me down a beer in his rathskeller. In the 1930s, little Bertie led the grain strike that shut down the elevator in Granite City. A Lutheran who defied civil authority—that was hard enough to imagine without these stories of forbidden love in New Cana.

His wife, Lois, wore spit curls behind the temples of her gilded eyeglasses and laughed softly all the time. She, too, had once played a leading role in the church, comparable to June Semanns's or Alma Buford's. Now, she and her husband kept close to their immediate family except for his cemetery business and her weekly quilting.

It was difficult to imagine these two shells of virtue acting spitefully toward a pregnant teenager. Every Sunday I found myself studying their faces as if they were death masks, searching for any trace elements of cruelty or vindictiveness. Perhaps I lacked the imagination for evil, but nothing came to the surface. Bertie and Lois were decent people in a community of good neighbors who, try as I might to imagine it, could not have moved with such fury against an "Oriental" girl and their own poor son.

"*It wasn't 'The Lottery,'* " Teri had said, "*but it was like it.*"

I'm sorry, Teri, but there are two sides to every story, including yours. Memory is not a camera.

"Say, we'd better get home," I said, snapping out of my own reverie. "We've got a baby-sitter to pay." A chill was coming off the river anyway, and Leonard gallantly put his jacket around June's shoulders. It was comfy in the car with the windows up on a cool summer night. The four of us drove back to New Cana without much conversation.

True to Teri's own premonition, when her father found out she was pregnant, he did hit her. Hard, in the jaw. I kept June Semanns apprised of the situation, and she and Leonard put it into the hands of the elders. The elders quickly located a shotgun house just outside town and helped move her in. It wasn't much, but it had three rooms, running water, a stove, and a propane tank. She agreed to pay fifty dollars per month rent.

June also informally collected an old couch, a bed, kitchen table, window fan, and various knickknacks, and within a week the place was furnished. It was a shelter where Teri and her baby could grow to term. Several months later June organized a baby shower in the parish hall. Alma Buford got the wives from the garage involved as well. It was mostly a young-to-middle-aged gathering. Only a few of the older women attended. Those who helped seemed to do so in deference to June's moral authority in the community. Only June and Alma appeared to have a clear understanding of why we cared about Teri.

One Sunday after church I found a sealed white envelope carefully centered under the glass top of the sacristy desk. "TERRY'S COLLEGE FUND" was typed on the envelope. Inside was $750 in cash. The words on the envelope bore the telltale imprint of the church's ancient typewriter. But who had given the money and typed the words?

In the ensuing weeks other envelopes followed, one marked "TERRY'S BABY," another simply "DOCTOR." I suspected Bertie and Lois were the source, but I never proved it. Their son Ronnie was a church leader and, therefore, had a key to the building. He could have typed the envelopes. But then practically *everybody* in town had a key to the church. And would he have misspelled her name?

What did the money mean? Was it guilt money to salve the bad consciences of two old people, or was it a genuine attempt to heal the past?

In November Teri continued the spell of *Teramis*, and gave birth to a girl. She would have delivered her baby alone, but for June, who stayed with her throughout, and in a few days brought mother and baby home to their cottage. Up until that point, Teri's secret had unfolded only barely beneath the surface of the community and was, therefore, subjected to ferocious gossip. Teri was never the speaking subject, of course, but always a mysterious, partially hidden object of the community's speculation or assistance.

All that changed when we baptized Asia Theresa and welcomed her into the church. Everyone was there in their familiar places—Leonard and June sat in front with Teri and the baby; Buster Toland by the window, Ernie Semanns in the back; Alma Buford took photos. Bertie and Lois were there, too, along with Ronnie and his family. They watched the proceedings as through a single set of narrowed shutters. Everything remained the same and yet, with the coming of Teri and Asia, everything changed. Every fixed position imperceptibly shifted in relation to all others. We were no longer quite the same church.

The pastor solemnly asks the congregation, "Do you renounce the devil and all his empty promises?," which is the liturgy's way of asking a gossiping congregation, "Will you give up telling lies about one another?" And my congregation replied thunderously.

We renounce them.

When I took Asia in my arms, I said, "Receive the sign of the holy cross both upon the forehead and upon the breast, in token that you have been redeemed by Christ the crucified." The words are a part of every baptism. I had spoken them to my colicky son several months before as I held him in my arms and baptized him. They have always struck me as a portent. If you think you live under no sign other than your own good luck, these words promise an ominous alternative.

Flannery O'Connor has a story about a little girl who loves to visit the convent and the sisters. But every time the nun gives her a hug, the crucifix on Sister's belt gets mashed into the child's face. The gesture of love always leaves a mark.

I know the theologians locate the miracle of baptism in the mysterious convergence of water and the word of God. But that morning the transformation occurred a bit later in the ritual. After the last blessing is given, the pastor asks the parents and child to turn and face the congregation to receive its welcome.

In the definitive act of church-breaking, Teri, radiant in her only dress, shyly turned and faced them all. For a moment, at least, the gossip *about* the outsider caught its breath and fell silent, until it would begin again on behalf of her daughter.

Finally, at long last, Teri was embraced by the church. But not without the mark. Not without being mashed and nearly crushed by the buckle. Bertie and Lois didn't escape it either, nor Ronnie, and certainly not the lost Ted. None of us had.

12

The Scarlet Letter

 During my first year at the Cana church I was called upon to do a great deal of counseling, especially marriage counseling. In seminary, we were exposed to a smattering of psychological theories, along with the then-standard assurances that religion and psychology share the same general values. The goal of both is to help the individual discover the resources for healing that reside at the core of each person. It was safe to assume that master therapist Carl Rogers's concept of a person was the same as Jesus of Nazareth's. When I was in seminary, my classmates and I all considered ourselves "Rogerians." Some of us smoked pipes.

We were trained to listen to our parishioners without judging their attitudes or behavior, to parrot their every comment, to elicit insight from their own words, and to refer difficult cases to a professional therapist. Some of my classmates wore white coats when they made their hospital "rounds." All we lacked was the stethoscope dangling casually from the pocket.

Oddly, we learned next to nothing about the role of prayer, scripture, confession, or spiritual direction in the counseling process. The church's practices in worship or its ethical teachings were thoroughly segregated from our counseling sessions. We didn't know *The Ladder of Divine Ascent* or Gregory the Great's *Pastoral Care* or the Ignatian *Exercises* or Teresa of Avila's *Life*, in which even she admits "I did not know how to practice prayer." It wouldn't have occurred to me to pray with an angry husband and wife or alienated parents and children—perhaps in a church service in the general confession or in a hospital room if they were sick, but never in a counseling session.

When religious people have problems, several studies have shown that more than 50 percent of them turn first to a minister, priest, or rabbi. In rural areas the figure runs closer to 80 percent. It wasn't that my parishioners distrusted psychiatrists or psychologists, but they were farmers, and farmers assume that anything can be fixed with the tools at hand, which in their case were the church and its pastor. They first turned to their "shepherd," but he either practiced his Rogerian clichés on them or quickly referred them to a secular professional.

In fact, I had followed that pattern with Teri. Initially, I viewed our counseling sessions as supportive of her "real" therapy with a county psychologist in Alton. I had arranged her sessions through Social Services, but the more she revealed of her professional therapy the more disenchanted I became. Her therapist brought nothing to the table for Teri. He offered no tradition, community, or authority larger or older than Teri's own experiences. They were spinning their wheels in the same unhappy material. Her therapy was isolating her from her newfound community.

I admit that I might have felt some jealousy toward the therapist in Alton, who intruded into the privileged space once reserved for Teri and me and who promised to fix things I couldn't understand. He seemed to plumb the depths while I remained on the surface. He was the professional, I was the country parson.

Whenever I met with her after one of her sessions in Alton, I invariably encountered a Teri I didn't much like. The edgy, open, impudent church-breaker was closing up, saving her sharpest insights for the professional. Her interesting self-awareness was turning into self-absorption. After a session in Alton she was less likely to trust anyone, including me. She wasn't turning the corner from her own unhappiness to reliance on her Deliverer, which is the pattern taught by many of the Psalms. Whenever Teri went with her own instincts, they led her to self-pity and resentment toward those who had hurt her. We never prayed for her persecutors because it was not healthy to do so.

The conflict that was brewing between us never came to a head due to a banal and now familiar reason. One afternoon Teri said to me, "I'm not going back to Thompson" (her therapist).

"Why not?" I asked.

"He's always hugging me or begging for hugs. Yesterday I thought he was going to try to kiss me. I am so sick of it."

And that was that.

If pastoral care yielded mixed results at best, presiding at worship offered the satisfaction I craved. When I opened my arms and said, "The Lord be with you," the congregation would chorus back, "And with thy spirit," which never failed to feed my spirit. When the service ended, the ushers would throw open the back doors to reveal greens and golds of corn in tassel and the faded reds of distant barns. Our little church opened on to the whole flowering planet.

Once you've caught a glimpse of the cosmos through the back doors of your church, it doesn't seem like such a big deal to suggest to a sweet young couple that they quit sleeping with other people.

Which is precisely what I had to say to the congregation's favorite "nice young couple," Steve and Susan Truly. Steve was big and blond to the eyelashes; Susan was small and dark, and sinewy in a way that had recently become fashionable for women. He was a part-time student and a kilnsman at the glassworks in Alton, and his wife had just taken a secretarial job at the same place. Susan was a child of the congregation, a transplanted Dullmann. I had baptized Steve shortly after performing their wedding.

As far as I know, their wedding was a historic first, occurring as it did outdoors, beside the stand of beech trees at the edge of the church's property. They had shown up for the rehearsal dressed in their usual overalls-*chic*, and barefoot—which got my dander up—but it was next to impossible to stay mad at two such attractive, likable people.

In their wedding ceremony the next afternoon Steve and Susan's recessional moved to a spoken rendition of a poem by Lawrence Ferlinghetti, "Wild Dreams of a New Beginning," which also had to be a first. The setting sun was sending a shower of sparks off our broken copper cross. The afternoon light cascaded through the trees onto cinched women in flowered dresses and men in starched white shirts. They sat in folding chairs rented from the mortuary in Cherry Grove. The groomsmen were dressed in pale lime tuxedo-style leisure suits. One of them recited,

> On the lawn among the trees
> lovers are listening
> for the master to tell them they are one
> with the universe.

Most of the guests were sitting "on the lawn among the trees" themselves, their mouths literally hanging open. But we got through it. I justified it to myself by thinking, "At least it wasn't Rod McKuen."

Actually, I didn't want Steve and Susan to get married in the first place. During our premarital counseling sessions, I couldn't help but notice that they fought constantly. They could not agree on a car to buy, a house to rent, or on smaller things, like bank accounts, credit cards, and wall colors. They had a terrible time agreeing on Lawrence Ferlinghetti. One of the most impressive fights they held in my presence was over the question of neutering Susan's cat. After six weeks of this, I called Steve and Susan to my office in the parsonage. It was a breezy spring afternoon, and I took them out on to the porch to break the news to them. They sat on the porch swing, while I balanced myself on the rail. A dragonfly buzzed us a couple of times and went on.

"I've been noticing something about you two over the past six weeks," I said, which was the wrong thing to say because they thought I was going to pay them a compliment.

"You have, Pastor?" Susan said. "What's that?"

"You fight all the time. You can't agree on anything. Remember Muffin? Even the wedding plans. It seems to me that, if you're arguing all the time now when you're supposed to be deeply and romantically in love, what's it going to be like after you've been married a couple years?"

"We are deeply in love," Susan pouted.

"We are romantic, Pastor," Steve assured me. "Real romantic."

"Oh, I know you're romantic, all right," I said, wondering why I had used that word. "But are you hearing me? You do know what I'm talking about, don't you? You fight. All the time. As your pastor, I am going to say something I've never said before: I am asking you not to get married."

Susan and Steve looked at one another and sighed. They were not shocked by my request, but, since the invitations were already in the mail and money had been put down on the VFW hall in Cherry Grove, cancellation was not an option. Still, they had recognized their problem and had already crafted a solution.

Susan said, "We know we don't really get along so good, but there are *some things* we like." She said this with awkward coquetry, as if to spare me embarrassment. Then, getting down to business: "So here's what we're going to do. I plan to work the first shift in the office, and Steve'll work the second on the floor. I'll get home around four-thirty in the afternoon, about an hour after he's left for work. He'll get home around midnight or twelve-thirty, after I'm already in bed. We'll never see each other. And if we don't see each other, we won't fight, will we?"

This was the logical premise upon which their young marriage was built.

Late in the fall Clara Dullmann put the bug in my ear to give Steve and Susan a call. They had attended church once or twice in the six months they had been married, and Clara suggested, barely veiling her concern, that I might invite them over for a "checkup."

They arrived like students at the principal's office. Steve had the sullen look of a twelve-year-old who sets fires and can't understand why everyone's upset. Susan looked guilty, too, but she harbored a more profound knowledge of transgression that smoldered darkly behind her eyes. She appeared ruined. This wasn't just another one of their fights. The nice young couple had fled the garden with some new and disappointing information about themselves.

I should have seen through their randy courtship into the moral vacuity of their souls. That's what comes from chattering with a nice young couple about wedding music and the custodian's fee. Six months after their sixties-style wedding, they were—also sixties-style—bedding down other people. Steve "started it," Susan said, sounding more like a little sister than a wife, with a woman at the plant, and then another. Susan retaliated by means of an accountant in the office. Now they were even—and miserable.

That day we began a long journey to marriage. I can't say *back* to marriage, for there had never been anything there to return to. We started with the present and worked step by step backward to their wedding, their covenant, courtship, their parents, upbringing, and their values.

These sessions helped me understand the classic interpretation of sin as *absence*. Their acts of infidelity had created real hurt, but everything they did to each other seemed to emerge from a mysterious vacuum that had somehow slipped in between them, an absolute void into which love and decency had disappeared like dead stars into a black hole.

For me, it was more than a passing question: Where did that big black hole come from in a little church like mine? And how had it invaded the hearts of such *nice* people?

In our second or third session, I began to doubt that we would make it. That's when Steve pulled out a copy of the runaway bestseller *Open Marriage* by Nena and George O'Neill and began reading whole passages to me. The book represented itself as a work of cultural anthropology. It was loaded with the sort of *real data* that would have appealed to college sophomores or anyone with intellectual pretensions. It contained case studies from other cultures and disinterested observations, all of which were reported with an insufferable tone of objectivity. The book's bibliography had doubtless been assembled by a graduate student with a sense of humor, for it featured entries like "Spouse-exchange Among the North Alaskan Eskimo."

The book's message was that if you want to grow as an individual, don't get trapped by the cultural hang-ups of a "closed marriage," that is, a covenant based on monogamy. Why be suffocated by the Victorian values of fidelity and parenthood? In an open marriage, each partner is free to cross the boundaries of convention. You can stay married, if that's what you want, and satisfy other personal and sexual needs at the same time.

I listened impatiently to the wisdom of the O'Neills for about twenty minutes until I could take no more (by this time Steve and Susan had me thumbing through the paperback). I slid the book across the desk at them and said, "This is so much shit."

That was a mistake because the word "shit" on the lips of a pastor deeply offended their moral sensibilities. Such was the state of things among us. They took grave exception to the word *shit*, while I was expected to remain noddingly neutral toward their adultery. *Well, shit*, I thought. Without apologizing, I tried to convince them I was merely "upset" by the prospects of their separation. Gradually, I achieved the clinical tone that they so admired in the O'Neills and evidently expected in their country parson.

In time, we survived *Open Marriage* and moved on to more profitable topics. We created a counterscenario of what Steve and Susan wanted for their lives and then began the behavioral moves that would enable them to achieve it.

In about our seventh session in my parsonage study—with my counselees sitting in the two captain's chairs in front of the desk, which was the only arrangement possible in the cramped space, and with my kids screaming to the beat of Abba pulsating through two sets of closed doors—Steve and Susan forgave each other.

At their suggestion, we walked over to church after our last session. I flipped on the altar spots, and the three of us somberly arranged ourselves for a wedding. Without benefit of poetry, leisure suits, or other folderol, Steve and Susan renewed their wedding vows. It was nothing we planned or rehearsed. I simply paraphrased the wedding ritual, inserting words like "continue" and "rededicate," while they grimly held one another, as if characters in one of Ferlinghetti's sadder poems.

The madness between them ended. They actually quit fighting. The void went away, or we peeled it away, poisonous petal by poisonous petal, only to discover that even nothingness has a center. Steve and Susan found reconciliation at the center, and I found the ministry of reconciliation that God had promised me and the whole church. Novice that I was, I felt like shouting, "It works! It really works!"

My euphoria didn't last long, however, because I still had to deal with Buster and Beulah Toland, and Bust and Beulah *never* stopped fighting, or "fussing" as they put it, ever. He yelled even in normal conversation, and she never stopped whining. With them it was not a matter of counseling but refereeing. Beulah's drug problems and Buster's disposition to financial ruin made it hard for them to maintain the infrastructures necessary to a marriage.

Sweet Max was a very slow learner who needed more attention than he was getting. Lacy was old enough and ready to go his own way. Little Angel seemed immune to the chaos, as though she belonged to another family and was only boarding at the Tolands.

Buster and Beulah never came to my office for counseling. Neither was capable of sitting down and holding a conversation. Besides, the crisis was always located in the house they rented next to Buford's Garage. Since Beulah refused to cook, the place was always littered with old fast-food cartons. Bust had a habit of leaving used engine parts around the house as well. Anyone who lives in the country has rats in the barn; Bust and Beulah had them in the house. I did my refereeing in their home, where the crisis slowly rotated like a stalled hurricane from pills, to bills, to Max, to filth, to Lacy.

The only members of the family I ever got into my office for a proper counseling session were not Buster and Beulah but Buster and Lacy. That happened only because Bust practically wrestled Lacy into the truck one day and brought him to the parsonage.

Lacy was struggling with school and didn't have a job. He challenged his father at every turn, and on one occasion took off with his old man's truck. Buster and Lacy could not tolerate each other's presence, but because neither had a way out they were obliged to share a madhouse and follow the same predictable cycle of violence. These two strapping men, one with a barrel chest above a beer gut, the other in a Dead muscle shirt that showed off his new tattoo, were together the picture of powerlessness.

I did not know how to solve their problem. This would have been a perfect time to make a referral to a trained professional (Teri's old therapist was most deserving), but the two in my office were in no mood for referral. They sat in the captain's chairs facing each other, tensed and ready to fight. Buster might easily have slapped his son across his "surly mouth." Lacy was ready to slug his father.

We talked about how mad they were right now, and why, and how neither could get the upper hand over the other. We rehearsed the everyday outrages between them. They had grown a little less tense when I decided to ask father and son what each wanted from the other. Any lawyer could have advised me never to ask a question to which I didn't know the answer.

As soon as I put it to Buster, "What do you want from Lacy?" I was sorry I had asked, because I knew the ex-Marine would have a litany of complaints. Doubtless he would say, "I want him to get a job, a haircut, some new friends, real clothes instead of costumes, a little religion—a whole fuck'n new attitude . . ."

I braced myself.

Instead, Bust looked at Lacy, who by this time was slouching like a normal teenager, and said as softly as I ever heard him say anything, "I want him to be my son."

The late-afternoon sun stole behind a cloud, and dusk seemed to settle inside the study. The room fell into a state of molecular peace. Everything stopped for a few seconds, then started anew. From the next room the TV said, *Won't you be, won't you be, won't you be my neighbor?* and someone turned it off. Then it got very quiet again. The two men sat facing each other, dumbfounded.

When it was his turn, Lacy rattled off his demands like a hostage-taker. He wanted everything but a plane to fly him to Cuba. His list ranged from "respect" to "a decent stereo," but you could feel that everything had changed. His heart was no longer in his performance. Even as he ticked off his demands you could see he was thinking about how to answer his father's eloquent prayer.

About half my counseling sessions were the result of family coercion, though few actually employed the hammerlock as effectively as Buster did on Lacy. Nobody in New Cana ever went to the pastor to work on their issues or to grow as a person. They came—or were pushed—because something was about to rupture in the community.

Bill and Nora Dullmann no doubt pressured their daughter Heather to see the pastor, though Heather never admitted as much. She came by appointment and sat defiant in one of my captain's chairs, dressed in faded jeans and an Illini sweatshirt, sleeves pulled as if prepared for arm wrestling. Her auburn shag coordinated perfectly with an embarrassment of freckles from the cap of her forehead to the tips of her fingers. She routinely blushed in casual conversation on most any topic. Although her parents and I had a cordial if not close relationship, Heather always kept to herself. I made small talk with her every Sunday but hardly knew her. In her eyes, and perhaps those of the other young adults, I had already been co-opted by the old people in the congregation.

Her given name was Harriet, but on her eighteenth birthday she had her name legally changed to Heather. None of the townspeople knew what to make of it, with the result that no one ever called her anything. That was two years before. Until now, changing her name was the most radical sign of her dissatisfaction with Harriet Dullmann and New Cana, Illinois.

"You know I am in love with a man, and I am not going to give him up," she said in a fury, her neck beginning to go rash pink.

I had actually seen Heather kissing a guy who looked like Elvis, with a pack of cigarettes rolled up in the sleeve of his white T-shirt. There were few discreet trysting places in New Cana, and they hadn't found one. One afternoon I walked out of Burley Means's store and saw them in the shadows of Buford's Garage leaning against the wall. What they were doing struck me as a pretty public gesture, but, not wishing to leer, I minded my own business. I had no idea that the Elvis-guy was thirty years old and had a wife and three kids.

Later, when Heather and I met in my office, I would have liked to ask her why, when it came to men, she and her friends were willing to settle for so little. Heather had been an A student in high school. According to her parents, she always had her nose in a book of poetry. Other young women in our community had ambitions to be nurses, technicians, teachers, agronomists. Yet they too settled for creeps like "Elvis," who had no ambition beyond working odd jobs and riding a motorcycle. They married when they were still girls, but, unlike their parents, their marriages lasted only long enough for them to get pregnant and give up their dreams.

The younger generation would have said that their parents stayed married only to conform to social customs. But I think their parents remained together because they had begun with the hope of a common venture—the farm—and that made the hard work and sacrifice worthwhile. At least, they had an opportunity to build something that would last. Their sons and daughters had long since given up that illusion.

In the past twenty years half the farms around New Cana had disappeared through consolidation. Even though the fathers spoke grandly to their sons about inheriting the family farm, their children knew that all they were inheriting was the right to rent land that had once belonged to their parents. They knew that they would continue to live in the "country," in tiny speed traps like Cherry Grove, Prairieview, or New Cana, but the country would have nothing to offer them. When they weren't "doing a little farming," which was code for hiring out their labor, they worked like dray horses in the mills in Alton or the refineries in Wood River. These boys were the sad outcome of the farmer's proverb, "Shirtsleeves to shirtsleeves in three generations." I suspect that Heather had never known a boy or a man who hadn't glimpsed the endgame. The result was old-fashioned, country nihilism where an outsider like me would have expected "community values."

But a thirty-year-old father of three, a married man! This affair was broadcasting destruction. What about the wife and children? What would this mean for them? Heather professed not to care. What about your mom and dad? Heather cared even less, or so she swore. What about you, Heather Sue Dullmann? *Would Harriet have done this?* I wanted to ask.

"This *is* me," she said through clenched teeth. She seemed furious that I condescended to tell her who she was. After all, she had named herself, hadn't she?

"It's my job to tell you who you are, Heather," I said half-apologetically. "We are members of this extended family . . . We are accountable to one another. We are accountable to God."

I was playing the heavy in this conversation, the tyrannical male authority who was trying to stifle her only hope of freedom. The *Herr Pastor* has the power of the word and his office. He represents the accumulated righteousness of the cemetery committee, the elders, and all the old people. She had nothing other than her own will, but even that was thwarted. She couldn't simply move in with him because, well, the guy has these *kids* running around the house.

Toward the end of our painful conversation Heather said, "I don't care what you say, Pastor, I am keeping him," as if he were a stray dog.

And entirely without premeditation, I replied, as if continuing her sentence, "Then you should not come to communion. This is between you and this church, Heather. As long as you are seeing a married man," I said, now trying to soften the judgment, "I don't think you should come to the Lord's table."

Her face lost its color. She hugged herself across her chest, then folded her hands primly, as if to compose herself, and placed them on her lap. She looked down at her hands, and tears the size of raindrops began to fall upon them. She didn't sob or make a single sound until she said, "It's not fair." She said that several times, and then she left.

Heather's response took me off-guard. I hadn't thought through my judgments, and didn't expect the tears. Why was she crying? She wept because something had been taken away from her, and she was already missing it.

Predictably, Heather and the guy she vowed to "keep" split up in a few months. It was quickly over and forgotten. It would have ended with or without my intervention. A rebellious young woman and an older, married man will not live happily ever after. But the affair left an open sore, and not a healed scar, between Heather and me. In typical Cana fashion she refused to speak of it again. She didn't need to be reconciled to me because I had only executed a function, like the person who cleans your teeth or bags your groceries. It was nothing personal.

What happened to Heather? Is she a middle-aged mom with two

freckle-faced teenagers in Peoria or Bloomington? Does she ever think of that day? It doesn't matter. What mattered was an unscripted conversation in my study that ended in loss, and that is over. The moment had meaning for Heather only because she loved her church and was nourished by the sacrament. She knew she belonged to this community and belonged at its table. When you are as sure of that as she was, there can be no greater penalty than banishment. She cried because she was ex-*communitied*. What happens when you send a family member away from the table? I shudder to guess.

If we were to insist on the purity of the church, where would it end? Where would it begin? Several weeks after my meeting with Heather, I ran into a hateful old bird named Buehner, whose everyday speech was riddled with complaints and innuendo about "the colored." I let him know that I didn't share his views, but I didn't bar him from the Eucharist or threaten to do so. Why not? Did his routine racism pollute the body of Christ any less than Heather's adultery? Or does sex, especially when it is brandished by a defiant young woman, still rule in the Christian hierarchy of sins?

When I form the name *Heather* in my mind, it comes out *Hester*, and I remember my own sins. I gave her a new name that afternoon, one that I never took back. *Then you should not come to communion . . .* I said. In the heat of the moment, I did not reckon those words as a punishment but an implication of her behavior, but I vested her in a scarlet *A* nonetheless. I draped it around her neck as surely as I took the stole of authority every Sunday, kissed the embroidered cross on its yoke, and placed it on my shoulders. Since I was the one who gave her the scarlet letter to wear, I should have removed it.

I should have, but I never did.

13

"He Hits Me in the Stomach, so It Won't Leave Marks"

I first got to know the Barnes family through Tex, the twelve-year-old boy in my Confirmation class. Tex was tall for his age with a mop of sandy hair over close-set eyes. He stood out in a class of misbehaving eighth graders because he was so quiet. At first I mistook his silence for a scholarly nature, but I soon discovered that he was no more interested in Luther's *Small Catechism* or the Missionary Journeys of Saint Paul than the rest of my pupils. He was thinking all the time—but about something far from church.

Like concentric rings in a pond, the members of the Barnes family unfolded themselves to me. I next got to know Tex's younger sister Millie in the sixth-grade class, then the two younger children in Sunday School. They led me to a passing acquaintance with their mother, Rose, a woman who in our first meeting appeared tired and, like Tex, preoccupied with distant problems. Eventually, events brought me to the outer circle and to a disturbed husband and father named Seth. The entire family pointed like the hand of a compass toward Seth.

The only word of gossip I had on the Barnes family was that "the Missus" is kind of "mousy" and that "Mister" "drinks." She keeps house near Blaydon; he drives a big rig. Beyond that I knew nothing until one morning after Confirmation classes Rose Barnes told the children to stay in the car and walked back into the parish hall and asked to speak to me. Since there was no private place to talk in the building, we walked into the sanctuary and stood in front of the altar, where Teri and I had first met, and there she asked me for help.

Her story tumbled out faster than I could comprehend it. Most of it revolved around her husband Seth, who had transformed their home into a chamber of horrors. One detail of the gossip was accurate: He was drunk a good deal of the time and even drove his sixteen-wheeler when he was drunk. He also suffered from paranoid delusions and carried a gun. He had once invaded the emergency room of the VA hospital, pulled a gun on a nurse, and demanded that she remove the electrodes from his head. Incredibly, Seth had slipped out of the hospital and through the bureaucratic nets of Social Services and the law and was never detained.

Another part of the gossip about the family was decidedly wrong: Rose was *not* "mousy," but she *was* beaten regularly. She was a strong, clear-minded person who simply had no avenue of escape. Her husband practiced physical violence in a systematic fashion.

"He hits me," she said, "and sometimes the children, especially Tex. Tex is big, but not big enough to stand up to him." I must have searched her face with my eyes—for bruises?—for she continued to speak matter-of-factly as if she were explaining a family recipe. "He hits me in the stomach, so it won't leave marks."

I begged her to call the police, and I reported his behavior to Social Services, but Rose would not swear out a complaint. When Seth was on the road, the family got some relief and deluded itself into believing that things would be different when he returned. Yet they lived in dread of his reappearance.

Early one autumn evening I picked up the telephone to hear Rose say, "Seth's back. He punched me again. We're scared."

I called the sheriff, who agreed to meet me at the Barnes house outside Blaydon, but he said, "Unless he's committed a crime, Reverend, there ain't much we can do."

The sheriff and his deputy and I arrived at the same time to a disorganized scene. Rose was standing at the front door of their bungalow, the children grouped in a tableau behind her in the living room. Seth was pacing near the road at the edge of his front lawn, fiercely looking first toward the house, then down the road, but at no one in particular. His face was sweaty and bloated, his hair greasy. He had enormous mahogany-colored eyes. They might have once been his greatest asset in courting Rose, but now they were his most frightening feature. He appeared to view his adversaries out of the corner of his left eye.

The sheriff consulted with Rose, who complained that Seth was threatening the entire family. But Seth, who could pretend rationality for limited periods of time, dismissed her fears, reminding the lawmen, "Look, boys, I'm standing here on my own property. Nobody's been hurt, I hahn't done nothing wrong. You can't arrest a man on his own front lawn for not doing nothing wrong, can you?"

The sheriff was stumped. "I reckon he's got us." Then summoning his full authority, he declared to Rose and me, "I cannot arrest a law-abiding citizen on his own land."

I said, "This man has used his fists on his wife and son repeatedly. Sure, he's standing on his own property. And when you leave, he's going to walk in his own house and beat the hell out of her. Can't you see that he is menacing her right now? Sheriff, I am going to hold you responsible for this. By the way, did I tell you he usually carries a gun?"

At this last revelation, the sheriff's eyebrow twitched. "Now look, Reverend, you can climb down off'n your high horse. It ain't my fault that this little lady has four kids and a crazy man for a husband, but it ain't no law against being crazy. If'n I arrest him for nothing, like *you* want me to, *you* won't bear the blunt of it. *I* will. Do you have a restraining order? Of course you don't. The man ain't *trans*passing on his own front yard."

"What if he were trespassing?" I asked.

"Then I could cuff him," he said with a chortle. "Let's say he was at *your* house and you didn't want him on the premises, then I could take him."

"Then let's go to the church office," I said, "and we'll let him trespass there, and you, sir, can arrest him."

Rose packed the kids into their old car, and pulled up behind my car. The sheriff and his deputy got in line behind them. To my amazement, Seth hopped in his truck and followed the patrol car. We formed a strange (and morally dubious) cavalcade as the four vehicles set off in a line for New Cana, the pastor taking the lead in an effort to entrap one of his flock and to have him arrested. By the time we turned off the hard road, night had fallen, and only four sets of headlights, proceeding with the gravity of a funeral cortege, illumined the last stretch of prairie road.

At the church I hastily opened the sacristy and arranged the desk and chairs as if for a counseling session. Rose quickly led the children into the parish hall and then entered the sacristy. The sheriff and his deputy stood to the side of the entrance. With Rose seated nervously in front of the desk, Seth, who by this time was focused like a homing device on his wife, walked up the steps and barged into the sacristy.

I said, "Seth, Rose and I are having a counseling session. It's private. I'm asking you to leave."

Seth said, "This is my church, and this is my wife. I'm not leaving without her. What are you going to do about it?"

I stepped to the door, motioned to the sheriff, and said, "He's trespassing. Arrest him."

The law entered the church and took him without a struggle. Seth glowered at me. "You Judas, you set me up." Then he added in a cloyingly exaggerated tone, "My own *pastor* betrayed me. Arrested for coming into my own church." And they led him away.

Exaggerated or not, his words were true enough to bother me. *So much for the concept of sanctuary*, I thought—and pastoral care. But Seth was a sick and violent man who was determined to hurt his family. By having him arrested, we were buying time and making certain that he would be given psychiatric evaluation and treatment.

Throughout the ordeal, the four children sat quietly in the parish hall. They were coloring pictures furiously when we came out of the sacristy, except for Tex, who watched the lawman push his father into the backseat of the patrol car. He studied the scene intently, as if memorizing it, and then followed the car through the darkened fields until it made the last T toward Blaydon and disappeared.

Within the prescribed seventy-two hours Seth was given a committal hearing before a magistrate in the county seat. His wife and doctors knew he needed treatment and asked the court to commit Seth to the state hospital in Gaston for a period of ninety days. When it was Seth's turn to speak, my heart sank as he addressed the court with cool rationality.

It was true, he said affably, that a combination of factors had put the entire family under strain. After a long absence from this part of the county, the family had relocated from Texas, where he had been in an Army hospital (*that might have been true*) as a result of a wound suffered in Vietnam (*that was a lie!*). In many ways he felt he hadn't ("hahn't") recovered from that ordeal. Now his job took him away from home too frequently, with the result that the family had a hard time establishing a routine. The children were not sure of their father's authority. They have to know that the mother stands square behind the father.

The judge nodded sympathetically. *(Oh, dear God, he's buying it.)*

Now Seth was speaking to the magistrate as if the latter were a bowling buddy. "Unfortunately, their mother hahn't helped the situation by turnin' the children against their father, bringin' other men into the house *[another lie]* where they and my wife have done godknowswhat, claimin' I don't bring home a big enough paycheck to support my own children, tryin' to tell me that the very house we own *[they rent]* is in danger from the jewboys at the bank."

If the judge had been nodding off, he was now giving Seth his complete attention.

"Go on, Mr. Barnes."

"I'm gonna *rule* in my house the way you do in yours, Judge. Whatever it takes. A woman shall be subject to her Lord. The Bible tells us that much. Spare the rod and spoil the child. That too." His voice was building toward an awful, ritualized climax.

"What was done to me could have never happened without the United States government—and, I am sorry to say, that woman sittin' right there," pointing to his wife, "and the Jews who own this nation's hospitals, including the military ones of 'em. I am caught, Your Honor. You are caught, too, but you probably don't know it." He spied me out of the corner of his left eye and began to say something more, then stopped.

After the court committed Seth for ninety days, I had to admit to myself that I had already heard most of his opinions from perfectly sane farmers and businessmen in our county who routinely used the Bible as an almanac of disinformation and prejudice and blamed everything from low prices to bad weather on the U.S. government. The Jews didn't come up that often because no one had ever met a Jew. The Jews were simply a branch of one subsection of the great *Them* that makes our everyday lives as miserable as they are. Outside family and friends, just about everybody is a player in some conspiracy or other.

On a crisp Saturday morning you can hear such talk from earnest men in overalls in any country post office. But if you put on a tie, slick back your hair, and express such views in a sanity hearing, you'll go to Gaston State every time.

A few days after the hearing, I made the mistake of trying to visit Seth at Gaston. I can't imagine why I thought that he would accept pastoral care from the man who helped lock him up, but I did. Perhaps I didn't want to admit that I had made a pastorally ambiguous decision and that, in his eyes, at least, I had hurt him badly.

I found Seth in a literal padded cell, which I entered accompanied by an attendant. He looked sideways at me as if a roach had just crawled out of his mattress ticking. He also seemed genuinely surprised to see me.

"You. What are you doing here?"

"I want to talk to you, Seth."

"Well, I don't wanna talk to you. You think you can screw my wife, turn my kids on me, call the cops, testify against me, and then walk into this shit-can of a room for a nice little prayer? God damn you," he said, savoring each word. "You get the fuck outta here."

Of course, the "system" didn't work (Am I beginning to talk like Seth?). "They" let him out in three months, no better off as far as I could tell than when we committed him. His time away had given Rose a chance to clear out of the house and get established in a new neighborhood with new schools for the kids. I wondered how many times she had moved under similar circumstances. The family was in need of intensive therapy, especially Tex, who grew quieter with every passing day.

Gaston State was not the last I saw of Seth by any means. He hadn't been lying when he said he'd been in a VA hospital in Texas. The benefits provided by the very government he despised got him stabilized on medication, kept him in an apartment, and allowed him to buy an old Buick convertible in which he endlessly cruised our county roads. He drove slowly and glared at everyone he saw, especially me.

Now the shoe was on the other foot. He really *wasn't* doing anything wrong anymore. He was not interfering in his family's life; he was not trying to hit his wife or threaten her. He was simply cruising in the neighborhood of sanity, daring us to deal with him again. Seth had become a visible symbol of the medical, legal, and religious failure to solve the problems posed by one violent, sick person.

Seth started coming to church again, but only on the Sundays when his family was absent. How he knew their schedule I don't know. Now, instead of the pastor paying the parishioner an unwelcome visit, he was dropping in on me. If he was trying to rattle me, he was succeeding. Or perhaps he was only acting out the same point he made the night I had him arrested: This really was his church.

Whatever his reason for coming, he spent virtually the entire service looking at me (*Now* who's the paranoid?). He would slip into the back pew on the pulpit side, measure me with his evil eye—his face glistening with sweat and berry-brown from cruising in his convertible—and glare maniacally at me for about forty-five minutes. He never participated in the service and always left before it ended.

Now it was my turn to become agitated. I remembered about the gun. "When he gets tired of punching me, maybe he'll shoot me," Rose had said.

I found myself worrying about the gun, too, and about getting shot— not your usual concern in a small rural congregation. I did not want to turn my back on Seth. I could imagine the story in the *Cherry Grove Gazette*, "FAITHFUL SHEPHERD GUNNED DOWN AT ALTAR," just beneath an account of Ethel Semanns's Tupperware party in the New Cana social column. In my scenario, as I turn to the altar, Seth jumps to his feet and pumps several bullets into my back while my congregation sits frozen in horror. The tumult in the church is followed by lamentation and communitywide bereavement. As it turns out, I was a much-beloved shepherd.

Seth was a Lutheran and knew that the service is divided into two parts, the sacramental phases in which the pastor faces the people and the sacrificial moments when the pastor faces the altar on behalf of the people. He had doubtless learned this in Confirmation class and would probably wait until the sacrificial part to shoot me.

I took my fear of Seth seriously enough to alert my wife to keep an eye on him. She was very sympathetic, but with two squirming toddlers she was easily distracted. So I turned it over to the elders. I filled them in on the background of the story and explained my fear. In place of the wandering, cigarette-smoking ushers I positioned two men of authority at the back door, Gus Semanns and Bud Jordan, and gave them this instruction: "If Seth pulls a gun, you yell, 'Get down! Get down! Hit the deck!' Something like that."

Seth never pulled a gun, and the Faithful Shepherd lived to tell the tale, but I never forgot how I felt on those Sundays when his eye was upon me. For their part, the elders registered an unsettling absence of astonishment at being told what to do should a member of the congregation begin firing on the preacher. They nodded gravely and took it in stride, as though these things happened every Sunday.

Seth gradually disappeared like a Polaroid in reverse. His menacing church attendance waned; sightings on the country roads became less frequent. After a few months he was gone, into a neighboring county, perhaps, or another world.

Some of us worried that Tex was becoming more and more his father's son. His journey into the shadows was just beginning. The brooding nature had been there all along, but now it was no longer offset by his father's madness. The congregation and I did our best to support Rose and Tex, but too many emergencies had taken their toll. The crisis had become their way of life.

What happened to the Barnes family? The word from Blaydon was this: One night Rose came home with a U-Haul and moved the boy and girl and the little ones out of their house. She had run this drill before. She left her rent on the kitchen table with no forwarding address. Neighbors think they were headed for Texas, only because the girl said something about it to a friend.

They left before dawn. The neighbors weren't certain where they were headed, but "the Missus" was driving. That much they knew, and this: Nobody was following them.

It wasn't until a year or so after Rose and the kids left that I heard how Seth died. The news came thirdhand, but it was mostly believable, with the exception of one detail. Seth had drifted south along the river through Prairie du Rocher and Chester, all the way to Thebes, where he continued his practice of cruising the country roads and intimidating the locals.

One day he and a pal got drunk, and Seth drove his Buick straight off the launch ramp and into the Mississippi. Witnesses said the convertible rafted down the river a good ways, doing a slow rotation or two like a toy boat on its way to Cairo and the delta, until the current took it, and the Buick with its two occupants disappeared beneath the waters. A few days later they found the body of Seth's friend downriver. Seth himself never turned up.

It's the way I'd always imagined he would go: raptured straight into the earth, where no records are kept and no one would ever find him or lock him up and tell him he was crazy. The only thing that surprised me was that he had made a friend.

With the Barneses on my mind, this church was beginning to feel like a shelter or a rescue operation. Then I spent some time with old Annie Wengert, who testified to another way of life.

Annie was a Semanns, who through a long and complicated series of deals and house trades within her family was dying in the same bedroom she had been born in. That was back in Grover Cleveland's first term in office. The Illinois of her childhood was the prairie and not yet the corn belt. She had walked with her brother behind a horse-drawn plow, and she had watched Neil Armstrong walk on the moon.

Annie could no longer stand to wear her teeth, with the result that her genuine aura of wisdom was somewhat compromised by toothlessness and shriveled gums. In my memory of her I digitally fill in the teeth for her sake—and mine. I visited with her regularly, and on her eighty-fifth birthday I brought her flowers and cake and said something pious about long life.

She looked out a wavy windowpane and said, "I have a sister who's eighty-eight. Oh, Pastor, what if that should happen to me! Enough's enough. *Alles hat seine Zeit. Verstehst du?*" She always addressed me with the German familiar form of "you," *du,* because we were friends.

"Yes," I said, "I do understand. Everything in its time."

She and her husband, Louis, had worked hard on their farm and raised a good family. Life had not been easy on Annie. Her Louie had fought in France in the Great War, and they were separated for nearly two years. When he came home, it took him a while to "become himself again." She had passed by opportunities to marry other, more successful young men and remained true to a shell-shocked boy with no land.

Annie and Louis had nothing but each other and a few acres given to them by an uncle. At first they grew only strawberries and vegetables. Annie raised her own chickens and worked for her relatives. When Louis wasn't trying to develop their own farm, he hired out his labor at fifteen cents an hour. Over the years they leased, bought, or inherited enough acreage to make a living. They filled marshes, built fences and outbuildings, and dug drainage ditches by hand. When they took over her father's dilapidated old house, they jacked up the floor, built on a lean-to eating area, added closets, and installed indoor plumbing, which Louie initially resisted as unsanitary.

Their lives were not given to them; they wrestled them out of the soil like unruly hickory stumps. Every day was framed and defined by hard work. They endured floods and drought as well as the Depression when farmers couldn't sell anything. Annie and Louis had five children in all, one of whom, a little girl named Dorothy, died of diphtheria. *"After the worst had passed,"* she always added formulaically. She was buried in our cemetery.

There was another child, George, who had his hand mangled in a baler. When Louis died a few years back, Annie came under George's and his wife Marge's wing. She was living in George's house now, or was he living in hers? It didn't matter. Her "nursing home" consisted of the home place and a family and congregation that honored her as a source of wisdom. Her retirement community was her neighbors, who looked in on her regularly.

If it is true that there are only two farm narratives, the one dwelling on the hardships of rural life and the other on its goodness and generosity, Annie clearly opted for the latter. Like a lot of farm women, she could say, "We never went hungry." "Hard work didn't kill us." "You can count on people around here."

Her age had finally released her from the woman's traditional burdens of defending her husband and bearing his children. An Isak Dinesen character says, "Women when they are old enough to have done with the business of being women and can let loose their strength, must be the most powerful creatures in the world." If that is so, Annie's last power took the form of knowing what she wanted.

"Enough is enough?" I said half-mockingly. "You don't want more life, Annie?"

"I think you know the life I want."

"But what about this life?" I asked.

She looked at me as if she were testifying in a court of law. "I am satisfied with my life as I lived it. There are some things I wisht wouldn't have happened and some things I wisht I hadn't done, but they are my life, too."

When she reviewed the events of her life, it was clear that she considered it an immense adventure. *What a ride!* she might have exclaimed, *all the way from baptism in Cana Lutheran Church to burial in Cana Lutheran Cemetery. What a journey my life has been!* Although her husband had seen the world "the hard way, courtesy of Uncle Sam," she herself hadn't got beyond Missouri. And now she lay on her ancestral land, almost within view of the cemetery where she would be buried. In the steely realism of country ways, her name was already chiseled into her headstone. All they needed was the date.

It was the open-ended suffering of the Barnes family that drew me closer to Annie. She was my counterpoint to Rose and Seth and Tex, who traveled their separate tunnels with little or no prospect of a homecoming.

For all I know, it's Tex who's doing the cruising now, looking for something his father never found, or maybe still looking for his father. And how desperately Rose needed Annie's sense of completion. Annie hadn't escaped suffering; she had borne her share and more. But she had arrived *somewhere* and with something intact. The entire arc of her life testified, There is a proper end of things after all.

She recognized the homecoming in herself and spoke eloquently about it from her iron bed. I needed her testimony that day, perhaps more than I knew, as we flirted away the afternoon, arranging her flowers and nibbling her birthday cake.

Whan that Aprill with his shoures soote
The droghte of March hath perced to the roote,
And bathed every veyne in swich licour
Of which vertu engendred is the flour;
  —Chaucer, *Canterbury Tales*, Prologue

14

Rogate *and* the Steel Mills

 When April's sweet showers had bathed the dry veins of March, callused palms the size of gourds would cradle a few hybrid seeds as if they were crystal, and our church would ask God to make the crops grow. At the end of the service, representative farmers would lead the congregation through the back doors of the church and across the road into Norbert Semanns's muddy field, which at this time of the year was as rank and sweet as black bread soaked in port. There we symbolically planted the seeds.

The seeds took their place among the sediment and minerals deposited there by the scraping and removing of prehistoric glaciers. They joined the deposits of flints and particles of iron left by every person who had ever cultivated the land or hunted on it. All the humors were present in the humus, including pieces of every bird and animal that ever fed off the land, burrowed into it, and died on it. The water, blood, meat, bone, gristle, hair, and ammoniac gasses left by their carcasses was joined by the good Lutheran humus up the hill in the cemetery, which, incidentally, was draining into our well and contaminating the parsonage drinking water. "Aw, Pestur, don't worry," Gus chortled, "they was all good people!"

That was the joke of my first year. We couldn't drink the water because of its abnormally high Lutheran content. I thought of Whitman's line from "Song of Myself," "If you want me again look for me under your boot-soles." Communing with one's ancestors is one thing, but drinking the dead was quite another. In reality, the vast underground river of nitrates and herbicides probably *was* killing us all, but we yukked it up about the cemetery. The field across the street must have belonged to someone—Norbert Semanns, Sr., once "owned" it—and yet it belonged to us all, and we would all live or die by the field. You couldn't stand in the field without being impressed by the kinship of humus and humans.

Ironically, the minister who pronounced a blessing on the land was a callow suburbanite who had once chafed at hoeing his father's vegetable garden. He hadn't known any better than to kill a harmless blacksnake behind the parsonage and then have his picture taken with it. His wife frequently sat in a bikini at the edge of the pasture and read Edith Wharton and Emily Dickinson.

The corn was in and already behind, but that didn't matter, for *Rogate* was observed the fifth Sunday after Easter, no matter what. The ritual of the fields had been going on throughout Europe since the eighth century. *Rogate* is the Latin word for "pray." Because Jesus is risen and now intercedes for us in heaven, we can pray on earth, and *for* the earth.

The Protestant church was already in the process of discarding the named Sundays of Lent and Easter even as we blessed and planted the seeds. Now they bear the evocative names "The First Sunday in Lent," "the Second Sunday in Lent," and so on. The fourth Sunday in Lent was once named *Laetare*, which means "rejoice." It was known in the church as Refreshment Sunday. On this Sunday rose paraments replaced the traditional purple of Lent, and, psychologically and spiritually, we breathed a little easier. The color rose seemed to say, There's light at the end of the tunnel. Even at the dead center of Lent, Christ is risen.

The Protestant church got rid of *Laetare* as well as *Rogate* and many of the other days for reasons I have never fully understood. It created a bland church calendar and liturgies *du jour* in the image of people who have been abstracted from place and history, who have no feel for the symbols and no memory of the stories. They live, work, and worship in climate-controlled buildings. They have largely adopted a digitalized language. Their daily routines override the natural rhythms and longings of life.

I can only say that the Latin words were not too much for my high school dropouts. The simple outline of church history didn't overtax their imaginations. The liturgy and church year made sense to the farmers in New Cana, for who better than a farmer understands the circularities of life? The church year had a rhythm, and so did their lives.

Some would argue that the observance of *Rogate* arose in an agricultural world and is, therefore, irrelevant to all but the 1.7 percent of Americans who still live on farms. But my congregation understood the metaphor that underlay *Rogate*, which is this: When we do any kind of useful work, we join the act of creation in progress and help God keep the universe humming.

June Semanns's day began in the kitchen at five-fifteen when she prepared scrambled eggs, pork sausage and gravy, a pot of farina, hashed brown potatoes, breads, biscuits, or coffee cakes, and coffee. She was responsible for feeding not only her own family of six but by the lunch hour ("dinner" in the country) a crew of hired hands, as well.

Dinner was served to men who had been working in the fields for six hours. It was simple and heavy—beef roast or fried chicken, mountains of mashed potatoes with gravy, peas, green beans, tomatoes, sweet corn from the garden, rolls and breads from her own flour, and at least two kinds of pie, all of it relayed from the kitchen to a large Victorian server with sideboards.

The family and hands sat at an oval-shaped golden-oak table. I was always struck by how quiet it was around the table at midday. There was no small talk. The sounds of consumption were accompanied by a few cryptic remarks about work that needed to be done or the occasional request for more food. "Meat," one of the boys would say with a flatness that conserved his energy for eating. On special occasions June served plates of deep-fried morel, which was a common fungus growing wild in the fields. Most everyone called it "steak," often with a wink. "You tell me it don't taste like filet *min*-yon, Pastor. I dare you," Leonard would say.

In between the first two massive meals of the day, June parceled out jobs to whoever was home, checked the brooder, called her market, went over the route with one of the kids, worked in the garden, and kept up with her sewing. Now that the farm was mechanized, she was exempted from running the farm's dairy, chicken, and vegetable business.

After World War II, the government decided to treat farming like any other industry, which entailed getting women off the tractors and back into the kitchen. The publications of that period promoted a new cult of domesticity, as farm wives became housewives once again. Old women like Annie Wengert had worked in the fields and on the threshing floor. By June's day, women were restricted to the still-enormous job of managing a household and cleaning the farmhouse—the "woman killer," as it was called by nineteenth-century farm wives. While their husbands surrounded themselves with the most advanced tools and equipment, the women continued to perform manual labor domestically. Down the road from us, Lottie Semanns kept a husband and four kids in clean clothes on the strength of a four-legged antique washer with a hand wringer and no dryer.

June Semanns still maintained local egg customers on the outskirts of

Blaydon, but the other domestic operations, such as the vegetable garden, had become big business. Now she tended garden only for her family's consumption. Early in the afternoon she drove up to Cherry Grove where she carried the mail that another woman had sorted in the morning. After the evening "lunch" for ten people or so, she paid bills and worked on finances.

You used to hear stories about farm men who drove their wives "like mules" or whipped their boys to make them work harder. I had my suspicions about a few in this regard, but not about Leonard. He and June completed one another as perfectly as any couple I have known. Economically, they complemented one another's work without coercion or resentment. Emotionally, her sweet reasonableness managed to calm his raucous ways, and his high spirit stirred her up whenever she looked tired or worried, which was often. Leonard could crease his handsome face into a rakish smile at will, like the actor Robert Duvall. June could laugh only if Leonard made her. They were in their mid-forties, but they might have been married fifty years.

Leonard and June operated a business that required technical and managerial acumen, to say nothing of the farmer's traditional knowledge of crops, weather, and soils. When I first met Leonard he had just gone deeper into hock to buy a $44,000 combine. His inventory of tractors, planters, pickers—and the tools to fix them—was worth a small fortune by farm standards. Leonard had to master the labyrinth of prices and subsidies and somehow keep himself abreast of recent advances in scientific farming. Physically, he had to be able to pilot a planter or combine for hours on end, breathe the dust and chemicals, and then, five days a week, walk away from it all at three o'clock sharp.

At three o'clock he threw water in his face, changed his shirt, ate his third piece of pie, and headed toward the steel mill in Alton for another eight hours of labor. Some of the men worked the graveyard shift, preferring to nap in the evening, work in town till six, and then join the morning chores in progress before crashing for a couple hours.

What Leonard and the other farmers found in Alton was a different world. The mill was a campus of rusted, corrugated sheds—scores of them—painted in faded and peeling greens, browns, and grays. In many of the buildings entire panels of siding were missing. Across the top of each building, small-paned clerestories were slathered with three-dimensional grime. Many of the individual panes were broken. The yard was veined by railroad tracks on which open cars of scrap sat rusted to their tracks. Piles of corroded pipe and twisted rods littered the yard.

The noise in the steel mill had no source or center. Each building emitted its own racket through the black openings in its siding; together they produced a Surround Sound of aimless, arrhythmic clanging, grinding, screeching, and hissing, like an enormous engine about to rupture.

Lean, unsmiling men in silver hard hats with stenciled numbers strode with great purpose through the maze, flicking suspicious eyes toward visitors. Everybody smoked. Nobody talked. The noise made ordinary greetings impossible. The racket of banging steel was violent and unnerving, not like the oceanic roar of cicadas or the comical din of cows blaring at one another across the pasture. We had no trouble sleeping to the drone of distant combines in the autumn night.

The silence of the men in hard hats was not the silence of the old men in Bertie's rathskeller, which was that of married people who no longer need words to express their love. For that matter, it was nothing like the stretches of quiet between Leonard and me. One couldn't imagine a setting more alien to the civilization of New Cana than the steel mills of Alton twenty-five miles away.

Leonard said, "It's as hot as hell, Pastor." We were in the cafeteria, cooled by several large electric fans, and it was not hot as hell. No doubt Leonard was reflecting on where he had been a few minutes earlier, inside his shop in Building 6, where the electric-arc furnace melts iron scrap at 6,000 degrees Fahrenheit. His actual job was to stir liquid steel, a process he explained to me as if I were a child.

Not that long ago, I had stood with him hip-deep between windrows of the first haying. It had been hot as hell on that day, too, with gnats glued to our arms and neck, but the hay and cow dung smelled deliciously sweet, and it was good to feel the land through our boots. We worked it around like barefoot boys. Now in the cafeteria Leonard himself looked as hot as a glowing furnace, flushed with a different-colored heat and putting out a very different odor than he did in the fields. The day's work appeared to have aged him several years.

We were there because one of my parishioners was in intensive care at St. Joe's, and I was running into town at all hours to minister to her and her family. Leonard and I had arranged to have a late supper together in the cafeteria. I quickly discovered that my visitor's badge did not admit me to the smelting and fabricating shops but only into the yard, where I was closely watched, and into the cafeteria with its chrome and Formica tables and rat-colored linoleum floors. The floors were the color of the meat we were eating. Leonard and I were polishing off our meat loaf smothered in chicken gravy along with canned sweet potatoes, canned corn, packaged rolls, and coffee with individual thimbles of powder.

It was a quiet night in the cafeteria. Only a few tables were occupied by men on break. Some chatted softly while they ate from lunch pails, others stared out at the night and smoked. The hum of the fans reduced all conversations to a single murmur.

Leonard said, "I'm thinking of going back to farming full time. This place . . . I will die if I stay here. Anyway, I've got it figured. Loren Roberts has eighty acres he wants me to rent, and I'm lookin' to buy Eldred's place outright. They're too old to farm, and the government won't pay you forever to grow nothing. I can expand my volume with no more capital investment—just labor—and get the hell out of the cattle business, not that I'm in it in a big way, but get out of it entirely. Simplify. So say the Smart Boys. The only borrowing I would do would be for seed and poison. I don't plan to do anything fancy. Soybeans, corn, maybe some sunflowers on the side. Did you know there's money to be made in sunflowers?"

It was like Leonard to calculate from his strengths and not from what "this place," the mill, was doing to him. He had come very close to saying, "This place is killing me," but that's not quite what he said. Not only did he never complain, Leonard was constitutionally incapable of complaining. The decision to return to full-time farming was a vocational watershed in his life, and he felt obliged to run it by his pastor.

Then Leonard said, "Did you know I had a heart attack? I have to think about the future."

I did know that he had had a serious heart attack. That had been one of the first items I learned about Leonard. The local formulas cast his heart attack in heroic terms, as if Paul Bunyan had suffered a coronary:

> Planted all day,
> Got his corn in first,
> Didn't even call June,
> Drove himself to Alton,
> Collapsed at the door,
> Too tough to die.

Leonard had a vocation to farm. When you lose your sense of vocation, like most of the boys in the county had already done, then everything you do is undifferentiated work. It doesn't matter whether you push a broom or make corn grow. Any unit of work is as good as any other, so long as it produces enough units of money. Most of us wind up working for money, not for the joy in the act of production or the goodness of the thing produced. But Leonard believed that he and God were partners on the land and that together they could feed the world. This was too romantic a notion to talk about, of course. If I had tried, he would have smiled his tired, Robert Duvall smile and shaken his head.

But he had mentioned the future. Farmers are guided by tradition more than most people, but they also worry about the future more than most. What if this dry spell continues two more weeks? What if the new $2,500 bull loses interest in sex? What if the Brazilians flood the market with soybeans? What if McGovern gets elected? What if I can't cover my taxes?

No one around New Cana was succeeding as a full-time farmer. Nixon had just frozen beef prices, which for many producers was the beginning of the end. Leonard was about to quit a sure thing in industry and start over as a full-time farmer. He wanted to make certain I would recognize an act of faith when I saw one.

On my second Rogate Sunday in New Cana my sermon was about work, and when I preached it I couldn't get Leonard and June out of my mind. I was considering the story of Jesus' encounter with the paralytic beside the great pool at Bethesda.

It is not a happy story. Jesus asks the man if he wants to be healed, and the man replies by whining about how neglected he has been for thirty-eight years. Jesus says nothing about faith or compassion but simply does the work of mercy that his own nature requires. To make a man whole is just another way for Jesus to be himself. Later, the man turns him in to the authorities.

Jesus' work sets off a huge fight with the religious experts because he healed the man on the Sabbath and commanded the man to carry his bed away, which technically was also a form of work. According to the law, no one is to work on the day of rest. Jesus got into trouble with the religious authorities not because of the words he spoke, but because of the works he did. No one will bother us if we say the usual nice words about Jesus, but when we do his kind of works we will look odd to the world.

Jesus said, "Yes, but my Father is working all the time, and so am I." He might have been echoing the proverb, "Like father, like son," which means we can discern the parent in the child. "She's stubborn—like her mother," or "He's got his daddy's temper," we might say, except about Jesus we would observe, "He's got his Father's mercy." Jesus was acting out that saying at Bethesda by doing the works that belong to the Father.

True, God did take a rest on the first Sabbath. But the rabbis knew that God is free to work whenever he chooses. In fact, if God doesn't work on the Sabbath, how will he keep the planet spinning? Sunrise, sunset, birth and death—this is a full-time job. Without a God who works seven days a week, twenty-four hours a day, the rabbis knew that the universe would fall to pieces.

I wish I could tell you to take your Sabbath rest, too, and do no work. Put your feet up. Sleep late like the preacher. Leave the chickens unfed, the cows unmilked; if the sow is farrowing, let her fend for herself. But the vocation you have chosen doesn't give you much rest. You cannot imagine a single day that is not callused by duties.

Some Christians think ordinary labor is a curse resulting from Adam's sin in the Garden of Eden, as if the reason we have to work hard is because God bears a grudge over a sin committed a million years ago. But this saying of Jesus sets the record straight. Work is hard all right, but it's not the result of a curse. In this story, the curse (if ever there was one) is removed forever. It's replaced by a partnership with God in the ongoing work of creation. Farmers, construction workers, nurses, teachers, steelworkers, but most of all, those who perform acts of mercy toward their fellow human beings—all do the works of God that sustain the universe. One principle remains: "My Father is working all the time, and so am I."

PASTOR (in the sanctuary): Let us now proceed to Norbert's field.

The congregation files out the center aisle in an orderly fashion. The people cross the road and walk unceremoniously into the dirt. There is no talking or laughter.

LEONARD SEMANNS (crouching on one knee as he places the seeds in their furrow): Neither the one who plants nor the one who waters is anything, but only God who gives the growth.

JUNE SEMANNS (flanked by her husband, several farmers, a nurse, and the body man at Buford's): The one who plants and the one who waters have a common purpose. We are God's servants, working together. You are God's field.

PASTOR *(from the midst of the congregation):* Lord, when you came among us, you proclaimed the kingdom in villages and lonely places. Have mercy on those who work hard at lonely jobs, where they can't talk to others or can't be heard when they do. Remind all country people that you are never far from those who plant and harvest. Help everyone in our nation to say grace over their food and to respect those who produce it. O God, hear us as we bless earth, sun, wind, and water, in the name of Jesus.

Amen.

15

"I Believe in Miracles"

 Kathryn Kuhlman was coming to town. Not to our town, of course, but to the civic auditorium in St. Louis. Kathryn Kuhlman was a faith healer and an evangelist. She had her own television program, and she traveled around the country holding services of healing and inspiration. She was not as flamboyant and controversial a figure as revivalist Aimee Semple McPherson, whose offstage escapades had brought her notoriety a generation earlier. Nor was Kuhlman another Billy Graham, who in those days never let up on alcohol, narcotics, promiscuity, and communism. Even when surrounded by the high-tech apparatus of her "ministry," Kuhlman appeared to be a gentle spirit who only incidentally possessed the gift of curing diseases like osteoarthritis and multiple sclerosis. A retinue of white-coated medical experts traveled with her and documented the cures.

Still, like every parish pastor, I was wary. "Who does she think she's kidding," I asked my wife, "with that diaphanous white, flowing gown she wears? That's not church, it's theater."

"But, honey, *you* wear a flowing white gown every Sunday. Okay, it's not 'di-*a*-phanous,' but you strut your stuff, too . . ."

"Never mind."

What made Kathryn Kuhlman a controversial issue in our congregation was the presence of thirteen-year-old Amy Friedens, daughter of Erv and Doris (nee Dullmann), a member of my eighth-grade Confirmation class, who like all the other children, was memorizing Luther's *Small Catechism* and the sixty-six books of the Bible but who, unlike any other child in town, was carrying the burden of cerebral palsy. It was as if every little ache, spasm, and infirmity in the entire community had been rolled into a single mass of suffering and fitted to Amy's narrow shoulders.

"So, Pastor," Amy said as I wheeled her through the parish hall after class, "Kathryn Kuhlman's coming to St. Louis."

"Yes, so I've heard."

Amy laughed as she always did in bursts that she could not contain. She had a sweet, perpetually quizzical smile and the most transparent facial expression of anyone in the parish. Her hair was pulled back from her forehead with a ribbon in the center and barrettes on each side, which accentuated the openness and goodness of her face. Never one for cutoffs or overalls, she was usually dressed like a Catholic schoolgirl, in a white cotton blouse and a tartan plaid skirt. Amy did not have a devious side to her, but I could sense that she was feeling me out on a matter of critical importance.

The *so* was the giveaway. It carried the force of "What do you think?" Of course, she knew I was aware of Kathryn Kuhlman's crusade, and she knew that I had heard the quiet but intense debate going on in the parish. Jimmy the Greek could not have set the odds on this one: Would she or would she not attend the Crusade of Miracles and try to get herself healed? Erv and Doris had let it be known around town that the decision was "up to Amy."

We all had a lot invested in Amy's decision. Her illness had stimulated the most concentrated act of love in New Cana's history. When she was four, her doctors at Shriners Hospital in St. Louis gave Erv and Doris the terrible news. They also prescribed a regimen of "patterning" for Amy. Every hour, eight hours a day, six and a half days a week, a team of four volunteers would stretch and manipulate Amy's neck, arms, hands, legs, and feet in an attempt to "train" her muscles to work together. Patterning would not improve individual muscles as much as provide a reeducation for all the muscles at the same time.

The regimen of physical therapy was, of course, more than Erv and Doris or their nearest relatives could provide. The Cana church delivered the therapy, along with many members of Lutheran congregations in Blaydon, Cherry Grove, and Prairieview.

In the old days, neighbors might have come together for a day or two to raise a barn, roast a pig, and dance to the fiddle and accordion. Amy's malady occasioned a different sort of barn raising. Eight hours a day, seven days a week, people with no earthly knowledge of physical therapy came to the Friedens house and quickly learned how to bend, pull, and rotate a little girl's limbs. At first it was the wives who came, but soon their husbands joined in the experience—farmers, mechanics from Buford's Garage, clerks from the implement store, retirees, teens, neighbors, strangers who read about Amy in their church bulletins, even a traveling salesman or two.

The women carried in Tupperware containers of homemade candy and chocolate chip cookies along with every conceivable kind of fruit bread and cake. When Irma Retzel took her turn, she always brought a tin of her county-famous fudge. Several of the older women brought their versions of Better-Than-Sex Cake. As the summer wore into fall, the entire community flowed through the Friedens' neat little brick rancher with the home-poured ramp out front, where friends and neighbors kibitzed over Amy and ate prodigious amounts of sweets. They say everyone gained a little weight that year.

Stove-up farmers with callused hands and big women in calico dresses knelt on the dining room floor where Amy lay in cruciform position. At first tentatively, but soon expertly, they synchronized the movements of her arms and legs. Doris remembered that whenever they performed their ritual, they said "nice" things to Amy and touched her unashamedly. "In their own way, I think they loved her," Doris said.

"That's where she gets her smile," her father says, but no one really understands how or why a little one who's never danced or walked should possess the most luminous face in the county.

New Cana continued the ritual until that Wednesday before Thanksgiving nine years before, when the doctors at Shriners said, Stop. The exercises have done all they can do for Amy. The human barn raising had ended, though the final product was far from complete.

The patterning had been a blessing to the whole community. It had allowed the church to practice the simple virtues of ministry without delving into the mystery of who caused Amy's condition and why. The patterning represented the church's best religious response to Amy and the Friedens family. Despite the congregation's prayers for God's "sustaining presence" and "healing grace," it was pretty much taken for granted that there would be no miraculous cure. In the folk theology of Cana, the miraculous cooperation that was evoked by the patterning was interpreted as the answer to our prayers. It *was* our cure.

Now Amy was considering going for broke in one last effort at a real cure. Kathryn Kuhlman was no quack. She appeared to be "a good Christian lady," as Erv put it, whose special powers might well be of God. It was not difficult to imagine these two gentle spirits meeting on an enormous stage festooned with thousands of white carnations. Kathryn gently strokes Amy's arms and legs, the way New Cana had done nine years before, and Amy, smiling radiantly, rises from the wheelchair and takes her first tentative steps. A massed choir is singing "How Great Thou Art."

The Friedens family understood the strain this dream had placed on New Cana and, now, on me. The community had performed its ministry heroically, and the church had offered its prayers faithfully. The young minister was trying his best to prepare Amy for Christian life under difficult conditions. His own theology was a little threatened by Miss Kuhlman's approach to healing. He had spent ten years learning that God works only through the church's channels and doesn't usually interfere in the processes of nature.

I suspected that Erv and Doris were already mending fences when they said, "It's Amy's decision." They were not pushing it. No one could criticize a little girl's desire to run and play, so long as her family did nothing to disparage the adequacy of Cana's ministry.

A luminary like Kathryn Kuhlman had the power to give a church and its minister something of an inferiority complex. When confronted by a spiritual celebrity of that magnitude, we couldn't overlook the marginal quality of our lives in New Cana. Suddenly, we seemed so *local*, like the second-string preachers who pick up the pieces after a Billy Graham crusade. We would play backup to one of God's true stars.

"*So?* So, I do know that Kathryn Kuhlman is coming to St. Louis, and I hear you're thinking about going," I said to Amy.

"I am." Amy laughed nervously. "Mom and Dad and I have been talking about it. We talk about it every night at dinner. We have a prayer about it before we eat, and then we talk."

"And so?"

"Well, we think it would be a good spiritual experience for all of us," Amy said in a rehearsed manner. "Miss Kuhlman is a real Christian. I've watched her on TV. She's *pretty*. She couldn't do what she does unless she was true."

"I know," I said. "If she is doing that, she is from God, or God is with her." I meant to say, "If she is *really* doing that," but I couldn't bear to cast a shadow across Amy's hopeful face.

Amy brightened when I spoke positively. "That's what Mom and Dad say, too. It wouldn't be a miracle, exactly." She paused and repeated herself, "It would be a good spiritual experience."

I said, "In other words, Amy, you wouldn't expect to be healed by Miss Kuhlman. You would go there for the prayer and music and the Christian fellowship. Think of all those Christians in one place. I imagine it would be a wonderful afternoon . . ."

Amy furrowed her brow and grew silent. "Not exactly, Pastor, no, not exactly." She pursed her lips with determination, like a child who has just said "No" to her parents for the first time, and is not a little proud of herself.

Now it was my turn to get quiet. We were sitting in the sacristy, where I had pushed her chair. The altar guilders might walk through with flowers at any moment. I closed both doors and felt like locking them.

"What about your mom and dad? What do they say?" I asked.

"It'll be a good spiritual experience for them," she said, repeating the family's phrase for the third time. Then she sat silent for a moment and smiled at me.

"You know, Pastor," she continued after this little dead spot in our conversation, "you're a real good pastor. That's for sure. And this is a wonderful church. We have learned a lot about Jesus and God and Martin Luther, what they did and all. Miss Kuhlman is doing that, too. But you are a real good Confirmation teacher."

She was letting me down easy. A thirteen-year-old was delivering pastoral care to her pastor from her wheelchair, and we both knew it.

She didn't come out and say it, but I had the distinct feeling she was not going to St. Louis for the Christian fellowship. She was going for the cure.

The first time I prayed for a miracle I had been Amy's age. The doctors had all but diagnosed my dad with cancer, subject to a biopsy report that would take a week. All week long I said my prayers every night while I listened to Cardinal games before drifting off to sleep. When the biopsy came in, it was negative. The next time I prayed for a miracle was for my baby son.

"Please, don't let it be hyaline membrane disease. Let it be . . . pneumonia." On each occasion I had presented God with a manageable range of options, but this was different.

If I encouraged her to go, I ran the risk of raising unreasonable hopes. If I did not encourage her, I failed to hold God to his promises—and let Amy down as well.

I reminded Amy that prayer is prayer, whether in an auditorium or in her hometown church. God doesn't listen more attentively to famous people or large groups. God never turns away from us, ever.

"If you go, I will pray extra hard for you. If you decide not to go . . ."

She said she understood and that I was a real good Confirmation teacher. As I wheeled her out of the sacristy, I felt she had made up her mind.

The collapsed wheelchairs, walkers, and crutches were stacked in mountains of wood and metal near the service entrances of the auditorium where the bus drivers had deposited them. Women in stretch pants and men in leisure suits picked through the equipment looking for their loved one's chair or walker. Inside, the murmur of anticipation was growing. It might have been a wrestling match or a basketball game.

An enormous pastel choir materialized on the risers. Almost all the women were champagne blondes. The director, pianist, and the male soloist wore iridescent tuxedos with ruffled shirts. The service would be conducted on an enormous stage uncluttered by altar, pulpit, cross, or any Christian symbol. A baby grand piano sat discreetly to the side. The runway was covered with white bunting as if for a wedding.

Kathryn Kuhlman was a fragile little woman in her mid-sixties with a mane of hennaed hair and a vulnerable smile. She didn't radiate charisma or star quality—until she moved. When she moved, she used the stage and filled it like an Elizabethan actor playing Lady Macbeth. But instead of, "Come, you spirits/ That tend on mortal thoughts! unsex me here," out came her signature phrase, "I believe in miracles because I believe in God," the husky *Gawd* emerging from deep within a set of smoker's lungs. Her trademark white dress, with flowing skirt and fitted bodice, swirled about her. Frilly trumpet sleeves gave her slender arms a life of their own.

She preached as if she had choreographed every sentence of her sermon. When she warned of Armageddon, she crouched like a soldier in battle; when she spoke of God's grace, she flirted the gospel with a Doris Day smile, as if each man in the audience were alone with her in the parlor. When she prophesied the salvation of Israel, she pointed a bony finger toward some imagined horizon and laughed her Lady Macbeth laugh. Then tears came to her eyes. She knew things—awful, terrible things—these farmers did not know, and saw things taking place on the rim of eternity that no one else could see. Long ago, when she was a country bumpkin herself, the star of an Iowa ensemble known as "God's Girls," she had let go of the gospel as a stuffy lecture and reclaimed it as the melodrama it is.

"Wonderful *Je*-sus," she said, "wonderful Jesus, I have no healing virtue. I have no healing power." Speaking of herself in the third person, she added with a throaty laugh, "I wouldn't walk across the street to see her. I was born without talent." The audience could identify with that and nodded appreciatively. These comments proved to be the bridge from her apocalyptic message of salvation to the service of healing. She added, "But if you can use me . . ." and gazed knowingly at the rafters of the auditorium.

The audience began to stir. This is what people had come on busses from as far as Arkansas and Oklahoma to receive. The members of her medical entourage shifted in their chairs. This was it.

"Something is happening in the wheelchair section, something, oh, oh, I don't know," she said in evident distress.

With that, a woman in a flowered muumuu walked haltingly on to the stage. Kathryn Kuhlman spoke to her with genuine affection, as to a puppy. "Come here, come, come." Suddenly, a great river of the afflicted surged across the stage. MS patients exercising their legs, stroke victims maniacally touching their toes, arthritis sufferers mocking their wheelchairs, children clapping their hands and running to their parents. All the while, people in white coats circulated among the victims to verify their healing. Some of the healed swooned on the stage as Kathryn Kuhlman, giggling in amazement, cried, "What is this? What is this?" She seemed to love her victims. After she healed them she often squealed with delight and kissed them. More than a hundred people were made whole that afternoon.

But not Amy.

Where did these lucky ones come from, and how were they chosen from the multitudes to be healed?

The next time I saw Amy she was still in her wheelchair, as cheerful as ever. I had already heard in the post office that she, her family, and a few neighbors had gone up to St. Louis for the service. Word was, it had been a "good experience" for everybody. Even those who remained at home prayed no less determinedly than, years before, they had massaged Amy's muscles and stretched her limbs. How many miracles can you expect in a lifetime?

When she spoke to me in the sacristy, I had worried that going for the cure would leave her disillusioned and bitter, as if a child with cerebral palsy is brimming with illusions in the first place. But then you never go broke risking everything on God. The act of trusting is itself a replenishing activity, like loving or farming or writing. You can't hold back your best for another occasion. If you give of yourself fully, there will always be more to give. Trusting makes for greater trust, not disillusionment or timidity. Amy taught me that. Or, I should say, I learned that from watching Amy smile.

Nobody in New Cana agonized over the healing service in St. Louis, but I did notice a change in Amy. She seemed more prepared to think about her future in a wheelchair and to get on with it. In the course of the following months, she became more vocal about her physical condition and more assertive toward the church. She told us that her dad shouldn't have to carry her up the steps into the parish hall. She was too big for that, and he was too old. Through her uncle, she petitioned the trustees for a ramp and a clearing for her chair among the pews. She announced her plans to become a counselor in a rehabilitation center and by the time she was in her first year of high school had already found a college with the program she wanted.

Would Amy make an effective counselor? I thought of our conversation in the sacristy when she disarmed me with a rare combination of tact and candor. It had taken her about ten minutes to prepare her pastor for a controversial act of faith. If that performance was any indication, our Amy had a brilliant future.

16

The Cleansing

 Three days before Christmas it began to rain. At first the rain cleansed the tin roofs and idle tractors of the year's oil, dust, and accumulated grime, and we welcomed it as though it were an April shower. By the morning of Christmas Eve, however, it was getting ridiculous. The rain seemed intent on flushing the entire cemetery and all its inmates down the notch and into the Brush where the Snake Road had become a raging river. It splattered with mud all that it had cleansed. The animals stood their ground stoically. Eddie Buford's celebrated

Charolais, the only white cattle in our part of the county, turned brown as sewage.

At midday the slope of the cemetery caved in on each side of the gravel drive, and while the dead did not literally come out of their tombs, their microbes did, and gleefully joined the torrent of muddy water pouring down the hill toward our well.

The rain would not have been enough to discourage attendance at the candlelight Christmas Eve service, but as the dreary day faded into night the rain turned to ice. The roads and power lines were freezing over.

A few families began arriving a little before eight. They represented the younger men, who had the strength and foresight to put chains on the tires of their trucks earlier in the day. The elderly either stayed home or piled into the trucks with their children and grandchildren. By the time the service was to begin, about thirty people had gathered in the front pews of the church. For Lutherans, they sat remarkably close to one another, probably because the furnace was not keeping up against the howling wind.

After I vested, I used the acolyte's taper to light the candles on the altar, including the two eucharistic candles, and all four candles on the Advent wreath. With no organ music in the background, the lighting of candles assumed the added significance of all acts performed in silence, like the dressing of a body or the first gestures of making love. I thought of mothers lighting the lights of Hanukkah and of vergers and priests illuminating ancient churches. I thought of my children, who for four weeks had sat solemnly on the parlor floor as Tracy, cross-legged before them, lit the Advent wreath and taught them to sing "O Come, O Come, Emmanuel." Now they sat attached to each of her hips, watching the ritual with astonished eyes. With the fourth candle lit, the entire church breathed. It was official: Jesus had come once again.

When I returned to the sacristy to put away the taper, I found Max Toland sobbing uncontrollably. It had slipped my mind that Max was to make his long-awaited debut as an acolyte on Christmas Eve. No one had explicitly decreed that a backward boy may not light the candles, but somehow he had never been included on the schedule. In the meantime, he had been wearing out the altar candles, practicing every Saturday as if for a decathlon—and now I had forgotten him. Beulah, of course, hadn't made the service, but Max and his dad, Buster, had ridden over with Leonard and June. I put my arm around Max, but he only reproached me with swollen eyes and "How could you?"

I helped him into his red surplice and white cotta and cleaned the snot off his face. He gravely placed his wad of chewing gum in my palm and waited in the sacristy while I returned to the chancel to extinguish every candle. Even before Max appeared in the sanctuary, everyone seemed to understand what was going on. No one minded in the least. We had had our little rush of Christmas awe; now it was Max's moment to shine.

He performed his duty flawlessly, addressing each candle the way a golfer addresses the ball before teeing off. He pointed to each candle before lighting it and said something like, "Number four, your turn." When he completed the Advent wreath, he turned to me, smiled beatifically, and arched his magnificent eyebrows one last time. Then he stole a look at his father, who was beaming as though his boy had just won the spelling bee, and took his place on the folding "acolyte's chair" across the sanctuary.

For my sermon I could do no better than to read from several of Luther's Christmas sermons.

"Let us, then, meditate upon the Nativity just as we see it happening in our own babies. I would not have you contemplate the deity of Christ, the majesty of Christ, but rather his flesh. Look upon the baby Jesus. Divinity may terrify man. Inexpressible majesty will crush him. That is why Christ took on our humanity, save for sin, that he should not terrify us but rather that with love and favor he should console and confirm."

What if we followed Luther's advice and subtracted *majesty* from all our conceptions of God? Would there be a remainder, or would God disappear? I think God would disappear, perhaps already *has* disappeared, only to reappear all over the world as a hidden presence in ordinary lives. As flesh. In my ministry the remainder was this small community of people whose very godliness had vanished, leaving only a collective of wounded and guarded hearts. I have created a formula for the disappearance of God's majesty, one that Luther might have approved: *God* minus (−) *majesty* equals (=) *Cana Lutheran Church.*

After the service the church emptied quickly, except for a woman named Jan. Jan wanted to talk. On Christmas Eve, no less, with my kids on a holiday-high, literally dancing a jig around the tree, Jan wanted to talk—about her husband Ralph, who refuses to come to church, about their twin boys, who are beginning to follow their father's rotten example, and about her mom and dad in Youngstown, who are getting up there in years and who can't possibly keep up that big house with the upstairs empty and oil being what it is thanks to the Arabs.

I was drifting into another of my endless postservice conversations with the Last Standing Parishioner. My wife was impatiently waiting; the kids were dying for their presents. Thinking of my own dwindling Christmas Eve, I said, "Well, Jan, I guess you'll be wanting to get home to your family." That was a mistake.

She gave me a hard look that said, *You are so perfect, with your little blond wife, two sweet children, and your cottage with a wreath on the door. You have no idea what it is to need the church as badly as I do.*

Jan looked over her shoulder into the empty sanctuary illumined by a beam of light on the altar. She could not conceal her bitterness: "This *is* my family," she said, as if I had mistaken a Buford for a Semanns. "Even if Ralph *hadn't* taken the boys up to Troy to go hunting with his daddy, which he *has done* this very Christmas, and which I do *not* appreciate, this'd *still* be my family. I can't help it." Then she excused herself. "Lemme get my ride."

I went home, and Tracy and I exchanged gifts. Mufflers for each, as it turned out. The sort of gifts you buy when your salary is $520 per month, and you are still paying off a master's degree and a cesarean section. We gave each child a big stuffed dog costing ten dollars apiece, which Tracy had put in layaway at the Venture Mart back in October. After we put the kids to bed, we had a glass of wine and ate some Christmas cookies. Then we went to bed in the darkest, coldest bedroom in Gaston County. We did not feel sorry for ourselves.

By Christmas morning a light snow had fallen to cover the ugliness of the past three days. Every branch and stalk was encased in crystal. The boughs of the oak and ash along the drive bent dangerously toward the roof of the parsonage. Rose canes no one had pruned and forsythia no one had planted were stunned by a new Illinois Ice Age no one had predicted. Hundreds of suns blazed in every angle and surface of the ice. Overnight, our trees, pond, and steeple had become a decorative scene on a plate or a teacup.

We bundled the kids into snowsuits and made our way to the Sacred Burning Barrel. Beyond the barrel we hoisted them and ourselves over a woven-wire fence and rolled them like snowballs down the ravine toward the Brush. Laced and snapped into their snowsuits, they moved like astronauts on the lunar surface.

Suddenly, all we could see of the church through the tangle of silver scrub and gnarled branches was the top half of the steeple. With a few more steps, all that remained in view was the broken cross, and then, nothing. We had come to a hollow in which we could see nothing of the human landscape and could hear no sound. In the stillness of the morning, nothing dripped, rustled, or sang. There was nothing to distract us from being alive. We sat like snowbirds for a few minutes and listened to the silence.

Then, with perfect coordination both children began to cry. We put them over our shoulders like little sacks of sand and climbed up the ravine toward our home for hot chocolate and more Christmas.

17

Working the Winkel

I had the notion that we should restore private confession in our parish, the idea being that our group confession every Sunday morning had grown perfunctory and routine. Private confession would be voluntary, of course, and it would work like this: Those planning to attend communion would be encouraged, not required, to stop by the church during the early evening hours of Thursday (before bowling league), Friday, or Saturday for a brief confession in the chancel. It wouldn't entail a recitation of sins but a "discussion of issues" with the pastor, a prayer of confession, and absolution.

I told everybody that the idea came from Martin Luther, but I think it actually came to me by way of my long talks with Teri. I had found that the area in front of the altar is not a bad place for a serious discussion.

No one came. Ever. Not even the most supportive members of the congregation could imagine such a thing. The idea died a painless death.

I was telling my colleagues about the idea and its demise at *Winkel.* Winkel is what German Lutherans called the small circuit meetings of Lutheran pastors. Winkel means "corner" or "angle" in German. It is both a place and a way of doing business. Winkel was designed to provide spiritual nourishment for the nourishers of parishes. Our cell of pastors consisted mostly of older men who served parishes in Prairieview, Two Rivers, Blaydon, Alton, Cherry Grove, and several other towns on the plain.

I loved the nurture and fellowship of Winkel. Never did I feel more like a pastor than when talking theology and gravely conferring with my white-haired colleagues. The only thing I didn't like about Winkel was the name, which sounded silly and rhymes with *tinkle.* When we pastors parted, we would earnestly shake hands and say without a trace of a smile, "If I don't see you before, I'll see you next month at Winkel."

Our Winkels consisted of three parts. First came the Bible study in which one pastor led the others through a rigorous exegesis of one of the appointed lessons. There was none of this "How did you *feel* when you read this passage?" or "Get in touch with your inner Pharisee" or other impressionistic techniques—we brought our Greek New Testaments and plowed through the sentence structure and verb tenses.

The second part of the Winkel was a service of Holy Communion. This was especially meaningful for most of the older pastors, who never received communion *except* at Winkel because Lutherans don't practice self-communion, and these men did not or would not receive from a lay person.

Then came great gobs of *Stollen* and coffee.

The third part of Winkel was what we called *casuistry.* In casuistry we let our hair down and discussed our most difficult counseling cases. Although we never named names, the families of our community were so interrelated that it was not difficult to discern whose lives were being sorted and assessed.

Our casuistry corresponded to our parishioners' gossip, although we insisted to ourselves that we were speaking theologically. What we ministers did in our monthly cell groups actually represented a healthy alternative to the private therapeutic model of pastoral care that still predominates in the church. In place of a therapist-patient relationship, our group's casuistry, like gossip, fostered a sense of the community's responsibility for healing.

I didn't say much in the casuistry sessions, mainly because I had little experience, and what few pastoral encounters I had had—like my late-night conversations with Teri or poor Seth's arrest in his own church—were such questionable moves that I was hesitant to report them.

It was in a casuistry session, however, that I told of my failed experiment with private confession. Everyone was sympathetic, but none more so than Cecil Johnson, my nearest neighbor to the north in Cherry Grove. Cecil's wife Geneva had died of heart failure shortly before we arrived in Cana. Everyone spoke of Pastor Johnson's devotion to Geneva throughout her illness, the depth of his mourning, and now his transparent loneliness—and men do exhibit their loneliness in a way women seldom do. His parishioners worried that their distinguished sixty-seven-year-old pastor was taking too many meals at the Dairy Queen. Occasionally, he neglected to shave. Tracy and I felt as if we had arrived late in the third act of an inspiring play, just after the decisive scene in Cecil's life.

Cece's eyes narrowed beneath unruly eyebrows that might have come from Wardrobe. He ran his hand along the side of his head, loosening long white strands of carefully plastered waves as he did so. He looked like an investment banker but talked like a philosopher. When he said something of substance, Cecil often footnoted his remarks by providing verbal attribution, as if he were a talking thesaurus. It drove his parishioners crazy because they had no idea how or why people named Calvin or Whitehead or Niebuhr were suddenly inserted into his sermons. "Which Niebuhr are we talking about?" they would ask. "The Prairieview Niebuhrs or the Cherry

Grove Niebuhrs?" Among his fellow clergy Cecil's compulsive footnoting was his most parodied trait.

"The people around here have done away with the spoken component. Their faith is so practical that they don't need to talk about it. Oh, sure, they emit an occasional grunt about the weather. But confession?"

Our Winkel nodded solemnly in agreement.

I thought of the wake-like atmosphere in Bertie's rathskeller, the long silences I'd endured with Leonard, and the moribund council meetings in which words were little more than pegs to hold the ship together. I hadn't noticed how accustomed to social aphasia I'd become.

"No," Cecil continued, gaining animation, "confessing takes you considerably farther than a feeling of remorse. You have to know yourself and your sins so well that you can find words to express them. We've buried them."

We? I thought. The repressed farmers or the repressed clergy?

Them? Our words? Or the sins themselves?

Our house had two front doors, a parlor entrance with a bell for pleasure, and a matching office door with a buzzer for business. Two Thursdays after Winkel, at the precise hour when no one ever showed up for private confession, Cecil Johnson rang the buzzer on the business side of the parsonage.

"What a surprise," I said, genuinely surprised. "Tracy is shopping with Sarah. She'll be upset to have missed you. Adam is upstairs asleep, and I'm minding the soup. Come on back to the kitchen. 'Set a spell,' as we say."

I poured some coffee and broke out the peach pie Tracy was saving for dessert. We had an Early American kitchen set, including an oval maple-look table with a plasticized top, four spindle chairs, two of which were fitted with booster seats, and a matching, skirted rocking chair. These sat on a crusty braided carpet we had gotten from Eldor Dietz's attic. Our carpet was strewn with raisins and lids to things. Tracy had painted the kitchen Sears yellow, added a border of fruit decals, forbidden the use of overhead lighting, and placed a couple of brass hurricane lamps in strategic locations, one on the dryer when it was not in use. She also spray-painted the washer and dryer pale green. The effect she achieved was that of a city-person's idea of a country kitchen. Every Saturday, after we put the kids to bed, we drank wine by candlelight and ate one of our free steaks from Ferdie Semanns. Sometimes we laid on a little Johnny Mathis and danced. The kitchen was our favorite room.

"Watch your feet there, Cece. Mind the LEGOs. What do you use?"

"Straight up, young man. You should know that by now."

"I'm honored that you made the effort to drop in on us, Cece, since no one just happens to be 'in the neighborhood' this far off the hard road."

"Well, for whatever reason, I am in the neighborhood," Cecil laughed, "and I thought it was about time that I call on you." We fell silent like the farmers and sipped our coffee. We made the same exaggerated "ah" sound in unison that men like to do when they're drinking something scalding or something strong.

Cecil said, "I do believe this pie is as good as Geneva's. You tell Tracy."

"Tracy and I were saying last night, I believe it was, that we were sorry that we never knew Geneva. Of course, we feel like we know her from the beautiful things everybody says about her—and about how you cared for her. You must be lonesome without her, man."

I wasn't trying to be therapeutic with my comment to Cecil. I was simply touched by his forlorn appearance, and I blurted it out.

Cecil worked his piece of pie around and said, "I do have Geneva on the brain, if you understand what I mean. It's not easy. Of course I miss her. But it's not just loneliness. We had forty-two years together. We were a team. We did everything in ministry together. Did you know that when I interned in Baltimore, we lived in the balcony of the church? Literally. We had a rollaway bed up there. Can you imagine such a thing? When I took my first church in Bentonville, she played one of those old-fashioned bellows organs, not much better than a *Doodelsak*. She organized the Sunday School and taught reading during the week, gave piano lessons, visited the widows, led the mission drive, and did it all for nothing above my ridiculous salary. We couldn't afford nice dresses for the girls or decent presents at Christmas. I know that hurt her, but she never reproached me.

"For years, we had no furniture of our own in the parsonage. There's only one thing worse than a parsonage, and that's a *furnished* parsonage. To tell you the truth, I never minded being a kept man. I only wish we had been kept in better style! When I got fed up with it all—and I did from time to time—who do you think it was who held my hand and told me to pray about it? Who do you think talked about 'our' call? Well, you know.

"You young guys think that you're the only ones who are a little maladjusted to the pastoral life. The seminary has always produced its share of idealists and misfits, no more today than ever. We were going to change things, too. You think the old guys like me have sold out to church bazaars in Bentonville and sausage suppers in Prairieview. No, we're just blazing a trail for you to follow through the same exciting territory!

"Geneva got me through my ministry. I hope Tracy helps you through yours. These women. My wife understood that men and women don't approach God the same way. Men think they have to wrestle with God and win concessions from him. We turn life into a three-fall event, winner take all. We storm heaven; women make heaven on earth. You understand me, don't you? She knew what I needed even when I didn't. I guess I wanted the kingdom of God. Instead, I got this parish. That's a joke, son. *Kierkegaard.*"

Cecil laughed a half-second too late.

I said, as though speaking at his retirement dinner, "At least you have no regrets. It's been a ministry filled with blessings from . . ."

"Oh, but I do. There's more to what I feel than loneliness. More to it than 'Poor Pastor Johnson, eating at the Dairy Queen again.' If I hear any more of that long-lipped pity, I'm gonna puke. I feel like saying, 'If you can beat the Deluxe Platter at the Dairy Queen, why don't *you* have me over and feed me yourselves.' Yes, I miss her, but I also have regrets. A regret. Perhaps I should say I have a question. About myself. I have a question about no one but myself.

"You know, she was in heart failure when I took her into Prairieview. She already had a pacemaker the size of a pack of Luckies tucked into her chest, but the veins were shot. Thank God, we got her out of there as soon as possible and took her to the university hospital in St. Louis. She had no distress, no pain, but no energy either, and she absolutely would not eat. She'd pick at the food, and I would beg her to eat just one more bite of Jell-O. 'Do it for Daddy,' I'd say, just like with the girls. I played a game with her. I'd work one of her favorite foods into the conversation, say, pistachio ice cream, and Geneva would say something out of habit like, 'That sure is good,' whereupon your servant here would rush out of the hospital across Grand Avenue to a supermarket and buy a pint of pistachio, dash back and put a bowl of the stuff on her tray. No dice. 'I don't think so, Cecil dear, not tonight.' It never worked, but I never quit playing.

"Geneva and I understood that she wasn't coming home. She was terribly afraid of going into one of these terminal nursing homes. One day I came to visit, and the nurse had curled her hair and put a pink ribbon in it. Makeup, rouge, the works. She looked like a dolled-up corpse. I asked the nurse what was the occasion, and she said, 'Oh, she was crying this morning, Reverend Johnson. She was saying things I wouldn't repeat to anybody. I've never seen her like this. It was all I could do.'

"Once we got it cleared up that she wasn't going into one of those warehouses, we could actually relax with each other and talk. We talked about everything, especially about the early years. When she was healthy, we reminisced very little. Thought of ourselves as avant-garde old people. But when you catch on that you're dying, you can't deny your own history any more. You have to recite it one last time. When your present gets as thin as hers was, all you have is a past. You are nothing *but* the past with a little rouge on it."

I asked Cece, "Were there differences between you and Geneva still to be straightened out? I imagine not everything gets forgiven in its own time. Maybe that's a foolish question . . ."

"Oh no," he said, "it's a wise question. Geneva and I—what should I say?—committed some real sins against one another in our day. At least by our reckoning. No," he quickly added, "don't get your hopes up, Reverend Father. No cheating or anything juicy. But hurtful things nonetheless.

"One day we decided to forgive 'em all. Clean the slate. Problem was, we were so blamed old, we couldn't remember the details, and we wound up laughing them off. With me lying on top of the covers, her taking oxygen, gasping and laughing at the same time. The nurse came in and just shook her head and walked out."

"So what's this question you have about yourself?" I asked.

Cecil acted as if he didn't remember that he had brought it up. "Oh that," he said, as if trying to decide whether to stonewall me or not. "There was one thing. There *is* one thing. You're a doctor of theology," he said with gravity, "perhaps you can help me with this little problem: Once Geneva got sick, I could not bring myself to pray with her."

I must have made an involuntary gesture of dismissal, for he countered with the most powerful word of the dwindling afternoon, "No."

"For our entire married life, we read the Bible and said our prayers together. That was who we were. That's why we had such a strong marriage. You can't stay mad at somebody you pray with. Every morning we prayed out of *Portals of Prayer* or at least recited Luther's Morning Prayer. Every evening we read a psalm together.

"You can imagine how surprised I was after Geneva died when I realized what had happened. I spent hours and days on end with her, but something had shut down in me. It was as if *I* were the one dying. Have you ever dreamed you were trying to touch something beautiful, you know, like a flower or someone you love, but you can't actually move your arms and get to them? It's as if you're wrapped in gauze. You can't reach out because you're paralyzed, and no one can comfort you because your nerve endings are dead. I couldn't break through to whatever it was that sustained Geneva and me for almost forty-three years. And nothing could touch me either. I never debated praying with my wife. I never consciously decided *not* to pray. I was so dead it never occurred to me.

"First they gave her a line of oxygen, then one of those masks that covered her mouth and nose. I'd look at Geneva's rouged cheeks behind that mask, and I could hardly breathe myself. It was my rage.

"A few weeks after she was gone it began to slip into my consciousness that I hadn't been able to pray. Now the enormity of it has gotten to me. Don't you see? I deprived my wife of the one thing that might have comforted us both.

"What good is the charade of being good old Pastor Cece, the beloved Sage of Cherry Grove, if at the time it mattered most I couldn't break through to the light? It feels like I've spent three lifetimes praying with people I don't care about—at least not the way I loved Geneva—but for her nothing would come. When I most needed to be a pastor, I failed. What good is it, if I couldn't use it myself?

"There's nothing I can do to change it either. That's the damnable thing about it. It's like when the government misspells your name. It will never be corrected. You might as well change your name. I can't tell you how badly I want to redeem those days with Geneva, but I'm blocked. I've tried every trick, but I can't get through. The way is closed to me."

I said, "Cece, you have absolved so many people of their sins. Now you have to absolve yourself. It's when you can't do anything to make amends that God does it all. That's the most powerful absolution there is. You say you can't break through to God. What if God is breaking through to you?"

Cecil said, "You are *such* a Lutheran."

"Aren't we all?"

Then he continued, "It's like *The Imperial Message*. Do you know it? Imagine a great emperor is dying in his palace. He summons his envoy and whispers into his ear a message meant only for you, Cecil Stem Johnson, and sends him on his way. But the passageways of the palace are jam-crammed with people, and the messenger can't get through. And even if he could, he would face the packed courtyard and after that the streets of the city itself, clogged with humanity. Never in a thousand years could that message get through to you. And yet, every Sunday we make the sign of the cross and dream it to ourselves. *Kafka*."

Cece could see that I was alarmed by this little parable. He said, "You can't make forgiveness that easy, friend. Else you make it cheap."

"I know. *Bonhoeffer.*"

"You see, Richard" (he could never bring himself to call me Rick), "I never fully subscribed to the Lutheran view of faith. It always reminded me of the old virtue of believing six impossible things before breakfast, if you know what I mean."

I waited for the *Lewis Carroll,* but nothing followed.

"Being a person of faith does not mean that we make decisions every day about what's true or false. Don't try to tell me that you have sat yourself under that oak tree and asked, 'Do I believe such-and-such proposition is true?' You know, 'Do I accept as a statement of fact that Jesus exorcised a demon or walked on top of the water?' We have made faith into a work of the mind, don't you see. *Luther.* These are impossible questions we force ourselves to answer. No wonder the most distinctive mark of our church is paralysis. We are always impaled on some question of fact.

"So, a long time ago I made up my mind that what really matters is how we live with one another in the church. The real subject matter of Christianity is not a set of truths but the whole checkerboard of our lives taken as a whole. Don't ask me if I *believe* in forgiveness of sins; just let me put my arms around you, don't you see, and *forgive* you. Don't press me on the composition of the body and blood of Jesus, but let's just meet at the table to eat and drink, and figure on meeting him there, too. I am a practical theologian, don't you see. A theologian of practice. If it doesn't work in real life, I'm not interested in it."

Now I could see where this Winkel was going.

"So where do I fail Geneva?" Cece continued, "In the simple practice of prayer. I get hoisted on my own petard. I work out my own theology of practice, and then I can't practice it. It's one thing to make a false move; it's another to dump the whole board."

Cece had worked himself into a terrible Winkel. He had cornered himself and now appeared finished. But a Winkel is also a slant. It is angular speech.

"I understand you, Cecil," I said. "You think the whole practice of the gospel has let you down because you let it down. You couldn't even pray with your wife. You believe that God hears prayer. But even more important, you know that the Christian life is a life of prayer. But you didn't practice it. I am so sorry for you, Cece.

"I couldn't agree more about the practice of faith. The church is full of practices and things to do. But you're not the only practitioner, Cece. Pardon me for saying it, friend, but you do tend to be the hero of all your stories. Enter Cece, *solus*. But here we are, the two of us, having this conversation. I am trying to be a good listener, but I can't possibly understand what's going through your head. And how can I even imagine what you had with Geneva? All I know is that forgiveness was meant to be practiced, but it was never meant to be practiced alone. When we can't do it, like you seem to think *you* can't, there are others around us doing it on our behalf. On *your* behalf."

Cece looked at me as if he had caught on to the angle I was taking. His eyes crinkled with admiration, like a checkers player who's facing a line of kings.

"You see, Cecil Stem Johnson, we have these sentences we say to one another, even when we can't get to the bottom of their meaning. Like 'I forgive you all your sins in the name of the Father and of the Son and of the Holy Ghost.' We even have gestures that go with the words, Cece, like this one."

He took his absolution like a child caught in a Big Fib. Poor Cece. He had concocted this long monologue about how, because he couldn't do *one* thing, God couldn't do *another*, and a mere boy masquerading as a father-confessor had shown him up for the liar he was. How humiliating.

I pulled down the rest of the peach pie from the counter. We finished it off in silence. We each had a second cup of coffee. By that time Cecil seemed anxious to leave before Tracy got home. He fussed with his raincoat as he moved quickly through the hall from the kitchen toward the front of the house. At the fork in the hall he chose to exit via the study and not the parlor. As he let himself out, he offered no parting aphorisms and therefore no final *Kierkegaard* or *Camus*. He simply left through the business side of the house.

179

18

Ashes, Ashes

 On Wednesday morning I dipped my fingers in a bowl of ashes and drew a cross on Buster Toland's forehead while saying, "Dust thou art, and unto dust shalt thou return."

Around noon he'd left Buford's Garage where he worked and went home next door for lunch. There was no lunch, and Buster apparently blamed it on Beulah. She was not his personal cook, she reminded him, and he reminded her that she was a doped-up mess. They had a huge shouting match but, instead of stalking out of the house in a roar the way he usually did, Buster dropped dead. In the blink of an eye, he simply ceased living. "He was dead before he hit the floor," Beulah said at least a hundred times to anyone who would listen.

Later, she would add that he seemed to fly momentarily before falling through the door. Given Buster's size, it was easier to imagine him exploding than flying, but that was how he died as far as she was concerned. Flying.

I don't remember how I found out about Buster, but by mid-afternoon Leonard and I were driving into Alton to break the news to Lacy, who was co-oping at Valley Steel. He was waiting for us at the guard shack, helmet tilted down over shoulder-length hair, eating a candy bar and smoking a cigarette. He had his lunch pail with him, which meant he had no plans to finish out the day. He knew something was up.

Leonard could relate to Lacy far better than I. He would crinkle his eyes and set his jaw in that perpetual smile of his, put a powerful grip on the boy's biceps, and say, "Sonny, I got somethin' to say to you." And Lacy would actually listen. That's the way it would have gone if Leonard had wanted him to be nice to his mamma or help him bale some hay, but this was different. So he took a half-step back and let the minister deliver the news.

I said, "Lacy, I'm sorry. Your dad died today."

"No shit," Lacy replied evenly, neither as a question nor an exclamation. He smiled an involuntary gesture of self-defense. It passed quickly, and he had little more to say as the three of us walked to Leonard's truck.

Buster's death made everyone in New Cana feel apprehensive. The entire community sensed that it had just acquired a new and heavy responsibility. Buster may have been a rascal, but he was our rascal. He was the one who held his family together, and he had left that family to us.

Now Beulah had no one to "fuss" with, and Lacy had no one whose authority he could challenge. She had only forgotten her self-pity long enough to attack Buster and trade insults with him. The same was true of Lacy, who now would become his own storm system with no walls to beat against. And with no one genuinely, goofily, proud of him, what would become of Max? And of Little Angel?

Our town was worried.

My part in all this began with the funeral preparations. In buying a funeral for Buster, Beulah was about to make the biggest financial transaction of her life. The promise of Bust's paltry insurance policies made her feel like a wealthy woman. I could sense an expansiveness in her when I picked her up to drive her to the funeral parlor in Cherry Grove to make the arrangements.

The town square of Cherry Grove was dominated by a few respectable businesses like the *Gazette*, a bank, and a chiropractor's office, along with three tap rooms, and Ed's Fine Dining. Downtown Cherry Grove had fallen considerably short of its original aspirations. Except for the block in front of the bank, the sidewalks were never completed. The back side of the square dissolved into a small parking lot. Cars and trucks were angled diagonally in the center of the main street, which widened to accommodate an island of tulips and a statue of Lincoln. An angel or muse knelt at his feet to inscribe on a scroll, "With Malice Toward None." Lincoln looks very sad and appears to gesture toward Metz's Mortuary, as if to say, "Whenever I'm in Cherry Grove, that's the place for me."

Architecturally, the mortuary's exterior achieved what its owner, Louie Metz, and his sons, Louis Junior and Freddy, did on the inside. Its colonial-style brick facade hid a large, decaying facility of wood and discolored stucco. Out back, a few bankrupt farmers in shiny black suits and silver ties spent their time tinkering with the hearses.

Louie met us at the door. This was not my first dealing with Metz, a man who always baffled and intimidated me, probably because he did not fit my stereotype of a funeral director. He was not mild-mannered or ingratiating. He did not fold his hands when he spoke of the departed. Never the self-effacing professional, Louie Metz was more the German butcher with a booming voice and guts on his apron who in a later decade could have passed for Helmut Kohl.

Once he got us situated in his office, he explained his firm's services and listened impatiently to Beulah's story of Buster's death, including the flying part. We talked about a "range" of services, including limo, escorts, embalming, and the restorative arts, but I knew this was prelude to choosing a casket, which is where the real money would be spent.

Louie ushered us into a windowless showroom adjacent to his office where twenty or twenty-five caskets were angled and posed in conversation groups beneath merciless fluorescent lighting. Wooden caskets were arranged in one group, mid-line bronzes in another, brushed-effect metals with fancy hardware in another, and so on.

"You want to know, 'Where do I begin?' don't you, Mrs. Toland?" said Louie. "I'll tell you where to begin. You begin with the man. He was your life-companion for nearly twenty years. Who was Buster Toland?"

"He was a Walnut," Beulah said without hesitation.

Louie appeared to be pleased by her response and gently steered us toward the wooden conversation group where an unnamed walnut casket was nosed in with a cherry "Last Supper" model and a mahogany "Going Home."

"On the other hand," she sniffed, "he did work with metal and steel his whole life. Carburetors, axles . . . shafts, you know, engines. He didn't mind grease. It's a different kind of man that works with wood, a patient man. You don't just clang away on a choice piece of wood. My brother was a carpenter. He rendered the finest woods—cedar, oak, ash, you name it. He always smelled like fresh-cut lumber. He smelled like whatever he was workin' on. Well, so did Buster, for that matter. But what he was workin' on was covered with oil and grease." Beulah pursed her lips and nodded to herself. "I think steel was his element. What do you have in steel, Mr. Metz, that's, you know, dignified?"

Louie sighed, an acknowledgment that the afternoon would be a long one, and adopted a more directive tone.

Leading us to a group of metal caskets, he said, "The 'Burning Bush' to your left has your husband written all over it, Mrs. Toland. It's reinforced steel, fire-forged, which gives it that rich burnished look. This one has what we call a vacuum seal. I don't have to tell you what that means. It means that this casket is absolutely airtight and waterproof, 'where neither moth nor rust corrupts.' Eh, Reverend? Just run your hand along that body. Feel the ribbing? Every one of those ridges reinforces the security of the compartment. Your husband will be safe until the Day of All Flesh, Mrs. Toland."

Beulah put her hands to her mouth as if she were about to vomit into them. She was obviously moved by the very possibility of keeping Bust safe until the resurrection.

"And inside," Louie continued, "this pillow-facing will be as soft a hundred years from now as it is right now."

"What is it?" Beulah asked.

"Pure satin," Louie Metz said. He asked, "Was your husband a working-man?"

"He was that," she replied.

"Then don't forget, the Sealy Posturepedic insures total comfort for Mister Toland's long rest."

Beulah all but gasped, "It has a mattress?"

I think she had a flashback of Buster coming in after a long day, dropping his gear, and sinking like the *Titanic* into the filthy chartreuse sectional they had gotten from a furniture outlet years before. You couldn't sit on it without falling through the cracks.

"He does deserve that," she said. It was obvious to Beulah even in the state she was in that we were looking at the top of the line in metal caskets. "Is it very expensive?" she asked.

"I can't price it out for you on the floor," Louie Metz replied. "Without figuring the services we talked about earlier, I couldn't give you an accurate estimate. But I can say that, the Lord willing, you will do this once and only once in your whole life. I can say, further, that you are about to make a temporal decision with eternal implications. And I can tell you another thing, Mrs. Toland," he said, as if to prepare us for one last profundity: "You get what you pay for." And he winked.

I said to Beulah, "Could we talk about this for a moment? The two of us. Pastor to parishioner." Louie did not offer his office or any space at all for our consultation. He didn't even remove himself from earshot. He took a step or two back and folded his arms.

"Look, Beulah, what are we trying to do here with this airtight container and this innerspring mattress? What are we trying to stop from happening? Can you tell me?"

"Well, Pastor, I just hate to leave him unprotected."

"I understand, Beulah. I hate to say this, but you can't protect him from . . . the elements." I meant the worms, of course, but I couldn't bring myself to say it. "Do you know how we say, 'Earth to earth'? Buster's element is earth. It's God's way. And then there's the matter of the resurrection. God promises to give us a new and transformed body. God promises not to lose track of our elements." I thought of the poet John Donne's metaphor, God knows the very drawer where every seed pearl is hidden, but I restrained myself. My sermon was already causing Beulah *and* Louie to glaze over.

"Besides," I added, "you can't afford it. Even on time, your payments would be—a hundred dollars a month." I pulled that figure out of the air. "You could be rich, or you could be strapped the way you are now. You could get yourself a Buick, you know the kind, cream on the bottom with the powder blue vinyl roof, or you can buy this coffin for Buster."

Beulah said, "I owe Buster."

"You can't make it up to him like this," I said. "That's why we have Jesus dead, buried, and risen."

Louie cleared his throat.

"Let's look at some others," I said. The three of us drifted toward a dark corner of the room where several cloth-covered wooden boxes were standing, stacked two-by-two. "We'll take one of these, Mr. Metz," I said, "won't we, Beulah?"

Louie looked at me with genuine hatred. Now it was his turn to ask for a private consultation. "Look here, Reverend, we need to have a few words."

We stepped through the doorway and around the corner, and he let me have it. "What right do you have to twist this poor woman's mind? She was depending on you for guidance. Reverend, you are a disgrace to your calling."

"Why, because I don't want her to buy a casket she can't afford? A *mattress*, Mr. Metz! Do you have any idea how poor she is?"

Louie responded in the vernacular. "And do you have any idea how badly she needs to put away her old man in style? Besides," he added, "Buster Toland would no more fit in one of those cardboard boxes than I would. Look at me, Reverend." He distended his gut like a frog. "Can you imagine me shoehorned into one of those goddamn things?"

I let my mind linger over the thought for a moment. "I'm sorry, Mr. Metz, you'll have to do your best. If that means 'shoehorning' him in, so be it. You people can do miracles with the dead. I've seen your work. You're good. It's settled. We'll take the one on top."

Early Friday morning, I learned it was not settled. Louie really meant it when he said I was a disgrace to my profession. Thursday evening he had telephoned each member of the cemetery committee to tell them the same.

At seven-thirty in the morning Tracy knocked on the bathroom door and said through the crack, "Walther Semanns, George Biedermann, and Bertie Semanns are at the front door. They want to see you."

They were waiting on the front porch like vultures. "We have a little problem," Bertie said, which meant a Big Problem.

The three entered the study. I arranged three chairs and said, "Sit," but they remained standing in a semicircle in front of the desk, with me standing behind it. They were dressed in neatly pressed overalls. Two of the men held caps at their waist. I stood there in my bathrobe.

"What's the problem?" I asked.

Bertie Semanns was the chief speaker. "Undertaker Metz called us last night, Pastor. It seems that you and Beulah got away yesterday without buying a vault for poor Bust."

"A vault?" I said, mistakenly thinking of a headstone.

"You know," Bertie said impatiently, "a box. A concrete liner that goes in the grave around the casket."

"Oh that," I said, almost relieved. "I reminded Mr. Metz yesterday that our old cemetery doesn't require a concrete box. It's just a convenience for these modern cemeteries. It keeps the ground from sinking around the grave and makes it easier to mow. But heck, our cemetery's already as lumpy as oatmeal. Most of those graves out there don't have boxes. Maybe that's why our water's so bad. Ha!"

No one smiled. Bertie looked at me the way he had in his rathskeller when he offered me the beer. "It ain't a matter of convenience, Pastor. You should know that by now. Undertaker Metz explained that nowadays decent people ain't buried without a vault."

"The people out there were all decent people," I said.

"Nowadays," Bertie bore in, "nowadays, decent people all have a concrete box. Mr. Metz said it himself: 'Only your poor white trash is buried without one.' "

I was stunned by the simple elegance of his argument. "Oh really," I said, "and I suppose you don't think Buster was 'white trash'?"

"Not no more he ain't," Bertie said.

"And I guess you, and you, and you, and your families didn't treat Buster Toland like trash when he was alive? You didn't look down on him, gossip about him and Beulah, and make sure he knew his *place* in this town?"

Bertie squinted a half-smile and said, "That may be so, or it may not. He's one of us now."

"I'll tell you what I think," I said. "I don't think you care any more about Buster now than when he was alive. All you care about is what Louie Metz says about you. You're afraid he'll call us all 'trash.' Don't you see, this is about money. Metz wants Beulah's money, that's all. It's just business."

Now George Biedermann chimed in in a reedy voice, "From what I hear, you and Beulah already saved plenty'a money on this funeral. I hear it'll be a cut-rate'n.'"

"It doesn't matter what you or Metz think. Beulah can't afford a concrete box. The law doesn't require it. Why start now?"

Bertie answered, "We're sorry you feel that way, Pastor. Buster Toland will be buried in our cemetery," he said, as if he had the authority to forbid it, "and he will have a box."

"Please don't do that," I pleaded. "If you do, Metz takes charge of our parish."

George and Walther had already put on their caps and stepped out onto the porch as I spoke. Bertie remained in the study and pushed the door to. The morning light shone through the small-paned glass of the study door across his smooth face. He really was a formidable little man with his bushy white eyebrows and great hawk of a nose. He looked at me in my bathrobe with contempt.

"Who *is* in charge, Pastor? You think you can come in here with all your ideas and change us, like this church belongs to you. Like the ministry belongs to you. But it don't. It's ours. You can irritate the community all you want and offend good people like Louie Metz just as you please, 'cause you'll be movin' on. But we stay."

His eyes flashed beyond me, penetrating the wall of my study and the back wall of the house to the cemetery. "Long after you're gone we'll be here. All of us."

I was astonished at what the tone of his speech revealed. "You mean you've been thinking of our ministry as a contest all along? Why must we push against one another? Why can't we have a partnership?"

"Why?" Bertie said bitterly. "Why, because *you* made it that. *You* started it, didn't you? Communion every Sunday, rock-a-billy music, removing the flag. They tell me you took the youth to the projects in St. Louis, and there was dancing between white and black. What do you say to that?"

"That's for another day," I said.

"Well, you get my drift, though, don't you?" Bertie clarified. "It's been one thing after another. We *could* have had a partnership, Pastor, but you couldn't accept us as we are. No, you had plans for us."

"What would you say then, that we've had a standoff?" I asked.

Bertie thought for a moment and narrowed his eyes. "Yes, I'd say that. You've done some things we didn't expect, but we've held our ground."

Suddenly I could feel the presence of Bust and Lacy in the stillness of this same office, and I could hear Buster say, "*I want him to be my son.*"

I felt very bad and, at the same time, not so bad, suspended between futility and peace.

As I saw Bertie out the door I said, "You men will do what you want."

We finally buried Buster on Saturday. Because our narthex was so small, the open casket was placed in the front of the church where early arrivers could view the body one last time. Bust was a snug fit in the cloth-covered coffin. But then his shirt was too tight, the tie too thin, the tie clip unnecessary, and when he was alive he never saw the need of pomade on his flattop. For once he was not perspiring. Many people remarked how dignified he looked.

Before the service began, the casket was closed and covered with a purple pall, and then wheeled back to the narthex for the procession. The pall covered the cheap coffin, the way the blood of Jesus covers our sins, and for a moment at least we could all forget our differences.

The gloomy prelude finished, the procession began in silence. Max carried the cross flawlessly, and I walked behind him, followed by the casket, the pallbearers, and the three mourners. The words that broke the silence might have been written with Buster in mind:

> *Man that is born of a woman*
> *Is of few days and full of trouble.*

The funeral service itself was a disaster, mainly because Beulah, who had received visitors and conducted her affairs with self-possession for three days, wailed at the top of her lungs throughout the service and my sermon. Lacy was occupied with Angela; her brother from East St. Louis had not shown up; she had no one. About halfway through my sermon, when I was comparing an individual's journey from baptism to the church's journey through Lent, June moved into the pew with Beulah, put her arm around her, and tried to comfort her. The more I said, the louder she howled.

Was this a hysteric compensation for twenty years of misery and fussing with Buster? After all, I was the one who had robbed Beulah of the last tangible means of making amends. Maybe Metz was right. Maybe she did need to put her old man away in style. The congregation was becoming annoyed. I didn't know what to do. I felt that I had an obligation both to Bust and the congregation to conduct a Christian funeral. If I stopped the service to comfort Beulah, *then* what would we do? Out of the corner of my eye I could see Louie Metz standing in my sacristy doorway with his arms folded.

I quickly concluded my sermon by reminding the congregation that Buster had been a good Marine, a good father, and a good member of the church, and now the church would assume a greater responsibility toward his family. At the mention of "Marine," Beulah's agitation increased dramatically. I must have looked like a man moving his lips in a gale.

After the service the procession made its way along the gravel path down the little dip and up the hill to the cemetery. We moved toward Buster's grave so slowly that I had time to daydream of happier days in the graveyard. Our family had reclaimed its gentle curves and perfect hiding places as a jogging track for me and a playground for the kids. Sarah and Adam had chosen Fred Buford's large flat stone at the peak of the hill as their "stage" for singing "Oh, How I Hate to Get Up in the Morning," a song Tracy's father had taught them from his military days.

We had also reclaimed the cemetery psychologically. When you live among headstones and plastic flowers, and the microbes of your nearest neighbors are giving your water a funny taste, it doesn't take much for daily life to lapse into dark comedy.

Like Prince Hamlet, I usually kibitzed with the gravediggers on the morning of a funeral. Perhaps it was my imagination, but it always seemed to me that the deeper the digger got into the grave, the more philosophical a turn the conversation took. Only a couple months earlier George Biedermann was standing deep in Orville Creed's grave, tossing out the last spadefuls of earth, all the while bragging about how much money he had made on his farm, when none other than Bertie (my new foe) leaned on his shovel and chimed in, "Yeah, George, and look where it got you."

When we passed Tillie Semanns's marker, I remembered an old shepherd mix named Luther that stayed down the road at Tom and Lottie Semanns's place, which was just in view out our parlor window. Luther found the pace of parish life congenial to his own. He spent most of his days hanging around the church, especially every Sunday when he suavely tried to blend in with worshipers entering the sanctuary.

The committee dug Tillie's grave just before Christmas. But when the rains came, we were forced to cover the grave with a tarp and postpone the funeral. Late one night I heard Luther whining pitifully. He had fallen through the tarp into Tillie's grave and was alternately paddling like a duck and thrashing like a deer against the slick muddy walls of the grave. One person couldn't simply reach down and pull the dog out without slipping into the grave himself. I called Tom, and he called the appropriate trustees, and together in the pouring rain we formed a human chain, first squatting and then lying end-on-end in the mud in order to pull Luther out of Tillie's grave. We got him out, but not without getting ourselves covered with mud and chilled to the bone.

The rescuers never talked publicly about the deed, since it did concern the grave of a matriarch of the congregation. But whenever the trustees and their wives were together, we *alluded* to the defilement with code words like "raining cats and *dog*" or "the Friends of Luther Club," and exchanged suppressed smiles and naughty glances.

From Tillie's grave you could see into the cleft where the ditch drained and the cattle came to drink. The electric wire separating the cemetery from Tom Semanns's pasture always drooped low, as it was on the day of Buster's burial. Sometimes the wire wasn't hot.

One day Tracy looked out the kitchen window and saw Tom's old bull standing motionless in the hollow of the cemetery. He was contemplating our children, both of whom were playing around a headstone with their backs to him.

Tracy slowly walked toward the children, quietly imploring them to come up the hill. Sarah must have sensed her mother's fear, for she looked over her shoulder toward the fence. When she saw the bull, she did a theatrical double-take and froze in horror, while her brother blissfully doddered around the stone. It was a tense situation.

In that moment, Tom and Lottie Semanns's fourteen-year-old, Donny, came galloping into the cemetery, followed by the ever-faithful Luther, and together they worried the bull back to the pasture. Donny rode his favorite horse as he always did, bareback, himself barefoot and bare-chested, clad only in a pair of jeans.

Donny Semanns not only saved my kids but several months earlier he had single-handedly inspired me to rethink my methods of teaching the catechism. At the public examination of confirmands on Palm Sunday, with the church bursting with relatives, it was Donny who had bungled the simple recital of Luther's explanation of the tenth commandment and then, as one of his classmates answered the question properly, added under his breath to me, *You're out to get me.*

What am I doing? I thought. *Not only does this kid not understand what it means to covet his neighbor's manservant and maidservant, he thinks I am orchestrating his public humiliation,* which, in effect, I was.

Until our moment of deliverance, that little exchange summed up my thinking about Donny Semanns, the slowest and most disagreeable child in catechism class. But since the episode in the cemetery, say *Donny*, and I see a beautiful, browned boy riding bareback across the field, over the ditch, and into the cemetery to save our children from his father's bull.

When we came to Buster's grave, we gathered as many of the mourners as possible under the canopy. When I peered into the hole, I could see that the concrete liner was in place, paid for by the members of the cemetery committee. That they bought it out of their own pockets only deepened the general corruption of the church and this ceremony. Now Metz was calling the shots in our congregation.

I suppose it was a small loss for me when compared to the defeat of death—only a flesh wound suffered in a parish squabble—but it was a defeat nonetheless. Louie Metz's sons were imperiously moving mourners around under the canopy with little wrist movements like parking lot attendants, pointing to the spot on the ground where they wanted individuals to stand. Louie stood to the side of the grave and shot me a triumphant look.

We brought nothing into this world, and it is certain we can carry nothing out. Beulah moaned loudly throughout the graveside service as she had in church. Within a few minutes I was making the sign of the cross with dirt on the coffin lid above Bust's forehead while commending him to the triune God:

> *May God the Father who created this body,*
> *May God the Son who by his blood redeemed this body,*
> *May God the Holy Ghost who by baptism sanctified this body—keep these*
>   *remains unto the day of the resurrection of all flesh.*

And it was over.

Actually, it was not over. The military phase was about to begin. Beulah, Lacy, Angela, and Max remained seated on Metz's fake-grass drop cloth, their folding chairs precariously balanced on the bumpy soil beneath it, while I solemnly shook hands with each of them. Max flashed me a big smile, and then looked guilty for smiling at his dad's burial.

Then I stepped aside, and Emil Johns, the senior veteran of World War II in our congregation and the secretary-treasurer of the VFW in Cherry Grove, presented a folded flag to Beulah. Emil was dressed in his neatly pressed Army uniform, displaying his sergeant's stripes on his left sleeve. He stepped smartly back and turned his attention to four uniformed veterans standing near the flagpole with their rifles resting languorously across their midsections.

I was never much in favor of mixing a military ceremony with a Christian ritual, but I knew Buster would have loved it, and in my heart this whole day had taken on a "Something for Buster" theme. When I saw the honor guard, a small alarm went off down my spine. As disturbing as the events leading up to the funeral had been, and as unsettling as the service had turned out to be, what was about to unfold bore an even greater potential for disaster.

The honor guard was composed of a veteran of World War II, another from the Korean War, and two from Vietnam. All four appeared uncomfortable in uniforms that pulled tightly across their chests and butts. The Korean War guy and one of the Vietnam vets were showing patches of bare stomach between shirt buttons stretched to the breaking point. One of the Vietnam veterans wore bleached shoulder-length hair and John Lennon-type glasses. The other—the big one—looked like a Hell's Angel in a Boy Scout uniform. He had a curved sliver of wire in the lower-left side of his nose. All four were armed and dangerous. None of their guns matched.

Emil barked his first order, "*Ready!*" and the guns made a cocking sound. When he cried "Aim!" the men raised the barrels of their rifles to a degree that did not satisfy Emil. "Get'em up," he added in a shouted stage whisper. They appeared to be aiming their guns at a point only slightly above the heads of the mourners. "I said *up*," Emil repeated in a more concerned tone. That's when it dawned on me: the honor guard was using live ammunition. "Get'em up, you sons of bitches," Emil shouted with more than a hint of desperation creeping into his best military voice.

"Aim," he repeated. *At what?* I thought. I worried about the peak of our garage, which had just been repaired.

"*Fire.*" The noise was deafening and not entirely simultaneous. They repeated it three times. Children held their ears and cried, but no one was shot, and nothing fell from the trees.

The men lowered their rifles, the smoke cleared, and we all stood there awkwardly waiting for the finale, which I assumed would be the playing of "Taps." I thought of little Adam standing on Fred Buford's flat stone and singing like a baby wren,

Some day I'm going to murder the bugler,
Some day they're going to find him dead.
And then I'll get the other pup,
The guy who wakes the bugler up,
And spen-n-nd the rest of my life in bed!

It seemed a fitting image for a day that had descended from tragedy to comedy into farce.

Everyone turned around and looked back across the cemetery, down the dip in the gravel road, and up the green, fresh-mown hill toward the back of our white garage. Moriah Semanns had found the only patch of sunlight about halfway up the hill and stood motionless as if in a spotlight on a stage. Behind her, the daffodils along the garage had just begun to bloom on a day that seemed to say, "It could get cold again." She was dressed in a pink jumper with a thin white sweater carefully draped around her shoulders. She had something pink in her blond hair as well. Her new cornet was catching and winking the sunlight, as if sending military signals to the mourners gathered across the valley. At twelve years of age, she was about to give the performance of her life.

Moriah's mom was standing beside her to hold the music and to steady her child for the performance. She wore a light blue dress and matching spring coat with a Jackie Kennedy pill-box hat. Like her daughter, she stood motionless. The two of them had more discipline in their little fingers than our entire honor guard and its commander. With her left arm extended, the mother held her daughter's music; she gently curved her right arm around the small of the child's back. They stood there like a doe and a fawn in the silence of the spring afternoon.

Then Moriah began to play. She did not play "Taps." She played four stanzas of "I Know that My Redeemer Lives," arcing each note across the ravine toward the mourners on the hill. The clear voice of her cornet reached us, it seemed, a half second after we saw her breathe, extend her neck, and puff her cheeks. It was as if her music were a time-delayed message coming to us from a saner and more beautiful world.

When she finished playing, her mother folded her hands, and the two of them recessed like acolytes up the hill, past the daffodils, around the garage, and out of sight, while everyone on the opposite hill stood motionless and watched them go. A few clouds drifted lazily away, and the entire hill was bathed in delicate sunlight.

When all was lost, Moriah and her mom had recomposed the scene and completed what none of us could resolve. As they disappeared from view, I heard myself whisper, "Thanks be to God."

All of Lent lay before us, but now, for the first time, I could stand in the lumpy mud of our cemetery and see Easter.

19

The Way It Was with Leonard and Me

 A couple of Sundays after Buster's funeral Leonard Semanns and I had a terrible falling out, and it was my fault, my own stupid fault. Church had just ended, the money-counters had finished up, and the elders had left the sacristy, when Leonard barged into the room and said, "You lied to me. You betrayed me."

I knew exactly what he meant. I replied, "I never lied to you. We never talked about it."

"Same thing," he said without hesitation. "And you know it."

"I cleared it with the elders," I said defensively.

"The elders," Leonard said, as if he were going to spit. "All they care about is that you show up on Sundays. How you thought you could take a second job, and not tell the whole congregation—and *me*, the *Presi-dent*—I can't understand."

"Well, *Leonard*," I said with mock consternation, trying to mask my rising panic, "it's not like I'm moonlighting as a cabdriver."

"A bunch of us is at Ed's in Cherry Grove, yesterday morning, havin' a good time. Marty Dullmann says, 'Well, now, I hear your preacher is teachin' classes at St. *Louie* University.' "

Since no one in the entire region calls St. Louis *St. Louie*, I assumed Leonard had something contemptible in mind.

"It's true, I'm teaching a course in religion."

"No," Leonard corrected, the way you say it to a dog when you don't want him to come in. "It's not just a course in religion, and you know it. It's for a seminary that has betrayed the church, left it, and started up a new school. It's a course at a new half-assed seminary that's got no building of its own and is so *piti*-ful that it rents rooms from the Catholics. You teach at an *illegal* school for preachers!"

"I'm sorry, Leonard, I had to follow my conscience. I *tried* to explain to the congregation some of the theological issues in this split. I tried to talk about the question of how we interpret the Bible. Remember the distinctions between history and myth? Some say Jonah got swallowed by a real fish, some say the story is a parable . . ."

Leonard dropped his arms to his side and let his mouth fall open. "There's more to it than that, Pastor," he replied. "You don't start a new school over a big fish."

"You're right. Exactly right. It's not about a whale or Adam and Eve. It's not even about evolution. Most churches settled that one fifty years ago." Leonard looked at me impatiently without conceding the last point. "It's about women."

"Women?"

"Sure. All this talk about interpreting the Bible literally is just a smoke screen for the real issue," I said. "The Lutheran Church doesn't want women preachers. The bigwigs are acting like this is a battle for the Bible, but what they really want to do is keep this church body isolated from other churches. And why? Because all the others ordain women, except the Catholics and the Mormons. Don't you see? If they can get you all riled up over Jonah and the whale, you won't even notice the real issue, which is women in the pulpit!"

"Don't give me all this talk," Leonard said. "I know you can talk. You're smooth with words."

"I'm telling you, Leonard, they aren't interested in defending your precious *Bible*. They're trying to protect their precious way of life, which includes, above all, The man is king in his castle. Look at the way this church is run: men preachers, men trustees, men elders, men voters. Listen to the way we talk: Alfred's Clara, Darryl's Betty, Leonard's June. So we find a few Bible passages to help us protect our way of life."

"Nobody's got a quarrel with it, including the women." Leonard spoke as if he had been preparing for this debate for years. "The women express themselves through their husbands. That's in the *Bible*."

My mind flashed back to wild-eyed Seth testifying at his own sanity hearing. *"I'm gonna rule in my house, Your Honor!"*

"But that's not the way you and June operate. She speaks for herself, and everybody knows it."

He paused to consider what I'd said. "There's an order to things," Leonard continued resentfully, "and it takes more than you to turn it upside down. You have no right to go off on your own and foller your own opinions."

"But when I try to explain the issues, you all table the discussion. It happens meeting after meeting. We don't talk about the things that are tearing our church body apart. We table *everything* around here."

"That's because we ain't *inter-est-ed* in the *issues*," he drawled, "and we ain't interested in being talked to like children neither. Besides, you're a fine one to worry about talkin' through the issues. When you decided what you wanted to do, you just did it, and didn't bother to talk to anybody."

"I cleared it with the elders . . ."

"The *elders*," Leonard said. He calmed himself, and some of the redness began to drain from his face. It occurred to me that I hadn't even worried that he might have another heart attack.

"Listen, Leonard . . ."

"You want to talk about *issues?* I'll tell you what the issue is. It ain't about Jonah and the whale, the Bible, or women preachers. Here is what it is: You went behind my back. You didn't have the courtesy or the guts to say, 'Leonard, I'm gonna deny what's right and go teach at an illegal seminary.' "

"Well, I'd hardly put it that way."

"You must'a known that you were doing wrong or you would have said something."

"You mean I have to account for my every minute?" I asked. "Why don't you install a time clock in the sacristy. I'm sure Bertie and the trustees would be glad to help."

"You are as free as the breeze, Pastor. You do what you please every day. You call when you want to call, and read your books when you feel like it. Except Sundays, you make your own day like none of us does. No, nobody'll ever expect you to punch a time clock."

"Well, then . . ."

"But you represent this church. You are not an independent day laborer. Not a hired man that we put to work, feed, and let go. That's just *it*. You represent *us*. This church is a Lutheran church. We've been tied to that seminary for more than a hundred years. Now you up'n decide you got *other* ideas. No, we ain't tellin' you to punch a clock. But we do expect you to— to . . . be *with* us." He said the words without a trace of sentimentality— or anger. "As far as I'm concerned—I mean, me, personal—I guess it don't matter . . ."

"Oh."

". . . but you are a part of this church."

Now utterly composed, Leonard turned slowly away from me toward the door. The fireworks were over. He looked at the doorknob with great deliberation as if it were the saddest or most complex doorknob he'd ever seen. He turned it and walked quietly out of the sacristy.

In the days that followed, I half-expected Leonard to call a general meeting of the congregation to air his concerns. After all, he was the *president*. The stalwarts in the congregation would declare their loyalty to mother church and her seminary, and I would be given the choice to quit teaching at the "illegal" school or to resign from the parish.

Of course, nothing like that happened. I might have known that we never did things that openly at Cana, and we were not about to begin. At least, I expected our falling-out would get around town, and I would hear versions of it in the post office or whispers at the quilting sessions. But again, nothing. A little gossip might have helped us all. But as it turned out, it was just between Leonard and me, which meant that he was badly hurt by my decision but was not about to use it to destroy me in the congregation.

He even took the chalice from my hand the following Sunday, but that did not mean we were reconciled. In fact, the *only* place we were on speaking terms was at the communion rail, and that was a scripted conversation. I said, "Take, drink, the blood of Christ," and he took it and drank it and said, "Amen." He never looked at me, but that was not unusual. Lutherans do not look deeply into the eyes of the communion server, smile, wink, say "Thank you," or offer any sign that this is a personal favor—because it is not. It's nothing personal. Leonard received the sacrament from me as he might have received a cup of coffee from a waiter in a restaurant.

It wasn't that long after my blowup with Leonard that Beulah Toland telephoned me. "Pastor?" she said. Her voice was thick and slurry. "I took my Seconal."

"What?"

"I took my Seconal."

"You did?" I said. "How many?"

"I took 'em all," she said. And she hung up.

I tried to call her back, but as it turned out she hadn't hung up. She must have dropped the receiver.

I felt an initial rush of panic at being alone with this terrible news. I couldn't face the responsibility by myself. Tracy couldn't leave the children, so I rushed out to the car and drove into town, to Beulah's house next door to Buford's Garage. But before I did, I telephoned Leonard. He was getting cleaned up to go into the mill. June had already left on her mail route.

"Leonard, meet me at the Toland's. Something's happened to Beulah." I called him because he was the president of the congregation and because he lived almost directly across the street from Buford's. I had entirely forgotten that we were not on speaking terms.

On the porch I said, "Beulah's taken a bottle of pills. We have to go in." The front door was locked. Leonard put a shoulder to it and, still without a word spoken, popped the door open on the first try.

The house was a shambles. A couple of Buster's engine parts still sat in the gloomy entrance hall. Newspapers and magazines were spread up the stairs toward the bedrooms. The morning's half-eaten eggs and toast along with an open stick of butter and a carton of milk sat on a card table in the parlor. The TV was blaring. The olive-colored carpet was frayed and greasy. The whole place was covered with dust and dog hair, and the room smelled of fried eggs and dogs, but no dog was to be seen.

We found Beulah sprawled on her stomach across the sectional couch. Her face was turned to one side, all squished and distended like a prize-fighter's who has just been knocked cold. Several enormous rollers held her streaky hair just so. Her flowered housecoat was bunched behind her. One arm dangled over the side of the couch above two empty plastic bottles, the telephone, and a few more rollers on the floor. Both the telephone and the bottles lay on the carpet just beyond her fingers' reach. If a director had wanted to compose the classic suicide scene, he could have done no better than this. We turned her over, and she groaned and mumbled something but did not open her eyes.

"Beulah, are you awake? Say something, please!" I said. Beulah made no response.

I grabbed one of the plastic bottles and dialed up the hospital. The nearest emergency care was located in Blaydon, which was a suburb of Alton. When I told the dispatcher about the Seconal, he said, "We'll come, but you'll have to treat her. If you wait for us to get there, she'll die."

"What can we do?" I asked, talking to the dispatcher but looking at Leonard. I repeated his instructions to Leonard. "Sit her up. Make her drink mustard and water. Get her to vomit."

Leonard held Beulah upright on the couch while I mixed the mustard and lukewarm tap water. Then we took turns patting her and trying to get her to respond.

"Beulah, can you hear me?" I asked. "Do you think you can drink this?"

For ten or fifteen minutes, it seemed, we cajoled her and tried to make her drink. She occasionally moaned but never opened her eyes or acknowledged us. "It's never going to work," I cried. "You can't make an unconscious person drink."

Leonard took her by the shoulders and said with great authority, "Okay, now, Beulah. Listen. Drink this!" He got a little down her throat, and she made a slight swallowing motion. With not a moment's delay, the Seconal along with the morning's breakfast came back at Leonard and all over Leonard, onto his chin and down his shirt. I was jubilant. "You did it, Leonard, you did it. Good job!"

"No, I'd say we did it." Leonard was not jubilant, but he appeared relieved and a little shaken. Perhaps he was remembering his own close call with the heart attack.

We bathed Beulah's face with cool towels and tried to comfort her until the ambulance arrived.

By the time the van finally showed up, Beulah was muttering about not wanting to go to the hospital and asking for Little Angel and complaining about her hair. She was clearly returning to her old self. I got into the back of the ambulance to ride into Alton with Beulah, and Leonard walked across the road to clean himself up and change his shirt. "Pastor," he said over his shoulder, "June'll be in to see her this evening, and I'll stop by after work."

That was the beginning of the great thaw between Leonard and me. Our manner of reconciliation reminded me of the way my father and I communicated on virtually all occasions. Always *through* something else, and that usually an activity: throwing a ball, catching a fish, planting a tree, but never direct from one heart to another.

We achieved approximations of feeling for one another, with the tacit understanding that the truth between people is cumulative. Everything will be sorted out at some mythical end point. Until then, extended conversation is premature at best. That is the way it was with Leonard and me, too, and for that reason I secretly put him into the category of my father, even though he was no more than seventeen or eighteen years older than I.

Leonard and I saw a lot of one another that spring. We also ate several suppers in his cafeteria at the mill until he finally worked his last night and turned in his helmet and his pass. He owned the helmet, but he said he didn't want it in his truck. We had a few beers that night at a little tavern in the Flats called The Wedge, next door to the Teamsters Hall, to celebrate the end of Leonard the Steelworker.

Only once did we talk about our little part in Beulah's emergency, and when we did it was pure county indirection.

All he said was, "Best way to shut a man up is to put him to work, eh?"

"So they say," I replied sagaciously.

Silence.

I was getting the hang of it.

A couple of times I rode into East St. Louis with Leonard to deliver beef cattle to a place outside the Yards. That was a dusty job but not a gory one, since it entailed no more than off-loading the cattle from the truck and signing some papers. I mentioned something about Upton Sinclair's classic exposé of the meatpacking industry, *The Jungle*, which prompted Leonard to say, "You have led a sheltered life."

Later that spring, on one of the last days you can do such a thing, Leonard took me with him to butcher hogs. A freak blizzard had ruined Palm Sunday, and the air felt crisp and autumnal. Leonard wasn't actually doing the butchering and neither was his uncle Wilfred, who, along with his wife Dorothy, was hosting the slaughter in their barnyard.

A young man named Billy Rod Hotop, who was widely known for his expertise in these matters, would butcher the animal, and we would encourage, evaluate, exclaim, and finally eat and drink together like priests in a mystery religion. As soon as I saw the setup in the yard—the smoking fire, the gallows-like contraption from which to drain the carcass, and the circle of men beginning to form—I knew I was taking part in an ancient ritual. We would play the chorus to Billy Rod's killing of the pig.

By my reckoning, the ritual got off to a bad start when the squealing hog was brought in, apparently more aware than I of what was about to happen, and Billy Rod shot it straight in the head with a big black pistol. That's not the way it was done in *The Jungle*. My chest felt as if someone was sitting on it, and I couldn't breathe. Even though we were standing outdoors, I felt the need to get *outdoors*, away from the oppressive odor of the barnyard and into some fresh air. I tried to glaze my eyes so as not to focus on the actual proceedings, but you can only block out so much without covering your eyes and making a fool of yourself.

Several workers hoisted the pig onto the gibbet, shackled his back legs, and pulleyed him into place, whereupon Billy Rod slit its throat and drained out the blood. For a moment, though, he simply let it hang and revolve slowly in the midst of the circle of quiet men. "*Behold the pig*," he might have said. "*Consider me*," he meant to say. Several helpers lowered the pig into a cauldron filled with scalding water to loosen the bristly hair, and then jacked it up again. He cut it again to bleed it out, and several women approached to claim the intestines to stuff sausage in.

Later, they would make cracklings by scraping the hair off the hide, cutting it into pieces with a little fat left on, and throwing it into hot oil. "You can just scrape off the fat with your teeth," Leonard advised. "Makes these Texas pork rinds taste like poker chips."

Leonard smiled knowingly at me. "Now you watch."

The show really began when Billy Rod proclaimed, "Anybody can't skin a hog in a half hour is loafin'." Then he had at the pig like a knife-twirling dervish, and, sure enough, in a short time, but an eternity to my chest and stomach, he had ripped the skin off the hog, eviscerated it, trimmed the head meat, separated what was edible from the offal, and skillfully hacked the carcass into hams, loins, rounds, ribs, and shanks. Soon, all that would remain beneath the scaffold would be a pile of four hooves and one snout.

Billy's arms and chest were covered with the hog's insides. His droopy mustache glistened with what looked like butterscotch pudding. Through it all he preened like the local matador while keeping up a stream of commentary, which he hissed through the vent between his cigarette and the twisted corner of his mouth. "Butchered me a Mulefoot a few months back. Big black Ozark Pig. Whattamutha'. Them's hooves I kept, I guarantee you."

"He's lyin'." Leonard leaned toward me and spoke matter-of-factly into the back of his hand.

Billy Rod said of a friend in the Brush, "When I butcher my own hogs, he gets flesh like a son. Knowwhattamean?"

"I don't believe he *has* hogs," Leonard whispered loudly.

The women were already rendering the lard and preparing to grind the pork sausage, when Leonard said, "Quite a show, eh, Pastor?"

I never knew whether Leonard was really bonding with me, or satirizing two men who pretended to be bonding with one another. He was perfectly capable of Cana-style friendship via shared activity, just like my father and me, but he was also capable of ironic distance from such a relationship. Was this the real thing between Leonard and me, or a spoof? I had my suspicions. He gave me his Robert Duvall grin and with a show of pastoral concern asked, "How are you doin' there, partner?"

I felt tight in the chest and queasy in my stomach and soiled by the rank odor of the yard. "No problem," I said.

"Good, because the women have really fixed us up a meal in the grove. I know you like chicken and macaroni salad, and I *know* you like your beer, but wait till you try Aunt Dorothy's pork sausage and head cheese. She puts dill in there. It's the dill. You slather you some of her ketchup or horseradish on there, and that's *eatin'*. The head cheese takes some gettin' used to, but it's something special, too. I personally have never boned a hog head, but . . ."

"*Leonard!*"

20

The Summer of
John and Mo

 *Watergate was a reve-
lation.* Not that it suddenly
unveiled the heart of darkness in Richard
Nixon. We had always known about that. No,
Watergate was a reminder of the microscopic
significance of our lives in New Cana.

Our year began with a series of epoch-
making events that affected us more than we
understood. The Supreme Court's decision
in *Roe v. Wade* meant that country girls like
Leeta or Teri or others like them, who found
themselves "in trouble," would have the option
of privatizing their problem by removing the
stigma of an unwanted pregnancy from the

eyes of the congregation. It wouldn't be necessary for the community to promise to help raise the child. The church would not have the opportunity to offer the hospitality of Jesus to a scared teenager and her family. Nor would it have a chance to fail to do so, as it had sometimes done in the past. No one would know. It was none of the community's business.

The same month, five days after LBJ died of a coronary, the war in Vietnam came to an uneasy end. Uneasy because most people interpreted the peace as America's first military defeat. The last of America's 45,948 fatalities was killed by a sniper and posthumously promoted to full colonel. We watched the POWs come home looking like ghosts and shadows.

Our congregation's Vietnam vets had for the most part already returned, angry and incommunicative to a man. Like birds with broken wings, some of them holed up in trailers and shacks in the Brush. Others returned to their parents' houses and moved into their old rooms still decorated for little boys with pennants and sports photos, where they watched TV and smoked pot all day and tried to figure out what to do with their newfound knowledge of good and evil. Unlike their fathers who had returned as heroes from Europe and the South Pacific, these returned as losers to no welcome at all.

Thanks to the energy crisis everything about farming became more expensive, and prices shot up accordingly. Nixon imposed a ceiling on the price of beef and pork, and our farmers were feeling doomed. The Secretary of Agriculture, a man named Butz, didn't help when he said, "Adapt or die, resist and perish . . . agriculture is now big business. Too many people are trying to stay in agriculture that would do better someplace else." Everybody waited in long lines at the gasoline pumps, and the trustees, following the Commander-in-Chief, mandated lower temperatures for the already-frigid parsonage. Both kids got ear infections.

But the event that riveted us like no other was Watergate. Of course we had known about it since before the election, but when the hearings went on TV we talked about little else. The televised hearings coincided with the beginning of what was promising to be a long, hot, and eventless summer in

New Cana. So when that "simple country lawyer," Senator Sam Ervin, shook his wattle and banged the gavel, we were all ears.

Even my parishioners, who had overwhelmingly supported Nixon over the Communist candidate, George McGovern, seemed to admire Senator Sam's ability to quote Scripture the way God intended it to be done, in the King James Version. Who but a true believer would dare reproach the imperious H. R. "Bob" Haldeman or the snarling John Ehrlichman with the word of God? Senator Sam's favorite peroration was, "God is not mocked! Whatsoever a man soweth, that shall he also reap!" We were Amen-ing all the way from New Cana, Illinois.

My personal favorites on the Watergate Show were John Dean and his beautiful wife Maureen. Dean was an Ivy-League type with a good chin, careful little spectacles, and expensive button-down-collar shirts. By all accounts, he had never excelled at anything. Here was a fellow no more than four or five years older than I—(I, who contemplated life from my office in a cornfield)—who enjoyed cigars and small talk with the people who ran the country, who screened candidates for the Supreme Court, and who discussed million-dollar payoffs to burglars with the President of the United States. This was a man who once told a reporter, "I would still like to be a writer. Maybe I will write a book. I love to play with words and twist phrases. I always play Scrabble." It was unimaginable to me how such an obvious mediocrity should have found himself in so great a position of power.

Even more fascinating to me was John's wife, Maureen. Mo Dean sat expressionless behind her husband during the Watergate hearings for days on end. Her blond hair was pulled back severely to reveal the features of a classic beauty. She seldom changed expression, even when a member of the committee challenged her husband's truthfulness. Her plastic demeanor reminded me of one of Alfred Hitchcock's heroines—perhaps Kim Novak in *Vertigo*. Just as I could not imagine John Dean in his Brooks Brothers suit burning his trash in a barrel at the corner of his lot, so I could not imagine Mo Dean without makeup, hair flying, as she bicycled two shrieking kids over country roads. Who *were* these people? How did they attain such power? And how had we so entirely and cleanly missed it? John and the beautiful Mo became emblems for the great gulf fixed between people like them and people like us.

There was nothing like watching the Watergate Show to make you feel like a real rube. To some extent, the entire nation experienced the same feelings of stupidity. We were all rubes. Americans seemed to say, "Here we were, going about our ordinary lives, paying our bills, taking the kids to Little League, while an amoral elite determined what we should see, hear, and think." The fascination with the Watergate Show reflected a deeper fascination with ourselves and our own lack of power.

I suspect such feelings were especially prevalent among Christian pastors, whose very title invites disparaging comparisons to political or economic power. A *pastor* is a shepherd. "I know my own, and my own know me," the Good Shepherd says of his own ministry, thereby setting the tone of intimacy and self-sacrifice that would characterize pastoral relationships forever. The pastor finds hidden spiritual meaning in ordinary practices, such as hospitality or friendship, and in normal life-cycle occurrences, like birth, sexual love, sickness, and death. The quality of any relationship is all important, and each is capable of transcendent meaning.

What has greatest meaning may have nothing to do with public opinion or the bottom line. Jesus said the widow who put two cents into the offering had given more than the rich, for she had given her whole living. He praised an unknown prostitute who anointed his feet with perfume and tears and dried them with her hair. He once said a good shepherd, as opposed to a cost-efficient manager, will leave ninety-nine sheep in the wilderness in order to find the one that is lost. We preached those ideas every week and, like fools, some of the saints even tried to live them. Watergate hosed down our precious *meanings* with contempt.

A minister may drive twenty-five miles to a hospital in order to recite a thirty-second prayer and make the sign of the cross over a comatose parishioner. Who sees this act and judges it to be good? The pastor may devote years of conversation and behind-the-scenes maneuvering in order to promote reconciliation among factions in the community. The preacher may invest fifteen hours of biblical research and reflection on a fifteen-minute speech for no other purpose than to make God a little more believable to the congregation.

Place this near-quixotic pursuit of *souls* beside the creamy power of people like John and Mo, and even a saint will doubt his or her vocation. Does the work of ministry really have the significance we attach to it? What is more important, the political power that openly rules the world, or the kingdom of God that secretly consecrates it?

As the summer of John and Mo wore on, Tracy and I watched the Show obsessively on a peanut-butter-and-jelly-smeared TV we shared with the children. They watched *Sesee'* (*Sesame Street*), we watched Watergate. All our activities and even our vacation were tolerated only as interruptions in the summer's regularly scheduled programming.

That same summer the Protestant churches of North America set out to reevangelize the continent. The plan was called Key 73, and it entailed a massive door-to-door effort among the churched and unchurched of the land. For the first time, the churches would cooperate with one another and not try to steal one another's sheep. If Lutheran callers stumbled across self-avowed Baptists, they were honor-bound to relay their names to the nearest Baptist church. The entire program still presupposed a shadowy Protestantism among Americans and made little provision for genuine secularism.

I recruited and trained a dozen teams of volunteers to go where no one from Cana had ever gone before—into the Brush and north toward Dempster. In my kick-off sermon I preached on the Sending of the Seventy in the Gospel of Luke. In that passage Jesus commissions seventy people to go into Gentile territories to bring word of the kingdom. When the new apostles return with great joy, Jesus exclaims ecstatically like a Pentecostal preacher, "I saw Satan fall like lightning from heaven!"

I told the people of Cana that we were privileged to participate in an ancient pattern of evangelization: calling, sending, witnessing, and returning, a pattern that is as old as Moses, the prophets, and Jesus himself. For us, Key 73 appears to be a last-ditch effort to salvage the institutional church, I said. To Jesus, however, who sees things we can't see, the pattern of Sending represents the beginning of the end of Satan. With his visionary cry, "I saw Satan fall," he is "remembering" a primordial time when Satan was cast down from heaven, and he is *seeing* it happen again and again whenever his people embrace outsiders and strangers.

My sermon nearly coincided with the appearance of new neighbors across the Loop Road from the church in the old Norbert Semanns home place. The rickety wooden house had been uninhabited for several years. Its two-story salt-box facade had turned battleship gray with peeling paint and mildew; the brick steps had crumbled; its faded green shutters banged in the wind. Wild spirea threatened to engulf the porch.

Initial intelligence supplied by postmaster Burley Means indicated that the new owners had a "foreign name." Indeed the name was foreign to New Cana—*Petranovic*, pronounced with a *vick* at the end to suit Midwestern ears.

Peter and Margot and their many children began transforming the property the day they arrived, first by the sheer energy of little ones laughing and running naked as chickens in the yard, and not long after by the addition to the house of a canopy with a pediment and three Doric columns, which Peter had acquired from a defunct mortuary. It wasn't long before Peter hung an enormous lantern from the ceiling of the canopy and replaced the old shutters with French louvers painted glistening black. He plowed the original driveway, which was largely overgrown anyway, and cut in a long winding road through the grove to the north of the house, adding a white-bricked serpentine entrance. Suddenly we were living across the street from

Tara, inhabited by dark strangers with a sense of beauty and style unknown to our region.

Everyone in the Petranovic family was beautiful in exactly the way no one in New Cana was beautiful: sensuously so. The teenage boy had the eyelashes and delicately sloped shoulders of his father. His sister flounced her hips and tossed her thick dark hair like no other woman in town except her mother Margot.

Their attention to color, space, and proportion made it clear they had abandoned our German inhibitions and, in a peculiar sort of way, our German theology as well. Most of us in New Cana would have said, "Beauty is okay so long as you don't overdo it, if it happens by accident. But if you work at it, it could lead to works-righteousness! Then it gets to be *too much* and starts to crowd out the things that matter, like . . . well, you know what I mean."

In the very summer we would be sending out teams of witnesses like shock troops in an invasion, God had planted a field of prospects at our doorstep. Of course, everyone understood that if they were *Catholic*—and with a name like *Petranovic* they probably were—we would have to write that name on a three-by-five card and send it to St. Mary's in Alton. Those were the rules of Key 73, and even in the case of Catholics we would play by them.

A week after the Petranovics moved in, the entire family visited our Sunday worship. At least we assumed it was a "visit," as if from aliens or Gypsies. But after church I made a startling discovery when I overheard Margot say to a circle of neighbors, "We don't *feel* like visitors. After all, *we're Lutheran*."

I had to restrain myself from ringing the church bell in jubilation. For I had not been optimistic about our program of saturation-evangelism, since our little prairie was already so crowded with churches that it qualified as a Lutheran "burnt-over district." Suddenly God was promising to transfuse our church with new blood. The Petranovics would crack the code of our community by dint of their sheer *difference*. I quickly imagined a new outreach brochure: *"Good things are happening at Cana!"* with my picture on the cover. I was a little shocked by my reaction to our new neighbors, by how badly I needed them to join our church.

Apparently I was not the only one who noticed the difference between the sensuous Petranovics and the insensate Semanns, Bufords, and the rest of us. For within a couple of weeks I heard by the grapevine that the Petranovics had decided to join the larger St. John's Lutheran Church in Blaydon. Even though they could stand on the front porch of their new plantation and gaze upon a perfectly decent Lutheran church and even *hear* our voices at worship as clearly as we could hear their rooster, they were willing to drive twenty minutes to Blaydon because they felt more "comfortable" at St. John's. I was crushed.

I received their decision as an indictment of my ministry. How could it be otherwise? I have clergy friends whose children have rejected the church, and they sometimes feel as judged by that rejection as I felt by our neighbors' decision. Why must our greatest failures occur among those who are closest to us? God had put some believers *across the street* from us, and we were (I was) unable to attract them into our community of faith. Where had we failed? Aren't we a "friendly church"? Does the organ sound that tinny? Are my sermons *that* boring? If the gospel won't *work* on people who are near to hand, like children, spouses, and neighbors, what's the use of sending ourselves out to far-flung places?

I took my disappointment out on my evangelism teams, lashing them for being unaggressive, unfriendly, insular, and, well, *themselves*. The whole group responded like a dog that's messed on the carpet, with shame and repentance. But then they, unlike their pastor, who was still wallowing in self-pity, decided to do something about it. They refused to take No for an answer. They would show me what they were made of. Within days, my entire Key 73 outreach program focused like a laser on the plantation across the road and upon its darkly beautiful but unsuspecting inhabitants.

Waves of visitors engulfed the Petranovics armed with carefully scripted conversations about the congregation, as if we hadn't heard about their decision to join another church. Our visitors included seldom-used words in their presentations, such as "community," "future," and "potential," when describing Cana. They even sang my praises, and Alma Buford reportedly called me "dynamic," a *most* unlikely word to be found on her lips or anyone else's in New Cana. We trained some of our junior highs to pretend that catechism classes with Pastor Lischer were "a blast." Our quilting group moved the Petranovics to the top of their waiting list and began working on a quilt for one of the older girls. Several women formed a car pool with Margot to take the little ones to the Montessori school in Edwardsville. The youth invited the new teenagers in town on a hay ride, which turned out to be even more fun than catechism class. One of our mill workers fabricated an iron gate in his shop with an enormous P at its center, and helped Peter and his oldest boy install it across the entrance to "Tara."

Not since the Crusades had any people been made the object of so relentless a program of evangelization. We simply wore them down. By the end of Key 73, the Petranovics capitulated and joined the church, our only conquest of the long hot summer.

The summer was also occupied with planning a celebration of the one hundred twenty-fifth anniversary of the founding of the church. The reclusive Henry Dire, a slight, graying man who sat in the sacristy every Sunday in order to tend our nonexistent PA system, was put in charge. Widely known to be a "nervous" man, Henry was the perfect choice to pursue the solitary work of archival research. He loved to pore over the minutes of ancient congregational meetings and possessed the added virtue of fluency in German.

He found the minutes endlessly instructive, and they transported him into a more interesting world than his own: "The Voters contracted with Wilhelm Nutzel to build a church 50 x 30 feet with a steeple 90 feet high for $3,100." "Pastor Schultz will journey to the Exposition to listen to the ringing of church bells." Later: "Our bell weighs 885 lbs and has been marked on the inside by Pastor S. School to be closed for the raising."

Around the turn of the century: "The Voters authorized the contribution of $35 toward funeral expenses for the Otto Semanns, Karl Semanns, T. Semanns, and D. Petersons in the recent Influenza." Which explains why we have so many stones in our cemetery marked *1900–1900.*

In 1916 with the Great War looming: "The congregation will attempt the English language one Sunday per month."

A dozen entries read, "The congregation voted to grant Pastor ———— a peaceful release," churchy boilerplate that referred to beloved pastors moving on to a "wider field of service" as well as those who had been fired for false doctrine, laziness, or high-handedness.

The possibility of my own "peaceful release" appeared unexpectedly in the form of a call to become pastor of another church, located in a vast resort city on the East Coast. My wife and I had lived in New Cana just long enough to find such a move unimaginable. We immediately began rhapsodizing about sunsets on the heath, the joys of burning our own garbage, and the wholesomeness of life in the country. Suddenly our rallying cry became, "Why would we want to leave Cana? Why would we trade all *this* for the plastic values of suburbia?"

Nevertheless, we seized the opportunity to deposit the children with our parents and to enjoy some sorely needed married-time together. We left the anniversary planning in the capable hands of Henry Dire and the committee, and, deftly converting a spiritual call into a summer vacation, we set off by Pinto to inspect this "wider field of service" in Virginia Beach, Virginia. We had no intention of accepting the call, but we desperately needed an adventure, and this was the best we could do.

Across the flatlands of southern Illinois and Indiana we chattered about the kids and the congregation, feeling a little guilty for escaping so easily from New Cana. We worried about the Petranovics, the fate of Key 73, finding enough teachers for Vacation Bible School, mimeographing the Sunday bulletin, and planning the big anniversary celebration.

By the time we got to Kentucky we quit talking about any church, the old one in New Cana or the new one in Virginia Beach, and settled into the vibrating hum of the highway as experienced through the wafer-thin floor of a '71 Pinto. We were exhilarated by the new landscape of rolling meadows in Kentucky and the rugged ugliness of gorged-out mountains in West Virginia. We stayed in the cheapest motels available and carried in breakfast from nearby McDonald's in order to watch Watergate in our room. A couple days we didn't get rolling until Senator Sam called a recess for lunch.

Everything seemed new to us, the way the outside world must appear to prisoners. We had lunch in a colonial tavern near Charlottesville, but to us it might as well have been a four-star in Paris. What was going on? The normal euphoria of parents temporarily on the loose? Or a more profound release from chains we hadn't recognized? Whichever, we were definitely having a good time.

We found a fifties-style motel on the boardwalk in Virginia Beach sandwiched between a pink stucco hotel and a turquoise stucco hotel, with a pancake house and a pizza parlor across the busy street. We had not laid eyes on a pancake house for many years, since before England, and ate our breakfasts there like anthropologists conducting field research. The street was lined with noisy fish houses and T-shirt shops filled with tourists like us. Young sailors from nearby bases roamed in packs all night along the boardwalk that was as bright and glitzy as Atlantic City.

The church itself was located several miles inland in a residential area bordered by strip malls, supermarkets, restaurants, and tony boutiques. The territory between the beachfront and the church seemed designed to obscure as much of the region's natural beauty as possible. Fingers of the Chesapeake Bay twisted arthritically through the city. At low tide the mud and silt was rank with bluepoints and teeming with snowy egret and heron. It was all beautiful, but more often than not the tidal water lapped at the loading dock of a supermarket or a souvenir shop. Even the ocean looked ugly when reflected in the plate glass of a pancake house. In other words, I was having aesthetics problems in Virginia Beach, similar to, but much more severe than those I experienced in New Cana, where it always vexed me to watch the sun set spectacularly over a landfill or a rusted Buick on blocks.

I formed my initial judgments based on first impressions of Virginia Beach, and what I first saw was the spoilage of nature by traffic, malls, and money. Genuine pastoral relationships would doubtless prove impossible in such a context.

When I met with the leaders of the congregation, however, I heard a different story. They were like a colony of believers in ancient Corinth or Thessalonica who, although they came together every Sunday in their little cinder-block first-unit of a sanctuary to sing the liturgy and share the Eucharist, did not really know one another. Almost everyone I talked to had recently been transferred into the area or was about to be transferred out. No one was *from* Virginia Beach. They didn't live in the same neighborhoods; their children did not attend the same schools; they never met in the post office, and aside from the accident of being Lutheran, they shared no common heritage in a world of Baptists, Pentecostals, and Pat Robertson, whose TV studio was only two miles from the church. If you can imagine a photograph of New Cana, this community was the negative.

I found it moving that they had sung hymns and prayed together before selecting me to be their pastor. They had not interviewed me or heard me preach, but entrusted their decision to the Holy Spirit. Because of this, they already considered me to be their pastor.

It appeared to take no effort on their part to feel comfortable with us and even to *like* us as persons. In a series of formal presentations, they spoke articulately of their desire to be faithful people in a sometimes inhospitable environment. One fellow said he was sure I could help them be better Christians. They actually salted their testimony with words like "community," "future," and "potential," words that didn't belong in New Cana.

Tracy and I left Virginia Beach dazed and perplexed. What had begun as a lark was ending in a wrenching decision about ministry and vocation. We had been so quick to judge the city's consumerism that we were unprepared for what we found in the church. I was so sure the people would turn out to be plastic reflectors of the plastic city; instead, we had all but bonded with people who were filled with love and eager to grow.

The journey west was a lot less fun than the trip east. No longer tourists, we drove hundreds of miles without speaking, each waiting to see if, as we turned onto the hard road and whizzed past Buford's Garage, Semanns Farm & Tractor Center, and the post office, our town of New Cana would still feel like home. It always had before. We were waiting.

Fortunately, there was no hurry. Lutherans fill their vacancies more deliberately than any of the churches in Christendom. Vacant congregations go months without thinking about choosing a new leader, and pastors, once they have received a call, may sit on it for additional months before hatching a decision. The time isn't used for negotiating more favorable terms; it is simply filled with prayer and dormancy. The President-elect of the United States names a Cabinet faster than the smallest Lutheran congregation picks a pastor, perhaps because Lutherans consider the latter process far more important. All is left to prayer and the brooding of the Spirit, and everyone knows the Spirit always works slowly.

I returned to a church whose summer activities were running at full throttle. The committee had Key 73 humming like a well-oiled machine. The Petranovics were visibly weakening in their resolve to join another church. Henry Dire's *History of Cana* had just passed its one hundredth page. But two additional tasks loomed before us.

No one could remember how long it had been since the hardwood floors in the church had been refinished, but now, with the anniversary celebration looming, the job had to be done. Our anniversary service would doubtless bring many visitors from other churches, and it wouldn't do to have them put their feet on our grungy floors.

There are people who refinish floors professionally whose names can be found in the Yellow Pages, but country people never pay a professional to do expertly what they can do recklessly for nothing. This was true of the chain-saw carnage perpetrated annually on our shade trees in the name of "trimming." Some of the sorriest cabinetwork and wallpapering I have ever seen was self-inflicted by people too cheap to pay an expert. Therefore, I wasn't surprised when the committee decided that we could easily sand and refinish the floors ourselves.

The trustees deputized several additional helpers, including me, and we all met in the church early on Saturday morning. We had rented several commercial-sized sanders and sets of goggles from Dullmann's Hardware in Cherry Grove. Three or four men had brought power tools of various sorts and were already unscrewing the pews while the rest of us drank coffee and quietly conferred like surgeons. To my astonishment, what no one had discussed was where to put the pews while the floor was being refinished. It was an overcast morning, and the weatherman was calling for light rain all weekend, so we couldn't carry them outside into the churchyard.

The committee arrived at the solution simultaneously, as if powered by a single brain. "We'll put them in the chancel, where it's carpeted," George Biedermann said.

"They won't fit in the chancel," someone objected.

But the committee, speaking as one, chorused back, "We'll stand them on their ends!"

We carried each pew into the chancel and laboriously hoisted it onto its end. Soon the chancel was clogged with standing pews poised precariously on their ends, like a cave filled with brown stalagmites. Unfortunately, our solution created an unimagined concentration of weight on a relatively small floor space. The wooden beams groaned underneath, and the floor gave out little popping sounds like rivets in a submarine that has dived too deep. A civil engineer, to say nothing of one rational person, could have seen it coming without doing the calculations.

Just as our committee had arrived at its brilliant solution simultaneously, it also recognized the imminence of disaster with a single, corporate gasp of foreboding. No one had to say, "With all that weight, the floor will surely give way, and our pews will crash into the basement!" That was the unspoken premise of Leonard's cry, "Get those things outta there! Quick!"

We did move the pews as expeditiously as possible outside into the churchyard, and it did rain, and the varnish on the pews turned to a milky paste. That is how our pews came to be refinished, professionally, in time for our anniversary service.

The more vexing problem, of course, was the matter of the broken cross. With the cross we moved entirely into the realm of oral tradition, and the oral tradition allowed for a great deal of speculation. Not only had the communal memory forgotten what materials the cross was made of or how it was damaged; no one could remember how long one of its arms had been dangling.

Some said the cross was made of solid copper, others said it was wood sheathed in copper. Those who adhered to the wood-sheathed-in-copper theory said that the wood had rotted within and brought about the collapse of one arm. Those who held to the solid-metal theory believed it had been struck by lightning, but they could not settle on the date of the storm, and their witnesses did not agree.

Both theories left something to be desired. Neither was symbolically satisfying from a religious point of view. One hundred twenty-five years of dry rot was not the message we wanted to convey; nor were we thrilled about a devastating lightning bolt, which is often the sign of a heavenly wake-up call. In either case, it had to be fixed.

We could not celebrate our catchy anniversary motto, "The Lord Hath Helped Us Hitherto, and Hitherto Will Help Us," beneath a cross that resembled a one-armed bandit and reminded some of dry rot and others of divine wrath.

Once again, our trustees considered how we might avoid the cost of a professional steeplejack and do the work ourselves. In the highly speculative conversations that occurred in the parking lot every Sunday, many a man had loudly offered a plan to climb to the top of the steeple and remove the broken cross. But as the day of reckoning approached, the farmer's well-known love of the earth prevailed, and we compromised by hiring an amateur to moonlight the job. Some Dullmann or other who worked as a lineman was recruited to "borrow" one of the county's cherry pickers on a Saturday morning, preferably near dawn. He and a coworker would remove the cross.

They did not come at dawn but instead arrived in the midst of Saturday catechism class. A group of interested spectators had begun to form, and I allowed history to repeat itself by dismissing the children from school so they could watch the historic cross-removal. Bobby Dullmann's pal maneuvered the cherry picker into place, and Bobby ascended the ninety feet as if in an express elevator. Within a half hour the mystery of the cross's composition and demise had been solved, and Bobby had removed what was left of it from its tattered crown. He capped the spire in another half hour's work, and by noon he had the borrowed cherry picker back in the county corral where it belonged.

Some of the older heads were a bit miffed that the mystery we had debated for several long winters had been solved in one hour by a nineteen-year-old kid from Cherry Grove.

The wood had rotted from within.

In the summer of John and Mo the corn turned crisp on the stalk, and by July it was fit for nothing but silage. There were no adventures left to distract us from the blistering silence of the fields. How much Watergate can you watch? We dreamed of a green and endless ocean.

When the summer reached its zenith, Leeta Weams gave birth to a boy, her second child in as many years. The child entered the world with what the doctors termed "multiple deficits" and was not expected to live. Leeta called me herself and asked me to baptize her baby.

St. Joseph's was no longer a mysterious fortress to me. It had become my shop, where I was accustomed to breezing in and greeting receptionists, orderlies, and doctors. Two of the nurses in the neonatal unit were members of St. John's, and others on the rotation were active in their respective churches. Over the years they had taught me a great deal about ministry in a hospital.

When I entered the unit, I found it arranged for a baptism. Dorothy Nix and Sharon Johnson were on duty and had agreed to act as witnesses. They had pushed the incubator to one side of the unit—healthy babies and all the joy they represent to the right, the baby with "multiple deficits" and all the numbing sadness he brings to the left. The lighting on the unit was usually blinding in its intensity, but someone had thoughtfully switched off a section of lights near the incubator.

A hush had fallen over the room, as parents of the other newborns stayed to themselves and softly cooed over their babies. On the shadow side of the room, the parents, two nurses, the resident, and the pastor stood in a semicircle about the incubator. Everyone was gowned, and the nurses were masked. Leeta and Shane appeared to be in shock. One of the nurses opened the end of the small white, humming cylinder, and I extended a moistened pinkie finger into the chamber. I made the sign of the cross on the baby's blue chest, which was puckered with tiny suction cups attached to wires.

"Receive the sign of the holy cross, both upon the forehead and upon the breast, in token that you have been redeemed by Christ the crucified."

Then, with my dampened finger I touched one of his downy eyebrows and said, "Shane Arlo Vachel Weams, I baptize you in the name of the Father, and of the Son, and of the Holy Spirit."

And the witnesses said, *Amen.*

That was an Amen on earth, choked out by five witnesses in an atmosphere of muffled sorrow; and, I believe, it was an Amen in heaven echoed by many other witnesses who see all things but, miraculously, no longer weep. We knew we were participating in something larger than ourselves, and so did the other parents standing respectfully on the far side of the unit. They also bowed their heads, and some made the sign of the cross. I could have baptized Shane Arlo many times over that day with the tears of the witnesses.

The Anniversary Committee determined that the new theme of our celebration would be "The Communion of Saints." Only now the committee and I agreed that the service would double as our farewell.

21

The Best Way
to Say Good-bye

But first **I** had some explaining to do to Max Toland, who was troubled to the point of agitation when I told him we were leaving New Cana. Perhaps it was because his life had already been disordered once that he assumed nothing else would ever change. His unhappiness took the form of compulsive questioning about the circumstances of the move. He never asked why we were leaving or how we felt about leaving or if he could visit, but only "How far is Virginia Beach? What's it like there? Who lives in Virginia? What is Virginia? Who will drive the car?" He asked these questions relentlessly, but no longer with his playful cock-of-the-brow and sweet smile.

At first I answered each question as factually as it was asked: "About a thousand miles . . . it's flat with an ocean . . . people like us," but something else was needed.

A few days before the big celebration, I took Max to the ball game in St. Louis, believing as I still do that baseball is the universal therapy.

Max had never been to a big-league game, and he was already capering six blocks from the stadium. We skipped along just above the surface of the sidewalk with a crowd of good-natured fans, many of whom were dressed in red shirts and Cardinal caps. Little boys clutched baseball gloves sized for the hands of giants. Max had his glove, too, a Bob Gibson model, which he had soaked in neat's-foot oil and wrapped in rags for three days and three nights in anticipation of our trip. Just in case. You never knew when Joe Torre or Lou Brock might hit a line drive with your name on it.

Max began shopping for souvenirs and snacks while we were still blocks from the gate. Clearly, no decision would be reached until he had tactilely inspected each kiosk and interviewed most of the vendors along the way. He meticulously fingered every cap, pennant, mug, and baseball, and surveyed every size hot dog, pretzel, and cotton candy on sale. Max was absorbing this day through his pores.

When I was a boy, my father and I used to walk through the shady residential streets to the old Sportsman's Park on Grand Avenue. The streets were lined with identical four-family flats—Scrubby Dutch, my parents called the people who lived in them. You could eat off their sidewalks and steps, my mother said. As dusk settled, the porches would fill with neighbors and relatives who chatted among themselves and paid little attention to the armies of fans trooping by on the sidewalks.

When we passed the YMCA on Grand Avenue, directly across the street from the centerfield fence, either my father or I would recite the legend of the Home Run, as if neither of us had heard it before. "Ruth broke a window on the fourth floor."

In those days I never asked for a souvenir because a baseball game was not a once-in-a-lifetime experience; it was woven into the fabric of my life. And I wasn't reduced to attending a single idealized baseball game with my minister, of all people, who was standing in for my once erratic and now dead father, because I had my own real father who would stay just beside me in the crowd and drape his arm around my shoulder while saying very little about anything except the game.

The new Busch Stadium was as symmetrical as the Roman Coliseum. It was perfect in its own way, with its graceful curves intersected by the plane of the Gateway Arch. The players wore dazzling white uniforms trimmed in red. They performed their languorous dance on a field as green and hard as a billiard table. The old Sportsman's Park was not symmetrical or dazzling; its living grass regularly browned out by August. Its grandstand and screened pavilion loomed darkly above the field, creating shadows and mysteries in sepia tones. What brilliance the old park possessed is now muted by memory and the palpable absence of baseball as it was and my father as he was.

Still, I could see the beauty in this place, too. Max nearly swooned at his first view of the field from our seats in the first row of the upper deck.

In the second inning we had hot dogs, in the fourth peanuts, in the sixth more hot dogs, in the eighth we split a German pretzel, and finished off the game with a torch of cotton candy. I matched his Cokes with beer until the sixth inning, and after that he lost me.

We did not talk about Virginia Beach. We did not talk about his father or his mother. We conferred about matters at hand: the wild pitch, the stolen base, the home run, the foul ball a few rows back, the quality of the peanuts, the location of the men's room.

After the last out, we remained in our seats as the rest of the fans filed out. The stadium was a haven where one could find peace, if only temporarily. The flags rested in the absence of an afternoon breeze. The field lay still and as geometrically perfect as a Burgundian garden, as apt a figure for eternal life as either of us could imagine.

Max studied the entire scene as if for the last time and said, "I could stay here forever."

"So could I."

And we left.

22

The Company
of Pilgrims

Harold Pringel hung on the rope as he did every Sunday at ten fifty-five and got the bell to ringing, and as its sound began to cross the prairie and slap against houses and barns, he slipped the rope into my hands and let me have the pleasure of the rhythmic pull and re-sistance, and permitted me to finish his job. It was something I'd always wanted to do.

In my sermon I spoke on the words of Hebrews: *"Since we are surrounded by so great a cloud of witnesses, let us also lay aside every weight, and sin which clings so closely, and let us run with perseverance the race that is set before us, looking to Jesus the pioneer and perfecter of our faith . . ."*

The night before, I had stood at the Sacred Burning Barrel for the last time to get rid of three years of trash and junk. I remembered all the sins I had committed as pastor of this little church: the inanities, failures, and missed opportunities. But most of all I remembered my pride, which weighted me down from my very first sighting of the church, impeded all my relationships with my parishioners, and never let me run with joy the race I might have run.

How I had despised Beulah, made fun of Buster, hated Bertie, distrusted Ronnie, betrayed Seth Barnes in his own church, underestimated Rose, avoided lonely Jan, crushed Heather, idealized my pal Leonard, toadied up to the elders, served myself, belittled everyone, confronted no one. I threw these memories into the fire, stoked it like a madman, and set off such a conflagration of trash that I nearly set the woods ablaze.

"Some things can never be fixed," Cece Johnson once told me. No more second chances. The nice thing about a boring sermon is that you can step down from the pulpit, say a silent prayer for forgiveness, and vow, "Better next Sunday." Not anymore. Now Cece too was gone and would not be available for absolution. He and Geneva no doubt having their final, eternal fling.

Let us run the race that is set before us. I remember Annie Wengert's marathon run to the Cana church cemetery, and I remember Seth Barnes's spooky rides on our county roads. And hadn't I jogged in circles on the gravel drive around the cemetery? But in three years I never met anyone who was truly *going someplace* as the world measures progress or success. Yet the entire congregation was rife with a sense of journey, doubtless the result of generations of unconsciously ingesting the Bible's language of pilgrimage.

JESUS: Behold, I cast out demons and perform cures today and tomorrow, and the third day I finish my course.

PAUL: One thing I do, forgetting what lies behind and straining forward to what lies ahead, I press on toward the goal . . .

Our journey in Cana was Pilgrim's journey, if not to the Heavenly City, at least toward the fullest expression of the life that had been given us. "The glory of God is humanity fully alive," St. Irenaeus said. If he was right, I saw the glory of God many times where I least expected it.

But what to make of *the inglorious sin that clings so closely?* We can only look to Jesus, the pioneer and perfecter of our faith. He was the first to run the course toward the fullness of life and complete it. We don't experience anything that he hasn't already endured or imagined. When he was raised from the dead, he perfected in advance the humanity of our dreams.

Follow him. There are no maps to point out the dangers in our lives, and the mapmakers—whether psychologists or politicians—have been discredited. But then, if you are lost in a dark wood, which would you prefer, a map that may or may not be accurate, or one trustworthy guide who knows every notch and trail because he's been there before?

When I was a boy and later a seminarian, I would have sworn that each person makes the race alone, like a long-distance runner who has separated from the pack and runs at his own pace. Religion was the most refined form of privacy available to me.

But now, as I looked out upon this cloud of upturned faces, each representing others already turned to the light, I was embraced by a wholeness I never before experienced. It seemed to me that I was looking at the church as God sees it, not as a series of individual quirks and opinions, but as a single heart of love and sorrow. The only thing that made us different from any other kinship group or society was the mysterious presence of Jesus in the community. We were his body, which is not a metaphor. The ordinary world really *is* capable of hosting the infinite Being. As I searched the face of my congregation on my last Sunday, I felt the theological point was proved.

When the service concluded, the ushers swung open the doors, and for the last time my view of the world was framed by the portals of Cana Lutheran Church: a half-mile of yellowed cornfields, faded red barns in the scrim of vapors rising from the land, a line of green trees on an oceanic horizon, a corner of the Petranovics' fancy white entrance.

Fortunately, there wasn't time for the finality to sink in, because the congregation was to recess to the cornerstone, where a time capsule was to be inserted and cemented for the ages. Would future generations speculate about the contents of the sealed box the way we had about the broken cross?

We didn't offer a great deal to posterity: a copy of the church constitution, a hymnal, a tiny Gideon New Testament, a pictorial directory of the congregation, a copy of the *Cherry Grove Gazette* with its society page, police blotter, and comments on the dreary Watergate business; a cassette tape of one of my sermons; a few hybrid corn seeds, and a plastic bag of dirt from Norbert Semanns's field.

Only the *Gazette* was a concession to "the world." The rest of our artifacts represented our church's testimony to the future. Had we wanted to capture our cultural moment, we would have included an antiwar tract by Daniel Berrigan; *Breakfast of Champions* by Kurt Vonnegut; a few Creedence Clearwater Revival and Stevie Wonder tapes; both reels of *Five Easy Pieces*, and in case our descendants were plagued by lack of self-esteem, a copy of *I'm O.K., You're O.K.*

We solemnly placed our capsule into the wall with absolutely no doubts that a new community would come after us and be like us, because made of us—our blood, faith, and stories. We were sure our great-grandchildren would someday eagerly rip this box out of the wall and find us infinitely interesting and important. With the capsule in place, the youngest member of the Sunday School, Bonnie Semanns, applied the last trowelful of cement, wiped the remainder on her jumper, and we were history.

———

After church the Anniversary Committee stayed on to put up tables and prepare for the afternoon's feast. The church owned enough folding tables to run a bingo operation, and we put them all out on the back lawn. Several we arranged end-to-end for the food, the others for dining. By the time church-goers and guests began arriving, everything was ready.

In both the Old and the New Testaments, the kingdom of heaven is compared to a banquet. That morning in the Eucharist we sang,

> Gather the hopes and dreams of all;
> Unite them with the prayers we offer.
> Grace our table with your presence,
> And give us a foretaste of the feast to come,

which was a suitable prelude to our church picnic.

On the main table the women laid platters of fried chicken (no Colonel Sanders) along with serving bowls of German potato salad made with bacon and bacon grease, vinegar, and no mayonnaise. Also, macaroni salads, deviled eggs with paprika, home-canned green beans, zucchini, summer squash, sliced tomatoes, raisin and carrot slaw, corn on the cob, baked beans with slivers of hot dog and brown sugar, generic "meat" casseroles, and many, many pans of Jell-O—some covered with baby marshmallows, some mounded with Dream Whip, others infused with Dream Whip and strawberries. Each version represented someone's key-signature Jell-O.

Bud Jordan was in charge of the grill, which Midwesterners call "the barbecue." He was grilling corn on the cob, hamburgers, and Dorothy Semanns's pork sausage, which is famous for its dill and enhanced, if such a thing is possible, by her homemade ketchup.

There was also a beer keg but not, of course, the customary Drunk Tent erected for wedding receptions and other affairs away from the church grounds.

Also desserts: strawberry shortcake with more Dream Whip, blackberry pie, banana cream pie, apple cobbler, chocolate cake, German chocolate cake, and Better-Than-Sex Cake, which was double-fudged with a line of peppermint through the middle and very moist. Gus Semanns was in charge of the homemade ice cream for the cake.

Everyone sat at long tables arranged haphazardly under the white oak and elm trees behind the church and parsonage. Families from Cana connected with relatives from Cherry Grove, Blaydon, Dempster, and Prairieview, and configured their tables into squares and triangles to make joking and storytelling easier.

The widows maintained their own table, as if they represented a registered guild in the congregation. Beulah Toland sat with them, drinking ice tea and gossiping like the older women. At long last, she belonged to an established group in New Cana. She looked as relaxed and comfortable as I'd ever seen her.

Susan Truly was obviously using the occasion to make a statement. The picnic marked her first outing as a mother-to-be. She looked skinny and radiant in an embroidered maternity smock she wouldn't need for months. She held court in a lawn chair while Steve hovered about her and proudly shared statistics of the pregnancy with interested parties.

Folks moved from group to group, but none more expertly than my son, who shuttled from table to table like a mendicant and ate off the plates of others.

In the front yard of the church, various contests were going on under the sponsorship of the Sunday School teachers. Old folks threw darts at balloons and rings at Coke bottles, while their middle-aged children kept cool under the canopied oak trees out back. The kids worked up a summer sweat competing in the one-legged race, the potato-sack race, the joined-at-the-hip race, and the Hula-Hoop contest. At nightfall, several hours after we were on the road, they would create informal games of hide-and-seek, as oblivious to me and my ministry as before we arrived.

On the side lawn of the parsonage, facing Tom and Lottie Semanns's place, the teenagers organized a pony ride for the little ones. Tom and Lottie's oldest boy, Donny, who regularly galloped bareback across our front lawn and who had distinguished himself in the Bull-in-the-Cemetery episode, was in charge of the two ponies. Smaller children got a ride around the yard; seven- to nine-year-olds were taken down the hill and up again, around the cemetery.

Our little girl, who had never been on a pony, was seldom off her spotted "Rosie" the entire afternoon. Sarah was just old enough to be very proud that such a splendid event was occurring in her own yard. My wife and I each felt a twinge of regret as we watched her and realized that she was losing the sort of community she would not remember and never know again.

When suppertime came and we were down to hot dogs, hamburgers, and the less-than-stellar Jell-Os, Leonard gathered the congregation under the tree and, standing on an overturned tub, made a little speech.

"We're here to celebrate one hundred and twenty-five years of this church, Cana church, and of course to get together and have a good time." (A murmur of approval at the mention of "a good time.") "We have been here a long while, and for the whole time God has been good to us. This church'n all has meant everything to us.

"We're also here to say good-bye to the Lischers, who have lived among us for nearly three years. Tracy has been a very busy wife to Pastor Lischer. If you don't believe me, just look at the size of the zucchinis and tomatoes just behind me! I would say that this is one impressive garden. We will miss you, Mrs. Lischer, and I know our Sunday School will miss your young ones.

"Pastor Lischer, Rick, you had your say this morning in the pulpit, and you get no more air time" (another ripple of approval). "It's not been long since you've been with us, but you have been our pastor in every way. Our lives are changed, somehow . . . *somehow*, because God sent you to us."

Leonard was a little choked up, and I was glad I had already had my say.

"Now the 'race' you talked about this morning continues. You and your family are headin' East, and you don't know what you will find. We hope it will be to your satisfaction. Most of us will stay right here, but wherever you go, you will be carrying a little piece of Cana with you. We will think of you as our pastor in the East. And we wish God's blessings upon your ministry. Amen."

My family and I left Cana cleanly and without delay, like circuit riders moving on to the next town. We didn't return to the parsonage for a night's rest or stop in St. Louis to visit relatives before heading East. Leonard's eloquent Amen was our cue to hit the road.

After his speech, a group of parishioners surrounded us and gently guided us toward the driveway of the parsonage and our yellow Pinto, which was almost fully packed. Sonny Buford had installed a luggage rack that week, and the elders were hovering about it, cinching and double-cinching the vinyl carrier to its corners. My wife said to Bud Jordan, "Be sure and use a Kenyon Knot," which stopped him cold.

"A what? I don't know how to make that one."

"It's my maiden name," she laughed, and he threw his arms around her and hugged her.

The elders were exercising their spiritual responsibility to the end, surrounding my car and ministering to it the way they had fussed and brooded over me in the sacristy every Sunday. Only this time, it was not a matter of getting me through a worship service without a hitch, but of delivering us all safely to a new community in Virginia. They patted the Pinto's hood as if blessing it.

The final items to be packed were the children. Once they were buckled into their car seats, they were in no mood for further good-byes. There was no time for one last turn around the cemetery or a walk-through of the empty parsonage. The sun was about to clot into the Brush, but I had no more sins to burn while we watched it go.

I wouldn't have minded slipping into my study for a moment to recapture Leeta and Shane's wedding or Steve and Susan's reconciliation, or even Bertie's hateful accusations. I could have listened one last time to Buster's eloquent prayer or Cece's confession. I never got tired of Leonard's blunt wisdom. Their voices are in the walls. That room once contained our community's version of faith, conflict, and love. But it really was time to go.

The poet-preacher John Donne said, "I date my life from my ministry." There is more to life than ministry, but I knew as soon as we pulled out of the driveway that I had needed Cana more than Cana ever needed me. I do make sense of my life from that ministry.

I also believe that pastoral ties cannot be severed, even when they are imperfectly remembered or forgotten altogether. If all our relationships participate in a vast network of meaning called "kingdom" or "church," they must have a richness we can't always savor and a permanency we can only imagine. They are eternal because God remembers everything and has engraved our names into the palms of his hands. The moment we hit the oil road, this ministry in the flesh was lost to me, and Cana became a story with voices and textures and a mystery all its own. For which I am grateful.

We followed the oil road whose right angles still conform to the history of families and their fields, past the familiar home places, until we came to the New Cana Road. From a distance the church appeared to be a ruin on the prairie or a ghost ship on the horizon, but we knew the folding tables and booths were already being dismantled, cleanup was under way, and the children would be playing like fireflies in the evening shadows. We turned right and drove through town, but it too was as quiet as a still life because everyone was at church.

Not a single person was to be seen walking along the road or rocking on the covered porches. A rolling door at Buford's Garage was half-raised—one of the boys tinkering on his own time, no doubt. Beulah's screen door still dangled by a single pin, exactly as Buster had left it the day he flew out. Wilfred's '56 Roadmaster sat rusted to its usual place in the tableau of ruined engines, ancient blades, and other debris.

We were the pilgrims now, the moving speck on a AAA map of the known world, excited and a little scared by the mystery of our open future. How daring we felt, to be setting out on a journey as the sun was setting!

How far can we go before bedtime? Will the motel have a color TV? A coffee shop? How can we be hungry already?

Even more unimaginable to us, we were on our way to a new church. Real friendships were waiting for us, but they did not yet exist. Stories of love and suffering were doubtless on the drawing board, but they had no real existence either. What would become of us?

We caught our rhythm on the hard road and, after the usual car songs and snacks, the children dozed until we stopped for gas near Freeburg on the old Route 15.

They opened their eyes with a start and asked in unison, "Are we there yet?"

"No," we said, "we are not there yet."

ACKNOWLEDGMENTS

Quotation from an anti-Alton newspaper editorial in *Freedom's Champion. Elijah Lovejoy* by Paul Simon, Southern Illinois University Press, 1994.

Quotation from the Alton Debate in *An Analysis of Lincoln and Douglas as Public Speakers and Debaters* by Lionel Crocker, Charles C. Thomas Publisher, 1968.

Quotation from letters of German immigrants in *Moving Frontiers*, edited by Carl S. Meyer, Concordia Publishing House, 1964.

Quotation from Flannery O'Connor's letter in *The Habit of Being. Letters of Flannery O'Connor*, edited by Sally Fitzgerald, Vintage Books, 1979.

Quotation from a Christmas sermon by Martin Luther in *Martin Luther's Christmas Book*, edited by Roland H. Bainton, Westminster Press, 1948.

Quotations about rural life in nineteenth- and twentieth-century America from *The Transformation of Rural Life: Southern Illinois, 1890–1990* by Jane Adams, the University of North Carolina Press, 1994.

Quotation from "The Times They Are A-Changin" by Bob Dylan. The Bob Dylan Music Company. Used by permission.

© CARTER ASKREN

Richard Lischer was born in St. Louis and educated in public schools. Following his graduation from college, he earned additional degrees from Concordia Seminary and Washington University, both in St. Louis, and the University of London. He returned to St. Louis for ordination in the Lutheran Church and his first pastoral assignment, a rural parish in southern Illinois. Following a second pastorate in Virginia, he joined the faculty of the Duke Divinity School, where he has taught for the past twenty years. His most recent book is the prizewinning *The Preacher King: Martin Luther King, Jr., and the Word That Moved America*. He is married to Tracy Kenyon Lischer, a lawyer in Durham, North Carolina. They have two grown children, Sarah, a doctoral candidate at MIT, and Adam, a lawyer in eastern North Carolina.